To Nancy:

MerryChristmas

Enjoy

Todd Davidson

(your 11th grade
Algebra student).

Legends of

LEHIGH - LAFAYETTE

... College Football's Most-Played Rivalry

By Todd Davidson and Bob Donchez

D&D

Publishing

Company

Illustrations: Tom Hayes
Cover Design: Dave Stevens
Cover Photo: Kris Eckenrode
Photography: Kris Eckenrode and Pam Lott
Editor: Evie Ishmael

Library of Congress Catalog Card Number: 95-92244
ISBN: 0-9640341-1-5

D&D
Publishing
Company
364 Kevin Drive • Bethlehem, PA 18017
1-800-FULL-MUG
Printed in the United States of America

To all those who call themselves friends or family of either school, and to college football fans everywhere.

Thanks for making Lehigh-Lafayette one of America's great traditions!

Being from Florida, I didn't truly understand the meaning of The Rivalry until many years after I graduated from Lehigh. One morning before The Game in Easton in the 70's, a group of young boys approached me and asked if I was a football player. I told them I played for Lehigh in the late '50's and my name was Harold Milton. They responded by saying, "Wow, I remember you. You were great. You caught a pass in the Lafayette-Lehigh game in 1960. You're a legend." Only then did I realize what The Game meant to me and the fans.

Legends of
LEHIGH-LAFAYETTE
... College Football's Most-Played Rivalry

By Todd Davidson and Bob Donchez

Contents

Second Quarter: Building A Tradition (1906-1949)

Halftime: The Traditions

Third Quarter: The Modern Era (1950-1983)

Fourth Quarter: Patriot League Years (1984-1994)

Postgame Wrap-Up

Acknowledgements

About The Authors

Co-author Todd Davidson (left) with Lafayette
coach Bill Russo.

Todd Davidson, a
Lehigh Valley native,
left his corporate re-
search and product
development position
at Procter & Gamble to
pursue *Legends*. Using
the skills acquired at
P&G, Todd spent many
hours researching and
writing a more passion-
ate endeavor. An
engineer by trade, his
creativity and design
skills are reflected
throughout the book.

Bob Donchez, a former
sports writer for the *Globe-
Times* and sports director
for WLVR radio of Bethle-
hem, left Wall Street three
years ago. He settled in
the mountains of Colorado
where he writes, creates,
and does other innovative
projects in the entertainment field. His first book,
*A View from the Stands — A
Season with Bob the Beer-
man*, is a light-hearted look
at life in the bleachers
during the course of a
baseball season and was a
regional best-seller.

Preface

The Lehigh-Lafayette game is an American tradition that dates back to 1884. To college football, it's the most-played rivalry. To fans, it's entertainment. Something to watch and enjoy. To players and coaches, it's something to sit back and reflect on, to uphold.

After two years of researching, interviewing, writing, and editing, we realized that for most, Lehigh-Lafayette is more than a football game. The spirit of competition that exists in every athletic contest is taken a step further to create not only a football game, not only a rivalry, but a way of life. The Lehigh-Lafayette game is an integral part of a college education. The game provides thrills and excitement and instills an attitude that is essential to succeed in all walks of life. Traditions, pregame hype, and celebrations are all as important as the football game itself.

No other football rivalry is quite like Lehigh-Lafayette. The traditions are pure and the festivities are genuine. Sportswriters are afraid to predict the winner, oddsmakers shy from a pointspread, and coaches don't have to worry about getting their players "up" for the game. Previous records, scores, and games against common opponents are meaningless. It's one game — all or nothing!

On the field, the action has been likened to a title fight. A hard-fought battle. A fight to the finish — like two heavyweight boxers exchanging blows and counterpunches. Cuts, bruises, scrapes, and scratches — no holds barred. A victor emerges, often times in a split decision.

Off the field, the events that some call "indescribable" fuel passion and rekindle memories of this college classic.

The challenges in writing *Legends* became apparent from day one. Chronicling a rivalry as impassioned as the one between these two Lehigh Valley schools forced us to develop some unique ways to split the billing between the two competing institutions.

Early in our explorations, Lafayette faithful pointedly noted that it wasn't appropriate to refer to the rivalry only as "Lehigh-Lafayette." Similarly, Lehigh supporters didn't take kindly to "Lafayette-Lehigh."

Faced with this dilemma, we struggled for a way to deliver an unbiased viewpoint. After dismissing several options, we finally settled on the terms "The Rivalry," "The Game" and "The Series" to collectively refer to the Lehigh-Lafayette or Lafayette-Lehigh game. For those times when this wasn't appropriate, we decided to start the reference with the school most closely tied to the related incident. Hopefully, we haven't offended fans or alumni of either college in the process.

Every effort was made to balance the headlines, billing, and stories of The Rivalry. Unfortunately, the documentation of some of the games was spotty at best. Soliciting testimonials from the early years was difficult, as was locating newspaper accounts of 110 years ago. Editorial commentary and sarcasm had to be separated from factual information. *Legends'* intent is to provide an impartial description of the events that capture the true essence of The Rivalry.

The idea of writing *Legends* originated in 1992 during a postgame tailgate at the annual sandlot Turkey Bowl football game at Bethlehem's Asa Packer Elementary School. Three years later, the idea became reality. We hope that reading this book is as enjoyable as the journeys we encountered in writing it.

Reflecting to the beginning of this project, we decided the first step of the research process was to define "rivalry." In *Webster's Tenth New Collegiate Dictionary* we found:

> **rivalry**\'ri-vel-re*n, pl* **-ries** : one of two or more striving to reach or obtain something that only one can possess.

For Lehigh and Lafayette, the "something that only one can possess" is a victory in the annual football matchup. History reveals The Game is a rivalry in the truest sense of the word. After completing *Legends*, it is our recommendation that Webster changes the definition of "rivalry" in the next edition to:

> **rivalry**\'ri-vel-re*n, pl* **-ries** : see Lehigh-Lafayette (or Lafayette-Lehigh).

Todd Davidson   Bob Donchez

FIRST QUARTER
The Early Years
(1884 - 1905)

The origins of the great institutions of Lafayette College and Lehigh University date to the 1800's. Lafayette College, founded by the citizens of Easton, Pennsylvania, was established along the Forks of the Delaware River in 1826. Shortly thereafter, in 1865, Asa Packer founded Lehigh University at the base of South Mountain in Bethlehem, Pennsylvania, just 15 miles across the Lehigh Valley. As the institutions developed over the years, so did their athletic programs. On an October day in 1884, Theodore L. Welles, the Founder of Lafayette Football, and Richard Harding Davis, The Father of Lehigh Football, organized their respective teams to meet on the Easton Athletic Grounds for the inaugural game of the historic series. Little did these football pioneers know they were about to start a tradition that would become "College Football's Most Played Rivalry!"

Here's the First Quarter of action. It promises to be an old-fashioned treat!

The First Game ... The Rivalry Begins!

"My teammates and I prevailed upon the college to pay $52 for 11 brown and white jerseys, and then we thought that what we did not know about the game was not worth learning. With this idea in mind we went down to Easton and played the first of those memorable games."

— Richard Harding Davis, The Father of Lehigh Football

The first encounter between Lehigh and Lafayette on October 25, 1884, was in sharp contrast to modern-day football. In fact, a modern-day football fan attending the first contest would be hard-pressed to identify if the game was rugby, Australian rules football, or a prehistoric version of American Gladiators.

Prepare to relive the action as the two teams kickoff the first Lehigh-Lafayette football game from the Easton Athletic Grounds. Here's how it all started:

Admission: $0.25 (No gate at the entrance, tickets purchased from a field officer along the sidelines).

The Field: 120 yards long with no end zones. Goalposts at the goal lines which marked the end of the playing field. Five-yard demarcations, but no hash marks (not part of the field until 1906 when the forward pass was introduced). Rocks, dirt (or mud), tree stumps, broken glass, and a few grassy patches were the forefathers to the astro turf and plush grass fields of today. It was vintage Little Rascals/Our Gang sandlot football.

The Stadium: The field was the stadium; no locker rooms, press box, or bleachers. The spectators, press, field officers, policemen, and players intermingled along the sidelines. At this time, the football fields were referred to as the Lehigh and Lafayette Athletic Grounds. The blueprints for Taylor Stadium and Fisher Field were merely design dreams in the minds of two architects.

Attendance: Literally, a "standing room only" crowd of 250 people lined the sidelines. No bleachers were available for seating.

Scoring: A touchdown scored four points, an extra point conversion two points, a field goal (then known as a drop kick) five points, and a safety two points.

Rules: Primitive at best. Each team had three downs to retain possession by gaining five yards or losing 20. The ball could only be lateraled backwards (no forward pass at this time). No tackling below the waist. The extra point attempt was kicked from the spot the ball crossed the goal line. Additional rules were developed, at the discretion of the referee and team captains, as the game was played .

Time of Game: In the Early Years, two 45 minute halves were played instead of four 15 minute quarters.

Referees: Whoever was available. It was not unusual to have a student, faculty member, or fan yanked from the sideline at game time to act as referee.

Equipment: There wasn't any! Matching shirts were a commodity. Some of the more innovative players had leather straps attached to their shoulders and hips so that other players could pull them forward in a pileup to net extra yardage. The football helmet was not invented until 1896.

The Ball: A rugby ball with a rounded appearance resembling a basketball more than a modern-day football.

The Center Snap: To start play, the center would "snap" the ball to the quarterback by rolling it along the ground with his foot. It was football in the true sense of the word.

The Players: Eleven warriors on each side. A substitute or two mixed in with the spectators and press on the sidelines in case a player became injured to the extent he could not continue in battle. In some extenuating circumstances, a non-collegiate fan or friend from the stands might be asked to play if no other substitute was available for an injured player. A player weighing over 200 pounds was a rarity.

Substitutions: The participants were truly iron men, playing offense and defense for the entire 90 minutes. If a player left the game for any reason, he could not return for the remainder of that game. It was not unusual to

No Complimentary Passes

The first Lafayette-Lehigh football game was not without controversy. The 150 Lehigh fans that accompanied the team to Easton unknowingly entered the Lafayette football grounds without paying admission. The situation was quickly remedied when the Lafayette field officers made them aware that tickets needed to be purchased to witness the game. Once this was understood, the Lehigh fans willfully paid their dues.

have a quarterback who was also a running back, punter, and field goal kicker, as well as a defensive lineman. Two-way men were a luxury. Four-way men were the rule. George Blanda would have had it easy.

The Coaching Staff: The Early Years were dominated by a hands-on coaching philosophy. Student-athletes acted as the captains and coaches of the teams until 1891, when Lafayette hired the first paid coach in The Rivalry.

Lafayette had a significant advantage over Lehigh in the initial confrontation. For Lafayette, the Lehigh game was the beginning of the third season of intercollegiate football competition. For Lehigh, the Lafayette game was the first kickoff in Lehigh football history. In fact, only three people on Lehigh's team had ever played football before the Lafayette game.

Lehigh's captain, Richard Harding Davis, had three weeks of practice to prepare his woefully inexperienced team for the showdown. Despite its inexperience, the Lehigh football team went to Easton with its new brown and white jerseys and fully expected to defeat its crosstown opponent. The Lehigh eleven began to think differently after the final whistle, as a powerful Lafayette squad shredded Lehigh's new brown and white jerseys to the tune of 50-0.

The conditions for the first Lehigh-Lafayette game were less than ideal. Richard Harding Davis described the playing surface as a "soft quicksand of mud." In fact, according to Davis, the field was so muddy that Lehigh's halfback Bish Howe would occasionally call out, "Don't pass that ball to me Jake (referring to Lehigh quarterback Jake Robeson). I'm stuck in the mud and I can't get out." Should have dialed 9-1-1 for help, Bish.

To say Lafayette taught the Lehigh men a lesson that day would be a gross understatement. The Lafayette players were prepared for the slippery conditions and wore strips (primitive cleats) on the bottom of their shoes. Only one player on the Lehigh team had cleats on his shoes,

You're Fired!

Mr. Uptegrove, director of the Lafayette gymnasium, was the referee for the first Lafayette-Lehigh game. Toward the end of the first half, his decisions became so unjust that the Lehigh players insisted he be replaced. Robert Wittmer, Lafayette Class of 1885, took over as referee for the remainder of the game and proved to be a competent replacement.

Batter Up!

The first recorded intercollegiate athletic competition between Lehigh and Lafayette was not in football, but instead was played on the baseball diamond on May 4, 1872 in Easton. Lafayette won by a score of 34-16. Later that same year, Lafayette again defeated Lehigh by a score of 88-20 (in four innings). No, sports fans, these were not football scores, nor for that matter basketball scores. They were indeed the scores of the first Lafayette-Lehigh baseball games, according to the archives.

and as Davis observed, "The rest of us slid over the worn grass as though we were on roller coasters."

Lafayette used home-field advantage in a way that would be praised by the greatest of modern-day coaches. The Maroon won the toss and wisely elected to kickoff so that Lehigh would face the sun, wind, and uphill slope of the field. By the time Lafayette switched goals in the second half, the wind had calmed and the sun had set in a way that provided Lehigh with no advantage.

From the first series of downs, Lafayette dominated both sides of the rush line in what proved to be a very long day for the Lehigh eleven.

Although Lehigh came out on the short end of the score, one Lehigh man was able to salvage this remark about the first Lehigh-Lafayette game: "We did not win ... but we gave Lafayette the worst licking she ever had in her existence and many, many a sore head went back to Easton that night." Lehigh must have returned to Bethlehem with many, many a sore ego and sore behind.

Lafayette and Lehigh met for a second time in 1884 on Wednesday, November 12th, at the Lehigh Athletic Grounds. The result wasn't much different, a 34-4 victory for Lafayette. Lehigh was much improved since the first game and even managed to score a touchdown — the first in Lehigh football history. The first player to cross the goal line for the Brown and White was appropriately, Richard Harding Davis.

Richard Harding Davis, The Father of Lehigh Football

Richard Harding Davis ... The Father of Lehigh Football

"Richard Harding Davis was a sturdy fellow ... a cracker-jack dodger and fast on his feet, a factor just as much in the old days as it is in the more open style of today. He was hard as nails when it came to bucking the line and it took an old-fashioned pileup to stop him."

— excerpt from 1925 New York Herald Tribune article by Frank Dole, coach of the University of Pennsylvania football team which met Lehigh in 1885.

Richard Harding Davis was born in Philadelphia, Pennsylvania in 1864. While at Lehigh, Davis founded the theatrical group Mustard and Cheese, Lehigh's student government Arcadia (eventually replaced by the Forum), and the football team.

For Richard Harding Davis, the first Lafayette-Lehigh games in 1884 were very busy days. In these games, Davis posed as Lehigh's founder, halfback, captain, coach, and sportswriter.

Davis not only played in the games but covered them in the student press. Davis certainly provided a unique slant to media coverage as he was able to live his own ESPN Sportscenter Fantasy. Unlike most sportswriters who get the scoop from the press box, Davis got his play-by-play accounts from behind the rush line where he had an uninterrupted view of the field. His observations both on and off the field provided picturesque accounts of not only the Lehigh-Lafayette games, but of football as it was played in America during the Early Years.

Davis did not stop with football. Later, he became one of the first war correspondents to see actual combat. Writing for the *New York Times*, *New York Herald*, and *Times of London*, Davis covered the major world conflicts of his time. In addition, Davis wrote over 30 volumes of fiction, including short stories, novels, and plays. He is noted for his most famous work, *Soldiers of Fortune*, written in 1896.

During his years as a correspondent, Davis became a close personal friend of Theodore Roosevelt. As President, Roosevelt greatly influenced the game of college football, saving the game from extinction in 1906 when he lobbied for drastic rule changes to deter violence and injuries.

Richard Harding Davis died unexpectedly in 1916 at age 52. He is remembered as a sportswriter, war correspondent, novelist, and playwright. Perhaps, he is best remembered, by Lehigh and Lafayette alumni alike, as a great football player who contributed to the start of one of the most celebrated traditions in college football history ... the Lehigh -Lafayette game.

The Rivalry Builds...

After Lafayette overwhelmed the Brown and White in The Rivalry's first year, Lehigh entered the 1885 season with vengeance. In the first of two encounters, Lehigh's center Pierce, the most imposing and dominant player on the Lehigh squad, was ejected for rough play. Lehigh's captain Frauenthal bitterly contested the call to no avail. With five minutes left in the first half, Lehigh refused to continue play and left the field with the score 0-0.

Later, football authorities awarded the game to Lafayette by a 6-0 score, stating that Lehigh had no right to protest the game on a referee's judgement call.

In the second game in 1885, Lafayette and Lehigh battled to a 6-6 tie, leaving only the bittersweet taste of a moral victory for Lehigh as it managed its first tie of The Series. Meanwhile, Lafayette enjoyed a 3-0-1 advantage over its cross-town opponent.

The Flying V Wedge

Lafayette and Lehigh were two of the forerunners of American college football. Lafayette kicked off its inaugural season in 1882 and Lehigh in 1884. As the game evolved, their football teams pioneered various innovative tactics and strategies. One such ploy, used frequently by both Lehigh and Lafayette in the Early Years, was the "V trick," also called the flying wedge, on kickoff returns. The players would amass into a V-shaped wedge with the ballcarrier in the middle and proceed upfield in a hodgepodge of human bodies, blood, guts, and whatever else happened to get caught in the melee. The only defense was to hit the wedge straight on and hope the blow would stop its forward progress. Although quite effective, the head-on approach often resulted in severe injuries.

Walter Camp, "The Father of American Football," credited Lehigh with the invention of the V formation. Lehigh football pioneer J. S. Ginson, Class of 1886, was the first to implement the "V trick."

Pudge Heffelfinger, an All-American guard for Yale who coached Lehigh in 1894, created his own method of breaking the flying wedge. Pudge stood 6' 4" tall and weighed 200 pounds — a virtual monster in his days. Instead of trying to undercut the wedge, Pudge would jump over the wedge, landing inside on top of the ball carrier. Pudge's kamikaze style of play earned him much acclaim. Most of the early football experts agree that Heffelfinger was the best guard to ever play the game. One football historian described Pudge on the football field as a "disembodied spirit." Even with his aggressive style of play, Heffelfinger was never seriously injured in his long-lived career. He played competitive football until age 66, and was a star player at age 55.

Rained Out

"For after all, the best thing one can do when it's raining is to let it rain."
— Henry Wadsworth Longfellow

Controversy brewed in both Lehigh-Lafayette contests in 1886. Two games were scheduled, two were played, neither was completed. Both were bitterly disputed.

The first Lehigh-Lafayette game of 1886 left a distinct mark in The Series' history as the first and only rainout. Fifteen minutes into the second half at the Easton Athletic Grounds, a torrential downpour halted the action by the mutual consent of both captains. According to the *Bethlehem Times*, the rain diminished the game to a point where "the players were rolling about the field." The game was called and the score stood in favor of Lafayette, 12-0.

In the weeks to come, there was much dispute as to whether the game was officially a victory for Lafayette since it was not played to completion. Before rendering a decision, Frederic Knorr, the game's referee, wrote Walter Camp, the leading authority on football at the time, for his opinion.

Camp responded: "The rules require two halves of 45 minutes each, so technically a game is no game unless full time is played. 'Rain or shine' is the custom among footballists, so the leaders might have insisted upon continuance of the game or forfeit. As they did neither, the referee must call it no game."

With Mr. Camp's response, Knorr declared the game a draw. Lehigh, in an act of true sportsmanship, did not wish to accept the draw and instead awarded the victory to Lafayette since Lehigh was clearly outplayed by its opponent. In the archives, the game is officially recorded as a 12-0 Lafayette victory.

The Controversy Builds ...

In the 1886 rematch at Lehigh's field, the controversy continued. Questionable officiating compelled Lehigh to withdraw from the contest with fifteen minutes remaining in the game.

From the opening whistle, it was apparent Lehigh would not get any breaks. H. L. Forceman, the manager of the Lafayette team, acted as referee. The Lafayette players were suspected by the Bethlehemites of playing unfairly throughout the game, breaking many rules and deliberately trying to injure the Lehigh men.

At one point, Williams of Lafayette intentionally kicked captain Pierce of Lehigh in the back when he was down. No penalty was called by the Lafayette referee and play continued. The one-sided refereeing became more apparent when Lafayette was consistently awarded four and five downs to Lehigh's three.

During the second half, a dispute occurred over what down it was for Lafayette. The referee went to the sidelines to consult with a substitute and a *Daily Times* reporter. According to one source, while the referee's back was turned, a Lafayette man picked up the ball and ran to Lehigh's three yard-line. After the commotion, the referee turned to the action on the field. Upon seeing the result, he cheered with undisguised enthusiasm for his team, allowing the play to stand.

Obviously discontent, captain Pierce of Lehigh protested the call and removed his team from the field when the play was not overruled. With many of the Lehigh players on the sidelines putting on their sweaters, a Lafayette player picked up the ball and crossed the goal line claiming a touchdown and 4-0 victory for Lafayette.

Lafayette sources argued the referee's decision was just and Lehigh was making a habit of "quitting" the game once the score was not in its favor.

"Lehigh's conduct reminds us of the boy who wouldn't play unless he could beat."

— excerpt from The Lafayette, 1886

The official outcome was hotly debated during the following weeks. Without television and instant replay, the arguments were based on hearsay and speculation. According to most sources, the game was officially scored a 4-0 victory for Lafayette.

Even today, the Bethlehemites still protest the game should be a 0-0 draw, which would make it the only scoreless tie in Lehigh- Lafayette history.

One reporter wrote, "It is indeed a most lamentable state of affairs when two colleges like Lehigh and Lafayette, situated so near each other, and whose relations ought to be of the most intimate kind, can not play a friendly game of football without causing so much ill feeling on both sides."

Amidst the controversy and season-ending dispute with Lehigh, Lafayette had developed into a respected football power, completing a fine season in 1886 with a 10-2 (or 9-2-1) record.

Lehigh's First Taste of Victory

"Winning isn't everything, it's the only thing."
— Red Sanders

Going into the 1887 season, Lafayette enjoyed a 4-0-2 advantage over Lehigh in The Series. Lafayette brought its team to the Lehigh Athletic Grounds hoping to maintain supremacy on the football field. Lafayette was so serious about defeating Lehigh that the Maroon cancelled its game with the University of Pennsylvania the week before to better prepare themselves for the Brown and White.

Lafayette lined up one of the strongest teams to date, while Lehigh was suffering from injuries to several key players. In an underdog role, Lehigh upset Lafayette by a margin of 10-4, giving Lehigh its inaugural victory over its rival.

A parade in the streets of Bethlehem followed the victory, highlighted by the students serenading Dr. Coppee and President Lamberton at their homes.

Lafayette, not accustomed to losing to Lehigh, barraged the media with excuses and accusations. One Lafayette professor went as far as preparing an affidavit for the press stating that he heard the referee say to the umpire, "We'll do Lafayette dirt this half."

The professor later withdrew his statement, citing he had only witnessed the referee and umpire talking but was not positive of the exact nature of the discussion.

Lehigh contributed to the media stir by stating that the only reason Lafayette was able to score a touchdown was because the Lehigh players made the mistake of drinking too much water when overheated, thus enabling Lafayette to score toward the end of the game.

The Maroon avenged the loss in the second game by defeating Lehigh 6-0 in Easton with a strong defensive showing. No doubt, the Lafayette trainers provided plenty of water for the Lehigh players to guzzle on the sidelines.

> **Knee-Knocker**
>
> Rule changes in college football permitted tackling below the waist for the first time in the 1888 Lehigh-Lafayette games.

The First Bonfire!

Lehigh's first taste of victory in 1887 took the edge off of its hunger, and the Brown and White continued to fulfill its growing appetite by defeating the Maroon twice in 1888.

The first game of 1888, a 6-4 Lehigh victory in Easton, was one of the most exciting in The Rivalry's history. Only one other Lehigh-Lafayette game, barring games ending in a tie, was decided by a lesser margin — Lafayette defeated Lehigh by a score of 13-12 in 1929. The game was so intense that fights not only broke out among the players on the field, but also among the spectators on the sidelines.

The end of the second game, played in Bethlehem, marked the beginning of a lasting tradition — The Bonfire. After the 16-0 victory, the Lehigh freshmen celebrated by setting fire to the grandstand. The torching of the grandstand was not only a victory celebration, but a way of demolishing the old grandstand so that a new one could be constructed — possibly the first hint of Taylor Stadium in its construction phase? The Lehigh students had long viewed the old grandstand as an eyesore and disgrace to the Athletic Grounds.

The bonfire created quite a stir in South Bethlehem that Saturday night, sounding a three-alarm fire that brought various Bethlehem fire companies to the flame. Once the companies learned it was the grandstand that was burning, they returned to their firehouses allowing the celebration to continue. Reportedly, the Easton Fire Company did not respond to the alarm after learning it was Lehigh's grandstand burning. They had previously heard of the intention to torch the grandstand if Lehigh was victorious and, according to the *Bethlehem Times*, copped the attitude, "It's only Lehigh, let it burn!"

In the shadows of the burning grandstand, Lehigh had gained the attention of the collegiate football world, finishing with an impressive 10-2 record in 1888.

Lehigh's "Iron Team" Wins Championship of Pennsylvania

Lehigh's 1889 squad was known as the "Iron Team" and was one of the school's best teams during the Early Years, compiling an 8-3-2 record. The nickname, the "Iron

Team," was coined after Lehigh defeated Navy, Johns Hopkins and Virginia the last three games of the season ... in three consecutive days!!!

In the Early Years, Lehigh, Lafayette, and the University of Pennsylvania played for the Championship of Pennsylvania. Each team would play the other two teams twice during the season. The team with the best record against its instate opponents was crowned "State Champions."

Historically, the University of Pennsylvania had the strongest teams and was regarded as the powerhouse of Pennsylvania football. However, in 1889, Lehigh mounted its own campaign to dethrone Penn. During the season, both Penn-Lafayette and Penn-Lehigh split their doubleheaders. In the first meeting with Lafayette, Lehigh emerged victorious by a score of 17-10. A victory over Lafayette in the second matchup of the season would earn Lehigh the state title.

On paper, Lehigh had the stronger team. The Brown and White lived up to its pregame billing by jumping out to an early 6-0 lead in the first half. Lafayette, on its home field, stormed back to even the score late in the second half. In a hotly-contested battle, Lehigh escaped from Easton with a 6-6 tie, and its first Championship of Pennsylvania. Against the Pennsylvania rivals, Penn finished 2-2, Lafayette 1-2-1, and Lehigh 2-1-1.

Lehigh's 1889 Team: Champions of Pennsylvania

Lehigh Misses Chance to Join the Ivy League

One of the more intriguing games of the 1889 season did not involve the Lehigh-Lafayette matchup. Instead, the game between Lehigh and Wesleyan would have an everlasting impact on the future of The Rivalry.

In the late 1880's, conferences and leagues did not exist. There was only the Intercollegiate Football Association consisting of Harvard, Penn, Princeton, Yale, and Wesleyan. Wesleyan was clearly the best team at the time. Of the other independents, Lehigh had won similar acclaim in its section of the country, compiling a 10-2 record in 1888. The Lehigh-Wesleyan game, scheduled for Thanksgiving Day 1889 at Hamden Park in Springfield, Massachusetts, was billed the "Battle for the Ivy" with the winner becoming the front-runner for consideration into what would become the Ivy League.

In the midst of a torrential downpour and a mighty sea of mud, Lehigh jumped to an 11-0 advantage by scoring a field goal, touchdown, and extra point (at the time, a field goal was worth five points, a touchdown four points, and an extra point two points).

No Mas!

Lehigh left a mark on the record books in 1889 by defeating Penn State 106-0. That's not a misprint — Lehigh 106 Penn State 0. And yes, that's the same Penn State in Happy Valley that became a national power under legendary coach Joe Paterno.

The 106-0 defeat of Penn State is the largest margin of victory in Lehigh football history. It also marks the worst defeat ever suffered by the Nittany Lions, a record that will likely never be broken.

By the way, the offensive scoring display by Lehigh (and lack thereof by Penn State) all took place in a little over three quarters of play. The Penn State captain submitted to defeat with 15 minutes left in the game! Upon returning to the Penn State campus, the team captain Charles Aull exited the train and made the following announcement to the welcoming committee: "We couldn't get to the son of a bitch with the ball."

The game was literally a slugfest with play being stopped every few minutes in the first half due to players fighting. One incident was so severe, the police had to come onto the field to break it up.

At the start of the second half, Lehigh lost three key rushers to injury. Rafferty's collar bone was dislocated. Dislocated? That's what the medical report read. Crane had a 1-1/2 inch gash above his eye. To complete the "crippled list" (as it was called in the Early Years), Riddick's nose was broken and lost some of its natural beauty due to a tremendous slug.

With time running out, Wesleyan was in jeopardy of losing its standing in the prestigious Intercollegiate Football Association. Fueled by an inspirational cheerleader, Wesleyan staged a dramatic comeback .

Historian Carl F. Price captured the play-by-play action: "Suddenly, from the Wesleyan bleachers, a man walked out in front, clad in heavy rubber boots and a raincoat. He shouted to the Wesleyan contingent, reproaching them for not cheering for their

Woodrow Wilson — a professor and cheerleader at Wesleyan who helped keep Lehigh out of the Ivy League.

"Woodrow Wilson couldn't keep the United States out of World War I, but he was apparently responsible for keeping Lehigh out of the Ivy League."

— Frank Claps, Lafayette alumnus and former sports editor for the <u>Bethlehem Globe Times</u>.

team; and at once, he began to lead them in the Wesleyan yell, beating time for them with his umbrella."

Perhaps the mystery cheerleader had soaked up too many spirits during the pre-game rain dance? Whatever, Wesleyan, inspired by the cheers, mounted its comeback and scored a touchdown and extra point closing the score to 11-6. Shortly thereafter, with darkness rapidly approaching, Wesleyan converted a field goal from 45 yards to even the score 11-11. The Wesleyan fans, led by their new-found cheerleader, exploded with enthusiasm. By the time the melee was brought under control, the game was called due to darkness with 17 minutes still remaining.

Lehigh was denied admission to the Intercollegiate Football Association. The Brown and White, along with Lafayette, would eventually become affiliated with the Ivy League in 1984 as members of the Colonial League.

The identity of the rubber-wearing, raincoat-clad cheerleader was eventually disclosed.

"After the game, the Lehigh men, inquiring about the magnetic cheerleader, were informed that he was a Wesleyan history professor," according to Price.

The gentleman's name — Dr. Woodrow Wilson, who would later become the 28th President of the United States in 1913.

Lafayette's Other Rival

Similarly, one of Lafayette's more bizarre games of the 1889 season was not against rival Lehigh, but was against its other instate opponent, the University of Pennsylvania.

The Penn contest more closely resembled a WWF wrestling match than a football game. Eventually, the chief slugging offender for Lafayette, Wells, was ejected from the contest. Although officially ejected, Wells was not through for the day. As a Penn rusher made a dash for the end zone along the sideline,

Wells jumped off the bench and tripped him short of the goal line.

After gaining his feet, the Penn rusher charged toward Wells only to be intercepted by a mob of Lafayette students who pummeled the Penn rusher. According to one onlooker, the Penn rusher left the pileup with "a pair of pretty black eyes, a battered nose, and torn ligaments in his leg."

Pandemonium ensued, and the Lafayette fans, armed with stones and clubs, chased the Penn team from campus securing the Maroon's 10-8 victory. It was sometime before relations were soothed and Penn returned to the Lafayette campus for a football game.

Incidentally, Lafayette's chances of joining the Athletic Association (Ivy League) were weakened when its relationship with Penn soured. As long as Penn was in the league, the Association was hesitant to vote in a team that exhibited such "rowdyism" as Lafayette.

Lafayette and Lehigh, facing similar fates in their attempts to join the Ivy League, continued to build the Lafayette-Lehigh football game tradition and rivalry. The wide-open tailgates of Lafayette-Lehigh games would never be replaced by the stuffiness of Ivy League mixers.

Lafayette Struck by Forked Lightning

The first true star of a Lehigh-Lafayette football game emerged in 1890. An exceptional individual performance by Lehigh fullback Hutchinson paced a 66-6 rout of Lafayette in The Rivalry's second matchup of the season. Hutchinson was unstoppable, accounting for 26 of Lehigh's 66 points, as he rushed for five touchdowns and kicked three extra points. Hutchinson scored one touchdown by faking a punt.

Hutchinson had his way against Lafayette that Saturday afternoon, using cutbacks to elude and bursts of speed to outrun the Lafayette defenders. After the game, one enthusiastic Bethlehem man exclaimed, "That Hutchinson, he's as quick as forked lightning." For reference, according to the most recent conversion tables, a bolt of forked lightning in the 1890's is as quick as greased lightning in the 1990's.

Hoop It Up!

By the time Dr. James Naismith invented the game of basketball in 1891, Lehigh and Lafayette had already played 14 football games in their historic rivalry.

Lafayette's First Head Coach

From 1884 to 1890, the captains of the Lehigh and Lafayette squads also acted as coaches. In 1891, Lafayette unveiled a secret weapon — a "professional" head coach. W. S. Moyle, a standout player for Yale, became the first paid coach for Lafayette in that year. The paycheck for his first season was $400, collected by passing the hat among alumni. Moyle also played halfback for the team his first two seasons as coach until the faculty disapproved.

After an era of student mentors, Moyle is credited with teaching the benefits of real teamwork to his young Lafayette football squads. Moyle's affiliation with Yale added a "big time" football flavor to the Lafayette program during his two years as head coach.

A Triple-Header

The addition of a paid coach to the Lafayette football repertoire in 1891 did not "pay-off" as Lehigh swept a triple-header from Lafayette. The teams lined-up against each other an unprecedented three times, instead of the customary doubleheader in previous years.

Lehigh defeated the Maroon 22-4 in the first game in Bethlehem.

At the rematch in Easton, Lehigh won a close contest, 6-2, on an error in judgement by Lafayette's March. With just 30 seconds left in a scoreless first half, March attempted an unsuccessful fake punt. Lehigh took possession and scored the game's only touchdown two plays later to end the first half. The touchdown was the deciding factor, as Lafayette manage only a safety in the second half.

The interest in the Lehigh-Lafayette rivalry spread, prompting the schools to add a third game scheduled for the day before Thanksgiving in Wilkes-Barre.

The Game attracted 3,000 spectators, the largest crowd to ever witness a football game in Wilkes-Barre at that time. The exuberant cheering students startled the Wilkes-Barre natives, who were not accustomed to a rivalry as intense as Lehigh-Lafayette.

The Wilkes-Barre contest stands as the only time in The Series' history that The Game was not played in the cities of Bethlehem or Easton. Lehigh completed the 1891 trifecta by outscoring Lafayette 16-2 at the neutral field.

Lehigh's First Head Coach

In the spirit of The Rivalry, Lehigh followed suit in the 1892 season by hiring its own head coach, J.A. Harwell. With both teams sporting head coaches, The Game took on a slightly different look. As the football programs became more organized, leadership and teamwork were exemplified on and off the field.

Lafayette and Lehigh split their double-header in 1892.

At the first game in Easton, Lafayette's Moyle used a "hands-on" approach to coaching. According to media sources covering the game, "Moyle, during a slight scrap in the second half, deliberately came up behind Lehigh's right end Van Cleve and kicked him, thus disabling him for a short time." Moyle's aggressive coaching style proved effective in Lafayette's 4-0 victory over Lehigh. Lafayette scored the game's only touchdown by forming a mighty "V" that carried Harry Rockwell over the goal line.

Lehigh escaped the wrath of coach Moyle and the mighty "V" formation in the re-match in Bethlehem and emerged with a 15-6 victory.

J. A. Harwell's coaching career was short-lived. Harwell lasted only one season in South Bethlehem. H. S. Graves took over in 1893.

In 1893 and 1894, Lehigh took three-of-four from Lafayette, including two victories on Lehigh's home grounds.

In 1894, a star emerged for Lafayette in its 28-0 victory over Lehigh in Easton — halfback George "Rose" Barclay. The future Lafayette Hall-of-Famer scored 24 of Lafayette's 28 points, including two 80-yard touchdown runs and four goals after touchdown.

Lehigh established home-field supremacy over Lafayette during the Early Years. After a scoreless tie in 1886, Lafayette did not defeat Lehigh in Bethlehem for the next eight years. In contrast, Lehigh compiled a 4-3-1 record over Lafayette in games in Easton from 1887 to 1894.

Lehigh's home field dominance was soon to end, due to the arrival of one man on the Easton campus — Parke H. Davis.

Lehigh's First All-American

As Lehigh made a name for itself in the collegiate football world, it was just a matter of time before one of its players received national attention. The recognition finally came when Walter Camp named Lehigh's D. M. Balliet to his All-American team of 1891. Balliet was a three-year starter at center for Lehigh and anchored the Brown and White's "Iron Team" of 1889 that finished with an 8-3-1 record.

A Record Setting Run!

In the second Lehigh - Lafayette game of 1892, Goodwin Ordway, the right halfback for Lehigh, made a magnificent 110-yard run for a touchdown on a fumble recovery. Ordway picked up a fumble on the 10-yard line and ran 110 yards for a touchdown! The field was 120-yards long at the time. The run marks the longest in the history of the Lehigh-Lafayette football series — a record that may never be broken.

TIMEOUT

Lehigh-Lafayette Games Played in Bethlehem (1887-1894)

		SCORE	
Year	Winner	Lehigh	Lafayette
1887	Lehigh	10 -	4
1888	Lehigh	16 -	0
1889	Lehigh	16 -	10
1890	Lehigh	66 -	0
1891	Lehigh	22 -	4
1892	Lehigh	15 -	6
1893	Lehigh	22 -	6
1894	Lehigh	11 -	8
TOTAL SCORE		178 -	38
RECORD		8-0	0-8

Lehigh-Lafayette Games Played in Easton (1887-1894)

		SCORE	
Year	Winner	Lehigh	Lafayette
1887	Lafayette	0 -	6
1888	Lehigh	6 -	4
1889	Tie	6 -	6
1890	Lehigh	30 -	0
1891	Lehigh	6 -	2
1892	Lafayette	0 -	4
1893	Lehigh	10 -	0
1894	Lafayette	0 -	28
TOTAL SCORE		58 -	50
RECORD		4-3-1	3-4-1

Parke H. Davis Arrives in Easton

"With the advent of Mr. Davis, little Lafayette stepped from comparative obscurity to a level with the football giants."

— Francis A. March, Jr.

Parke Davis made his coaching debut at Lafayette in 1895 after coaching Wisconsin and Amherst. Francis A. March Jr. in his 1926 book, *Athletics at Lafayette College*, called Davis the "first of Lafayette's great coaches."

As an undergraduate, Davis played tackle for the Princeton eleven, where he was coached by future President of the United States Woodrow Wilson. While Davis was coaching Amherst, one of his student-managers was another future President, Calvin Coolidge. Davis coached Lafayette from 1895-1898 and also served as Athletic Director in 1896.

As coach at Lafayette, Davis jump-started the football program, working the student body and town of Easton into a football frenzy. He instituted college student body meetings, the forerunner to "smokers," known later as pep rallies. Davis, showing he was a true disciple of Woodrow Wilson, invented new cheers and composed songs, including "Ring the Bells of Old South College," to build morale and support for the football team.

He was a masterful innovator of plays and motivator of players. As March revealed, "Davis was able to make his players think they were invincible." His colorful personality and charisma lured hundreds more fans through the turnstiles. For Davis' first contest against Lehigh, the game-time jam at the ticket window was so great that several men had to be sent into the mob to expedite ticket sales.

During his years at Lafayette, Davis firmly established a system for conducting athletics at Lafayette. Mr. Davis not only coached football, but coached year-round for all sports. He established the training table and recruiting program on College Hill.

After his coaching days at Lafayette, Davis became an expert on the history of football. He covered games for the *New York Herald* and other newspapers, wrote numerous magazine articles, and authored the football section in *The Encyclopedia Britannica*. He kept volumi-

The First "Smokers"

Lehigh helped fuel The Rivalry by holding its first "smoker" in 1895.

A "smoker," held the night before the game, was the Early Years' version of a "pep rally." Some of the activities associated with the "smoker" included wrestling and boxing matches, speeches by the coaches, faculty, and players, and singing of fight songs and football cheers. The use of tobacco products was prevalent during the "smoker," hence its name.

"Smokers," held by both schools, became a traditional part of the pregame festivities.

Lafayette held its first official "smoker" in 1898 devoted solely to raising enthusiasm for the Lehigh game.

nous records and edited historical sections of *Spalding's Guide,* the annual official football publication, until his death in 1934. A recognized authority on football records and statistics, Davis also served on the National Rules Committee for College Football with Walter Camp from 1909 to 1915.

Lehigh, caught in the jetwash of Lafayette's newly constructed football machine, wished Davis had stayed at Amherst. Lafayette's rejuvenated football team came to Bethlehem in 1895 and did what no other Lafayette team had been able to do for the past eight years — beat Lehigh on its home field. Davis and Lafayette defeated the Brown and White both games in 1895 by a score of 22-12 in Bethlehem and 14-6 in Easton. During the game in Bethlehem, halfback George Barclay rushed for an 85-yard touchdown, the longest run from scrimmage to date in The Series' history.

The Year Without a Lehigh-Lafayette Game

By 1896, the twelve-year, 25-game rivalry between Lafayette and Lehigh was as strong as ever. At this juncture, Lehigh had won 13 games to Lafayette's 10, with two deadlocks. The schools were looking forward to the two games scheduled in 1896.

A week before the first game, Lehigh questioned the eligibility of Lafayette halfback George Barclay, who had ripped through Lehigh's defense for eight touchdowns in the past two years. Lehigh authorities claimed Barclay had previously played professional baseball and therefore could not participate in collegiate athletics.

Lafayette argued that although Barclay had played for the Chambersburg semi-pro baseball team the summer before, he had not been paid. Chambersburg covered only legitimate expenses associated with his travel. Lehigh countered with evidence that Barclay had received from Chambersburg: (1) round-trip railroad transportation from Easton to Chambersburg, (2) room and board while at Chambersburg, and (3) $35 cash, which Lehigh construed as a salary.

Through the course of committee examinations, cross-examinations, and re-examinations, Lafayette and Lehigh failed to settle their dispute before the first game. The Lafayette-Lehigh games for 1896 were cancelled, thus interrupting what would have become the longest, consecutive rivalry in football history. As it stands, the Lehigh-Lafayette game is still the most-played rivalry in football history (130 games played from 1884 to 1994). Fueled by the controversy of 1896, the Lehigh-Lafayette rivalry was restored in 1897 and has been played every year since.

A difference of only $35 kept Lafayette and Lehigh from maintaining the longest, continuous rivalry in college football history. Perhaps, a plea-bargaining lawyer could have worked a deal with the committee so that Barclay would only play "half" of the Lehigh-Lafayette football game since he had only played "semi-pro" baseball.

Lafayette – 1896 National Champions

"... To Lafayette belongs the distinction of being the first small college to beat a member of the so-called Big Four. This red-letter event occurred on October 24, 1896, when Captain Walbridge's 'Davids' stoned Pennsylvania's 'Goliaths' on Franklin Field."

— excerpt from George Trevor's <u>New York Sun</u> article, 1931

During the year without a Lafayette-Lehigh game, the Maroon produced one of its finest football teams in the school's history. The squad finished the season undefeated with a 11-0-1 record, earning a share of the National Championship with Princeton.

The two national football powers in 1896 were Princeton and Penn of the Big Four (Penn, Princeton, Yale, and Harvard). Lafayette fought Princeton to a 0-0 tie early in the season. Later, under the leadership of coach Parke Davis, Lafayette upset a Penn team that was riding a 34-game win streak and had not been defeated in three years. To understand just how dominating the Penn football program was at this time, after the Lafayette defeat, Penn went on to win 31 in a row. That's a 65-1 record over six years.

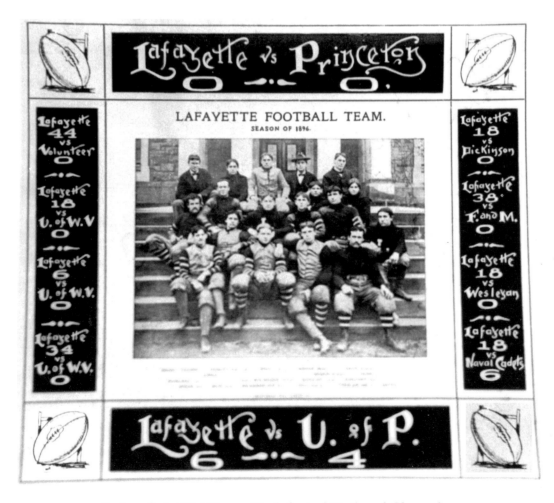

Lafayette's 1896 Team: Undefeated National Champions

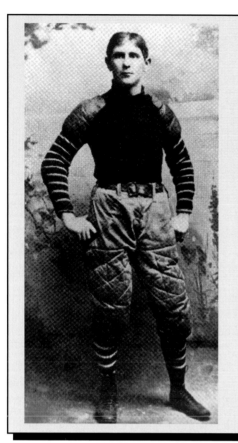

The First Football Helmet

George Barclay, halfback for Lafayette, is credited with inventing the first football helmet in 1896, when he wore leather strips on his head to prevent cauliflower ears.

Barclay's prototype helmet, called a "head harness," was made by an Easton saddlemaker from harness padding and rivets.

In the Early Years, players that donned helmets were considered "pansies." Barclay, who was nicknamed "Rose" because of his good looks and keen eye for the ladies, chose to take the abuse in return for protecting his tender ears and pretty mug.

Barclay's prototype helmet was dramatically improved over the years, prompting the NCAA to make helmets mandatory in 1939, and the NFL in 1943.

Lafayette provided the only blemish on one of college football's most impressive win streaks!

During the late 1800's, there was no love lost between Lafayette and Penn. The early Lafayette-Penn matchups nearly approached, but certainly did not exceed, the intensity of the early Lafayette-Lehigh games.

An unfortunate situation confronted Lafayette before the 1896 Penn game. Enroute to Philadelphia on the team train, halfback and captain George Walbridge was stricken with acute appendicitis. Before going to the hospital, Walbridge delivered a "pep" talk to the team, giving Lafayette its own version of "Let's win one for the Gipper!"

The pep talk inspired the team, which proceeded to defeat the mighty Penn Quakers by a 6-4 score. Lafayette's only touchdown was set up by a George Barclay fake punt, which advanced the ball to Penn's five-yard line. Two plays later, Barclay rushed around right end for Lafayette's only score, then kicked the game-winning extra point.

Lafayette's firm stance on Barclay's playing eligibility in 1896 paid dividends as his tremendous play against Penn almost single-handedly won Lafayette the National Championship.

During the Penn contest, Barclay unveiled his newly-found football helmet invention to prevent cauliflower ear. Barclay's crude football helmet was made of leather strips that were attached to the side of a player's head.

With Penn's victory over Harvard later the same year, Lafayette, along with Princeton, claimed its share of the National Championship. Even in the Early Years before

The Babe

The 1897 season brought an end to the outstanding collegiate career of one of Lafayette's finest linemen, Charles "Babe" Rinehart. Standing 6' 3" and weighing 225 pounds, the native of Phillipsburg, New Jersey, was a giant in his time.

Rinehart was picked as a guard on Walter Camp's All-American team in 1897, a tremendous honor for a small-school player during the Early Years when All-American status was rarely given to a player outside of the Big Four (Harvard, Yale, Penn, and Princeton).

In 1964, he was inducted into the Hall of Fame of the National Football Foundation. In 1969, he was named to the Eastern College Athletic Conference All-Star team of the best players during the first half century of college football. In 1976, Lafayette selected The Babe as a member of the Maroon Club Athletic Hall of Fame.

Lafayette's Charles "The Babe" Rinehart and a Friend.

"Charles R. Rinehart, guard at Lafayette...was the peer of any player who ever wore a cleated shoe. He stood 6'3" high, weighed 225 pounds, and was solid thew, bone, and muscle. ... His feet were as fleet as as those of Perseus. He knew every detail of football technique and his mind was a flashing dynamo of football wisdom. He could make openings and hold them open; he could lead an interference around either end and block one tackler after another. He could cover kicks and carry the ball around the end, send the kick-off booming up the field, and in practice drop-kick goals at 65 yards."
    — Parke Davis's Memorial to Rinehart in the Football Guide of 1934

Associated Press, United Press, and coaches' polls, "Who's Number One?" and co-champion controversies were commonplace.

Lafayette truly deserved part, if not all, of the 1896 National Championship. Lafayette, with a 11-0-1 record, allowed only 10 points on defense the entire season — a remarkable performance during any football era. The only ingredient missing from Lafayette's 1896 National Championship season was a victory over Lehigh. Unfortunately, one can only speculate what the outcome of a Lafayette-Lehigh matchup would have been. With the National Championship at stake for Lafayette, it would have been an old-fashioned donnybrook!

A special cigar, the "Lafayette Stonewall," was named in honor of the 1896 Lafayette team, and a team picture was attached to the cigar box lid. A new fight song titled "Rah! Rah! Rah! Lafayette!" was dedicated to the 1896 team.

Parke Davis carried his success into the 1897 season, blanking Lehigh by scores of 34-0 and 22-0. Five different players scored touchdowns in Lafayette's 34-0 romp. Gus Weidemeyer scored all three touchdowns for the Maroon in the second game.

In the first game of 1898, Lehigh responded by reversing the score 22-0 in Lehigh's favor. The victory was highlighted by James Ross's 100-yard punt return for a touchdown on a playing field that was 110 yards at the time.

The stage was set for the rematch in the season finale which would be the last game of the Parke Davis's illustrious coaching career at Lafayette and The Rivalry's first Snow Bowl.

The Snow Bowl

"Sunshine is delicious, rain is refreshing, wind braces up, snow is exhilarating; there is no such thing as bad weather, only different kinds of good weather."

— John Ruskin

On Thanksgiving Day, November 24, 1898, Lafayette and Lehigh met for the 29th time. But this would be different than any other game previously played in The Rivalry. The entire contest was played in a blizzard, thus earning the distinction of being the first Snow Bowl in The Series.

The driving snowstorm dumped four inches of fresh powder on the field during the course of the game. A brave crowd of 1,500 spectators at the Easton Athletic Grounds weathered the storm, which at times made it impossible to distinguish the players of one team from the other.

In the first half, Lehigh took advantage of a strong wind at its back and a poor punting performance by Lafayette's inexperienced kicker, Carter, to score a touchdown on a 20-yard punt return. The point-after-attempt failed and the half ended with Lehigh leading 5-0 (in 1898, the scoring system was changed making a touchdown worth five points instead of four and the extra point worth one point instead of two).

At the start of the second half, the weather and field conditions had deteriorated to a point where both teams were forced into a kicking contest. With this in mind, Parke

Davis exercised his coaching brilliance by inserting fullback Ed Bray, who had sat out the first half because of a badly strained shoulder, to take over the kicking chores for Carter.

With Bray, Lafayette's masterful punter, in the lineup, captain Best gave the signal for Lafayette to punt after every first down. The strong wind and blinding snow made the punts very difficult to handle. Eventually, after several punt exchanges, a Lehigh back mishandled one of Bray's booming kicks, and Lafayette secured the ball on Lehigh's five-yard line. On the next play, Lafayette pushed the ball over the goal line and kicked the extra point giving Lafayette a 6-5 advantage.

Bray's magnificent punting kept Lehigh out of scoring range in the second half. Late in the game, Lafayette reached Lehigh's 45 yard-line and attempted the near-impossible task of kicking a field goal.

Captain Best, the holder, and Bray, the kicker, scraped away the four inches of slush and snow so the ball could be placed on the ground for the attempt. The big fullback's foot booted the ball over the Lehigh line and into the vast whiteness of the snowstorm, true to its mark between the goalposts.

The visibility was so poor that the crowd at first was silent, not knowing exactly what had happened. Several minutes later, the word spread that the kick was good, and the crowd exploded with applause for the amazing feat (or foot) of Ed Bray. His kick gave Lafayette an 11-5 advantage, which is how the game ended.

Parke Davis's strategy, Ed Bray's foot, and an old-fashioned blizzard sent Lehigh home, a bitterly-cold loser.

The 1898 Snow Bowl was the last game coached by Parke Davis at Lafayette, but his coaching legacy continued. Davis embellished a football tradition at Lafayette that influenced the long list of coaching greats on College Hill.

The First Placement Kick

The drop kick had been the preferred field goal kicking method during the Early Years. Dr. Randolph Faries, a track man from the University of Pennsylvania, invented a new method — the placement kick. During Penn's game against Harvard in 1897, the Quaker's Bill Morice held the football on the ground, and John Minds kicked the ball through the uprights for the first successful field goal by placement kick.

The First Indoor Football Game

While Lehigh and Lafayette were battling the elements in Pennsylvania, two northern schools found a different way to brave the weather — by playing indoors. In 1892, the University of Chicago, coached by football immortal Alonzo Stagg, played Northwestern inside Tattersall's Riding Academy using an electric lighting system. The field was a tanbark floor 20 yards short of regulation.

Ed Bray's miraculous field goal during the 1898 Snow Bowl.

From 1895 to 1898, Davis compiled a 29-12-2 record at Lafayette. Next in line was Dr. Silvanis Newton, who took over as head coach in 1899.

Dr. Newton Takes Charge at Lafayette

"Dr. Newton was the cleverest coach the college ever had."
— *Francis A. March, Jr. in his book Athletics at Lafayette College*

Easton's football enthusiasts welcomed Dr. Newton to Lafayette in 1899. The new Maroon coach was a Phi Beta Kappa scholar, a renowned physician, a master of the theoretical aspects of football, and an inventor of new formations.

Newton is credited with perfecting the art of placement kicking at Lafayette and implementing the "guards back" formation which proved to be too powerful for the Lehigh eleven. A Lehigh football player observed that with the "guards back" formation, the Lafayette line could pound through the Lehigh defense with the force of a battering ram. Newton was also a great improvisor. During one season, the coach lost his starting quarterback to injury, so he recruited a baseball player, scratched a few useful plays on the recruit's well-starched jersey cuff, and sent him onto the field.

S.B. Newton — the only head coach to lead both Lehigh and Lafayette to victories in The Rivalry.

Newton's Lafayette teams dominated Lehigh from 1899 to 1901. In three seasons, Lafayette defeated Lehigh six straight times by a combined score of 174-0. Halfback Harry Trout provided the offensive firepower for the Maroon in 1899 and 1900, scoring eight touchdowns in four games. Lafayette recorded its fifth and sixth consecutive shutouts against the

Brown and White in 1901 by scores of 29-0 and 41-0.

During his three-year coaching career at Lafayette, Newton compiled an overall record of 30 wins, 6 losses, and 0 ties, including a 12-1 record in his first season.

If You Can't Beat 'Em, Hire Their Head Coach

"They made me an offer I couldn't refuse."
— Dr. Newton's response to becoming Lehigh's new head coach

Lehigh, tired of being defeated and out-smarted by its local rival, decided to make some changes for the 1902 season.

The first step was to find a way to get rid of Newton, who had successfully led Lafayette to six straight victories over the Brown and White. Lehigh not only got rid of Newton, but did itself one better. Offering a very attractive salary, Lehigh lured Newton away from Lafayette and hired him as its head coach for the 1902 season.

Walter "Scrappy" Bachman

The backbone of Newton's successful Lafayette teams was center, Walter "Scrappy" Bachman. Bachman is credited with developing the roving center concept on defense. During his senior year, he captained the 1901 Lafayette squad that finished 9-3, including two victories over Lehigh.

In Bachman's four years as Lafayette's starting center, the Maroon defeated arch-rival Lehigh seven of eight times.

Walter Camp selected Bachman on his All-American teams of 1900 and 1901. Bachman was inducted into Lafayette's Athletic Hall of Fame in 1977.

The second step was to play The Game one time each year, instead of the customary two games a year. Both schools agreed that a rivalry as fierce as Lafayette-Lehigh should be contested only once a year at the culmination of the season. The single-game format was in the best interest of the players, since serious injuries occurred frequently in the Lehigh-Lafayette match. Playing at the end of the season would give the coaches more time to prepare for The Game and offer a fitting climax to the year. The new schedule would also concentrate into a single day the visits of Alumni and friends to the campuses.

And so a historic change to the Lafayette-Lehigh rivalry was instituted. Since 1902, the schools have met once a season. The lone exception was during the World War II era when scheduling and travel restrictions forced the teams to play twice a year in 1943 and '44.

The changes paid off instantly for Lehigh. A crowd of 5,000, the largest in The Series' history at the time, flocked to Easton to witness the 1902 game. Lehigh's fans arrived in a 17-car train to watch the ex-Lafayette coach lead his Lehigh squad to a 6-0 victory.

"After Hours" Smoker

In 1903, some of the "smoke" from the Lehigh smoker escaped to downtown Bethlehem. When the smoker ended, the Lehigh students were not through preparing themselves for the Lafayette game. Upon leaving the gymnasium, the students lined-up four abreast and marched to the Grand Opera House in Bethlehem, singing and yelling football cheers. Impassioned, the students sought to perform the Lehigh fight songs on stage in front of a live audience.

As the ensemble approached the Opera House doors, the manager, Mr. Goodwin, promptly informed the students that he could not allow them to interrupt the night's performance with football cheers.

The enthusiastic students did not take kindly to the denial. The crowd of 200 stormed into the lobby and crashed the doors of the Opera House. Mr. Goodwin, overwhelmed by the melee and obviously not pleased with the quality of the show, notified Chief of Police Kelly who immediately showed up with reinforcements.

After several minutes, the students were dispersed, but only after they had given the Opera House one of its more memorable performances.

Lehigh's First Mascot

During the 1903 Game, Lehigh unveiled its first mascot. The freshmen on South Mountain caught a goat which they dressed in brown and white blankets with ribbon trimmings. The goat, paraded on the field during pregame, created quite a spectacle. One photographer, trying to capture a Kodak moment, got a bit too close for the mascot's liking. The goat stood his ground and bucked the photographer head over heels, giving new meaning to the word "kick-off."

Unsportsmanlike Conduct

In 1903, Newton again performed magic by coaching Lehigh to a 12-6 victory over his former Lafayette team before a record crowd of 10,000 in Bethlehem.

The game was notorious for a brawl between team captains John Ernst of Lafayette and Andy Farabaugh of Lehigh. According to *The Lafayette*, Farabaugh became upset after Ernst scored on a spectacular 25-yard run. "After the ball had been downed, Farabaugh made a cowardly attempt to put Ernst out of the game by jumping on his back, without any provocation whatever. The action was very unsportsmanlike ... and especially deserving of censure coming from the Lehigh captain." Ernst recovered from the blow to kick the extra point and tie the score 6-6. Lehigh regained its composure after the scuffle to score a late touchdown and a 12-6 victory.

Wherever Dr. Newton went, victories in The Rivalry followed. Newton coached in eight Lehigh-Lafayette games from 1899 to 1903 and did not suffer a defeat, even though he switched schools. Newton holds the distinction of being the only person to coach both Lehigh and Lafayette to victory in College Football's Most-Played Rivalry.

Postponed

The 1904 Lehigh-Lafayette game was postponed one week due to the untimely death of Lehigh's President, Dr. Henry S. Drown. Dr. Drown served as Lehigh President from 1895 until his death in 1904. Previously, Drown was a professor of analytical chemistry at Lafayette from 1874 to 1881.

Penalty-Free Game

In 1904, Lafayette and Lehigh played the entire game without a penalty being assessed — a first and probably last in The Series' history. Despite the intense competition, not one infraction occurred.

Perhaps, the Lafayette and Lehigh players had a change of heart and decided to play a clean, fair contest? More likely, it was a lack of officiating.

Newton's luck ran out in 1904, when another doctor, Alfred Bull, a former Penn All-American center and new Lafayette coach, handed Newton his first defeat in a Lehigh-Lafayette game. Dr. Bull's squad performed surgery on Dr. Newton's eleven, sending them to the emergency room on the short end of the score, 40-6. Lafayette's James Van Atta scored three second-half touchdowns and was a perfect six-for-six in the kicking department.

The Lehigh students unleashed a new fight song entitled "Yow, Lehigh!" for the Lafayette game. After Lafayette jumped to an early lead, the chant was noticeably absent from the Lehigh student section in the second half.

The loss wasn't due to a lack of effort by Dr. Newton, who tried every play in the book to propel his Lehigh squad to victory. On the first play of the game, Newton called for an onside kick, the first in The Game's history. The onside kick was unsuccessful against a well-prepared Maroon squad. Later, Lehigh attempted a lateral backward pass 20 yards across the field on a kickoff return. It, too, was unsuccessful, as one Lafayette player was not tricked by the play and stayed at home to make the tackle. It appeared that Lafayette was almost expecting the trick plays from Lehigh. Perhaps, they knew their former coach too well.

Lafayette Leaders Support The Rivalry

During Lafayette's smoker in Brainerd Hall before the 1905 Lafayette-Lehigh game, ex-coach Parke Davis delivered an inspirational speech to the students and predicted a big victory for the Maroon. Professor March ended the smoker by defending college football and the Lafayette-Lehigh rivalry. During an era when football was under tremendous scrutiny by school administrations because of violence and injuries associated with the game, March's stance was a bold and important one. March stressed the positive aspects of the sport, describing football "as a manly game with an excellent appeal for clean, straightforward playing."

Dr. Bull's Lafayette team bullied Lehigh again in 1905, this time by a score of 53-0, Lafayette's largest margin of victory in The Series at the time. The Maroon was led by

Frank Newberry, who scored two touchdowns and kicked eight goals after touchdown. *The Lafayette* reported that the Brown and White did not provide an offensive threat all afternoon, and "Lehigh's defense, although plucky, was extremely ragged."

With his luck run dry, Dr. Newton retired from football after the 1905 season to pursue a medical career full time. The doc's retirement was short-lived, as Newton came back to Easton one last time in 1911 to coach Lafayette to a 11-0 victory over Lehigh, this time officially ending his Lehigh-Lafayette coaching career on a winning note.

First Quarter Wrap-Up (1884-1905)

Lafayette-Lehigh fans, the referee's whistle has blown signalling an end to the first quarter of play in The Series.

In the Early Years, there have been highlights, lowlights, record-setting performances, and performances that some would rather forget. Traditions were established, hard-fought football games were played, and controversy prevailed — all building the foundation to one of sport's greatest rivalries.

A recap of the first quarter of play reveals there is not much that didn't happen in the Lehigh-Lafayette series during its first 22 years. Here's what happened:

- ✔🖎 There have been Founding Fathers, Sportswriters, Authors, War Correspondents, friends of Presidents, Presidents posing as cheerleaders, and even a handshake with The Babe.

- ✔🖎 After a series of blowouts, shutouts, close calls, and comebacks, things got so heated that a break in the action was necessary in 1896.

- ✔🖎 There have been student coaches, professional head coaches, coaches who were doctors, and an ex-coach of one team coaching the other team.

- ✔🖎 Games featured good officiating, bad officiating, and apparently no officiating in the penalty-free game of 1904.

- ✔🖎 Record-setters, stars, and a goat contributed to the pageantry.

- ✔🖎 History was made when a professional baseball player invented the first football helmet.

- ✔🖎 On the field, there was line-bucking and goat-bucking.

- ✔🖎 Off the field, there were smokers, parades, and a bonfire.

- ✔🖎 Uninvited guests crashed a rare Opera House performance.

- ✔🖎 The Games were filled with excitement, controversy, ejections, and injuries — and a "crippled list" determined how the teams were handicapped.

✔✎ In the medical reports, there have been fractured body parts, broken noses, and a dislocated collar bone.

✔✎ An inspirational pregame speech ended with an emergency appendectomy.

✔✎ The courtroom was visited to review an affidavit that influenced the verdict of the 1887 Game.

✔✎ Fans with ringside seats were treated to fights on the field, fights in the stands, fights among players, fights among fans, and fights among players and fans.

✔✎ Season ticketholders of The Rivalry witnessed single, double, and even triple-headers.

✔✎ Lehigh got poison Ivy in 1889. Lafayette got struck by forked lightning in 1890.

✔✎ A State Champion was celebrated and a National Champion with an undefeated record was crowned.

✔✎ Inclement weather doused The Rivalry with a rain out in 1896 and a Thanksgiving blizzard in 1898.

✔✎ But most of all, the first 39 games and 22 years of College Football's Most-Played Rivalry have just been relived.

There's more to come. Three quarters of football action remain along with the Halftime show and Postgame Wrap-Up.

Coaches' Notepad

First Quarter (1884-1905)

Lafayette Coaches: Records vs Lehigh

Coach	Seasons	Wins	Losses	Ties
Student Coaches	1884-1890	6	6	2
W.S Moyle	1891-1892	1	4	0
P.G. Haskell	1893	0	2	0
Janeway/Vincent	1894	1	1	0
Parke H. Davis	1895-1898	5	1	0
Dr. S.B. Newton	1899-1901	6	0	0
D.L. Fultz	1902	0	1	0
Dr. Alfred Bull	1903-1905	2	1	
Total		21	16	2

Lehigh Coaches: Records vs Lafayette

Coach	Seasons	Wins	Losses	Ties
Student Coaches	1884-1891	9	6	2
J.A. Harwell	1892	1	1	0
H.S. Graves	1893	2	0	0
W.W. Heffelfinger	1894	1	1	0
L.T. Bliss	1895	0	2	0
L.N. Morris	1896	0	0	0
S.M. Hammond	1897	0	2	0
H. Thompson	1898-1899	1	3	0
Walter Okeson	1900	0	2	0
J.W. Pollard	1901	0	2	0
Dr. S.B. Newton	1902-1905	2	2	
Total		16	21	2

First Quarter (1884-1905) Summary

Year	Where Played	Winner	SCORE Lafayette		Lehigh
1884	Easton	Lafayette	50	–	0
	Bethlehem	Lafayette	34	–	4
1885	Bethlehem	Lafayette	6	–	0
	Easton	Tie	6	–	6
1886	Easton	Lafayette	12	–	0
	Bethlehem	Lafayette	4	–	0
1887	Bethlehem	Lehigh	4	–	10
	Easton	Lafayette	6	–	0
1888	Easton	Lehigh	4	–	6
	Bethlehem	Lehigh	0	–	16
1889	Bethlehem	Lehigh	10	–	16
	Easton	Tie	6	–	6
1890	Easton	Lehigh	0	–	30
	Bethlehem	Lehigh	6	–	66
1891	Bethlehem	Lehigh	4	–	22
	Easton	Lehigh	2	–	6
	Wilkes-Barre	Lehigh	2	–	16
1892	Easton	Lafayette	4	–	0
	Bethlehem	Lehigh	6	–	15
1893	Bethlehem	Lehigh	6	–	22
	Easton	Lehigh	0	–	10
1894	Easton	Lafayette	28	–	0
	Bethlehem	Lehigh	8	–	11
1895	Bethlehem	Lafayette	22	–	12
	Easton	Lafayette	14	–	6
1896	No Game	No Game	No Game		No Game
1897	Easton	Lafayette	34	–	0
	Bethlehem	Lafayette	22	–	0
1898	Bethlehem	Lehigh	0	–	22
	Easton	Lafayette	11	–	5
1899	Easton	Lafayette	17	–	0
	Bethlehem	Lafayette	35	–	0
1900	Bethlehem	Lafayette	34	–	0
	Easton	Lafayette	18	–	0
1901	Easton	Lafayette	29	–	0
	Bethlehem	Lafayette	41	–	0
1902	Easton	Lehigh	0	–	6
1903	Bethlehem	Lehigh	6	–	12
1904	Easton	Lafayette	40	–	6
1905	Bethlehem	Lafayette	53	–	0
			584	–	331

	Wins	Losses	Ties
Lafayette	21	16	2
Lehigh	16	21	2

SECOND QUARTER
Building a Tradition
(1906-1949)

College football suffered a dark year in 1905. The *Chicago Tribune* reported 18 deaths and 159 serious injuries during the season. The game had become a test of brute force and broken bodies. There was a swell of public outcry and demands for abolition of the sport.

Columbia College faculty outlawed the game. Stanford and California abandoned football for rugby. Other colleges suspended play for a year.

President Teddy Roosevelt, a strong believer in the values of athletics, summoned representatives from Yale, Harvard, and Princeton and instructed them to find a way to save college football by removing its brutalizing features.

"Brutality and foul play," Roosevelt declared, "should receive the same summary punishment given to a man who cheats at cards."

In January of 1906, a newly-appointed rules committee met with the old governing body headed by Walter Camp. The two organizations merged, forming the American Intercollegiate Football Rules Committee, which would become the National Collegiate Athletic Association in 1910. The committee adopted a reform program that saved the game by opening it up, legalizing the forward pass, and banning dangerous activities.

After commissioning the committee to save college football, President Roosevelt spoke at Harvard University. His remarks set the tone for college football rivalries for years to come.

"Our concern should be most of all to widen the base, the foundation in athletic sports; to encourage in every way a healthy rivalry which shall give to the largest possible number of students the chance to take part in vigorous outdoor games."

With college football rejuvenated, a new era dawned on the Lafayette-Lehigh rivalry.

Holy Cow!

The hijinks off the field continued, unencumbered by the rule changes. Prior to The Game of 1906, a group of Lehigh seniors coaxed a cow, not only into Packer Hall, but up the stairs into the Lehigh President's Office, which was then located in the bell tower.

The First Forward Pass

In the first year after President Roosevelt intervened and helped establish a safer and friendlier football game, Lafayette blanked Lehigh 33-0 in The Game of 1906. Lafayette's Edward Flad threw the first forward pass in The Rivalry, a ten-yard completion to Chalmers, who scored two touchdowns on the day.

As the rule changes settled, a new style of play swept college football in 1907.

In the Lafayette-Lehigh game of that year, won by the Maroon 22-5, a series of firsts was recorded involving the forward pass.

The Forward Pass

Today's football purists would hardly recognize a pass play in 1906. The ball carrier (not necessarily the quarterback) was required to run five yards to the left or right of center and five yards back from center before attempting a pass.

An incomplete forward pass was considered a fumble. An incomplete pass was also a 15-yard penalty and a loss of down. The 15-yard penalty was discontinued in 1907.

A forward pass longer than 20 yards was illegal.

Initially, players passed the ball "end-over-end" like shooting a basketball, making it difficult to catch. The teams that perfected the overhand spiral pass had a distinct advantage over the "end-over-enders," which made for some severely lopsided scores during this era.

Another major rule change in 1906 required the offense to net ten yards in three downs to retain possession. Previously, the offense needed only five yards.

The first interception of a pass returned for a touchdown occurred, as George McCaa picked-off a Lehigh toss and returned it for a Leopard touchdown. And H. G. Lee of Lafayette was on the receiving end of Edward Flad's six-yard heave for the first touchdown pass in The Game's history.

Former Maroon standout George Barclay took the reign as Lafayette coach in 1908 and hoped to expand the passing attack. His troops finished six up and two down. Unfortunately for the Maroon, one of the losses was to Lehigh by an 11-5 score. The season-ending victory capped the Brown and White's second successive winning campaign, as Andrew Brumbaugh tallied two touchdowns.

A near-riot occurred as Lehigh faithful were leaving the Easton campus after the game. Cheering and chanting as they left College Hill, the South Bethlehem undergrads raised the ire of a number of Lafayette freshmen.

Newspaper accounts reported that "they (Lafayette frosh) rustled out in their shirt sleeves with the apparent intent of doing injury, but cool heads and superiority of numbers prevented the seeming danger of a riot on the steep steps."

The Year of Scandal

The undefeated Lafayette squad overpowered Lehigh 21-0 in the 1909 contest.

The 1909 game was notable for a record-setting circus touchdown pass of 50 yards by the Maroon. Quarterback William Dannehower took the snap at his own 45-yard line and pitched to tackle Aaron Crane in the backfield, who then hurled the ball downfield to Frank Irmschler for a touchdown.

In a controversial decision, Lafayette's first-year coach Bob Folwell did not allow third team All-American fullback George McCaa to participate in the Lehigh game because of an eligibility issue. Apparently, McCaa's four years of toting the ball for the

The 1909 Lafayette-Lehigh game ball which was used to score Lafayette's 50-yard flea-flicker touchdown pass in the Maroon's 21-0 victory.

Scalpers Prevail!

During The Year of Scandal in 1909, controversy hit even the Lehigh Administration, as complaints were filed against the University by Eastonians who were not pleased with their seat locations. Scalpers obtained choice seats, traveled to the confluence of the Lehigh and Delaware Rivers, and gouged the locals for tickets.

This did not deter Lafayette faithful from paying the inflated prices, as a special train on the Lehigh Valley Railroad was booked for game day. Additional trolley cars were scheduled for those desiring transportation to Bethlehem for The Game.

Maroon had expired before the Lehigh contest because of his participation in the 1905 season-ending match against Bucknell. McCaa almost earned a reprieve when it was discovered that he was technically eligible to play until November 26, six days after the Lehigh game. In the spirit of sportsmanship, Folwell followed the intent of the rule and sat McCaa.

The victors completed the season with a 7-0-1 record and the nation's number three ranking. Only a touchdown to Penn prevented Lafayette from finishing undefeated, untied, and unscored upon.

"Betting upon the game is not very brisk, for the Lehigh adherents, while hoping for a victory, do not seem to possess the courage of their convictions. It is probable that what little betting will take place will be upon the score, of upon Lehigh's chances of making a score."
— *Easton Express'* 1910 pregame editorial

Lafayette won its second straight over Lehigh by a 14-0 count before a capacity

Flag Day

A stadium tradition was unveiled by Lafayette during the 1910 season. School flags were raised and flown for each game, with the American flag in the middle. Lafayette was the first to establish this college football tradition.

Lafayette's school flag was developed by the Class of 1894. The flag is a field of maroon with a white cross forming four rectangles. In the top right rectangle appears the shield of Marquis de Lafayette.

crowd in Easton. Two long runs by John Spiegel set the stage for the Maroon's victory. Six thousand patrons attended the 1910 version at a soggy March Field, which had been covered with straw until game morning to absorb the rains of the prior days. By modern standards, the attendance proved small. But the seams were bursting at cozy March Field.

Winningest Lafayette Coach Resigns In Mid-Season

Coach Folwell departed for personal reasons after opening the 1911 season with five straight wins. He finished with a 19-2-1 record. All 19 of the triumphs were by shutouts. His .886 winning percentage leads all Lafayette coaches.

In *Athletics at Lafayette College* by Francis A. March Jr., Folwell expressed his farewell sentiments. "I took my last supper at the training table and the boys pledged me that if I went anywhere else to coach, and I wanted them to play for me they would. Spiegel afterwards did and made a great sensation in the football world at Washington and Jefferson."

Folwell resigned prior to Lafayette's game against the legendary Jim Thorpe and the Carlisle Indians. Thorpe's athletic exploits — as a track star, pro baseball and football player, and Olympian — were well-known and tickets were in high demand for the game at March Field. The man voted the outstanding athlete of the first half of the 20th

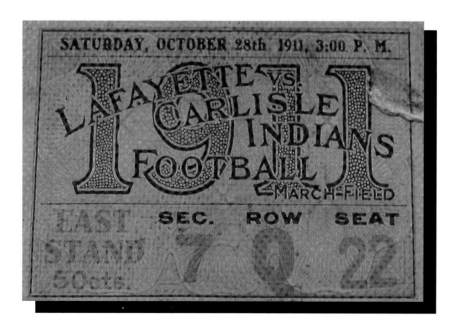

This ticket stub for the Lafayette-Carlisle football game in 1911 was found lodged in a door casing in an old house on Easton's Ferry Street. Preserved for several decades, the ticket was discovered by Mike Lucykanish in the fall of 1992 when he was renovating a room in his historic house.

century led the Indians to a 19-0 whitewashing of Lafayette in their only football contest against the Leopards.

Thorpe did make another appearance in Easton a year later. Competing for Carlisle in a track meet against Lafayette, the Indian scored 30 points by capturing first in six events. However, Thorpe finished third in the 100-yard dash, losing to Lafayette's John Spiegel, a halfback on the Maroon football team.

All-American V.J. (Pat) Pazzetti, Jr. leads Lehigh to victory in 1912.

S.B. Newton, who coached the Maroon from 1898 through 1901, returned to handle the chores for the balance of the 1911 season.

In a battle of present and future greats, senior captain William Dannehower out-dueled Lehigh All-American V.J. (Pat) Pazzetti Jr. In quarterbacking the Maroon for the third consecutive victory over its archrival, Dannehower passed for a score and kicked an extra point in the 11-0 whitewashing.

Lehigh's athletic grounds were modified to accommodate what promised to be the largest crowd ever at Taylor Field. The grandstand was moved back and raised, with additional bleachers placed in the front. Huge bleachers were also placed on the baseball diamond at the east end for general admission use. Thus began the blueprint for overflow seating which would mark the Taylor Stadium years.

The Rivalry Loses Ten Yards

Three major rule changes were implemented in 1912. First, a touchdown was now worth six points instead of five. Second, the offense had four downs instead of three to gain 10 yards. Third, the length of the field was reduced to 100 yards from 110, and end zones were established. The goalposts remained on the goal line until 1927, when they were moved to the end line.

Lafayette brought back S.B. Newton as an advisory coach to assist rookie coach McCaa in his first contest against Lehigh in 1912. This was the same Newton who coached Lehigh from 1902-1905 and Lafayette from

The Evolution of the College Football Scoring System

Year	Touchdown (points)	PAT (points)	Field Goal (points)	Safety (points)
1884	4	2	5	2
1897	5	1	5	2
1904	5	1	4	2
1909	5	1	3	2
1912	6	1	3	2
1958	6	1 (kick) 2 (run or pass)	3	2

1898-1901 and who played eight years of college football, for what could be the longest redshirt in college history. Newton played four seasons at Williams, and four more at Penn.

First-year coach Tom Keady directed Lehigh to a 10-0 triumph over Lafayette's coaching tandem. The Brown and White capped the year at 9-2, its best record since the 1888 team that finished 10-2. Meanwhile, the Maroon finished below .500 at 4-5-1, its worst season since the 3-8 squad of 1898 — coached by Newton.

All-American Pat Pazzetti Jr. led the Brown and White to victory. Known as one of greatest open-field runners of his time, Pazzetti threw the first touchdown pass in Lehigh history to George Sawtelle during the Lafayette contest.

Once again, it was bombs away in the 1913 contest. Albert Chenoweth replaced the departed Pazzetti at quarterback and duplicated his predecessor's performance in the 1912 game. The little 137-pound Texan tossed a game-winning touchdown to halfback Jim Keady, who was playing with blood poisoning. The Lehigh defense stifled Lafayette, blanking its guests 7-0.

The 78 Bethlehem police officers had their hands full as they tried to manage over 1,000 automobiles, 12,000 guests in the stands, and 500 gate-crashers who charged into Taylor Field in the fourth quarter when exits were opened in an effort to control the crowd.

Taking advantage of seven home games at the newly completed Taylor Stadium, Lehigh's 1914 team came into the Lafayette contest with a 7-1 record and a chance to claim the championship of the East. Coach Keady assembled a stellar cast of assistants to help make the Brown and White into a major power. Pat Pazzetti coached the backs. Line coach Sam "The Dopester" Strauss became the advance scout on game day, traveling every Saturday to watch the next team on the Lehigh schedule. And Lehigh's all-time great wrestling coach Billy Sheridan was the team trainer.

Meanwhile, under new coach Wilmer Crowell, the Maroon stopped a two-year sub-.500 slide and tallied its first points against the Brown and White in three seasons. Though the Lafayette scoring drought ended, it wasn't enough. Lehigh's Chenoweth returned from a five-game probation and connected with Sawtelle on a 60-yard touchdown — a four-yard pass and 56-yard run after the catch. Coupled with a 25-yard touchdown gallop around right end by All-American halfback William Cahall behind 150-pound guard F. N. Becker, Lehigh posted a 17-7 victory in Easton.

The Rivalry Invades Taylor Stadium

The first Lehigh-Lafayette game to be contested in Taylor Stadium highlighted the 1915 season.

Saving his best troops for the Lehigh game the following week, Lafayette coach Crowell permitted Penn State to run up a larger score than deserved. In addition, the Maroon and White had been practicing behind closed doors for weeks. Not even the College's President was permitted to observe. However, one scribe reported that Crowell utilized a dummy team method. Contrary to stories, Crowell did not import illiterate jocks from renegade football programs to practice against.

The coach used reserve players as pawns, running the scout team through offensive and defensive plays frequently used by Lehigh.

Another Bethlehem journalist, showing Lehigh's true engineering roots, used an algebraic equation to analyze and forecast the final results using comparative scores, Pythagorean's Theorem, a slide rule, and a primitive pocket calculator. The final prediction: Lehigh 6-0. The actual score: Lafayette 35-6 before a record setting-crowd in the new Taylor Stadium. Ironically, the Maroon was led by a quarterback named Taylor, with an assist from John "Bodie" Weldon — who completed 10 of 28 passes for 130 yards and three touchdowns.

The first touchdown in the inaugural Lehigh-Lafayette game at Taylor Stadium was scored by the Maroon's Donald Mummert on a 20-yard run with a fumble. Fred Hazeltine scored Lehigh's first and only touchdown late in the fourth quarter.

The loss to Lafayette ended Lehigh's 13-game home winning streak as the Maroon handed the Brown and White its first-ever defeat at Taylor Stadium.

The best move by Lehigh during the inaugural Lafayette battle at Taylor Stadium occurred at halftime, when a contingent of black-clad students paraded a casket across the field bearing the inscription "Lafayette." The Eastonians had the last laugh, as the College Hill boys buried Lehigh deep into the Taylor Stadium turf during the second half.

Taylor Athletic Complex

The new athletic facilities built on the South Bethlehem campus in 1914 were made possible by a gift from Lehigh alumnus and trustee Charles L. Taylor of Pittsburgh. Taylor Stadium and Taylor Gymnasium field house included a swimming pool and a large gymnasium with modern athletic equipment.

"The successes of the football program were directly attributable to the development of a system of physical training that required every student in the university to exercise regularly," reported the *Globe-Times*.

Golden Anniversary

The Series contested its 50th game on the gridiron in 1916. Interest was so great that special trains were scheduled from Bethlehem, Allentown, and New York City to Easton. Lehigh University also commemorated its 50th year of higher education in conjunction with the contest. The Brown and White blanked its neighbors from Easton by a 16-0

Bots Brunner — the vagabond of Lafayette-Lehigh football.

In winning, Lafayette demonstrated that it has perhaps the most powerful attack of any team in the country."

Lawrence Perry, working for Consolidated Syndicate, in a column in the *New York Globe*, said in part about the Lafayette team after viewing the game with Lehigh, "A final opportunity to see in action a team which has been spoken of as one of the greatest football outfits in the country came Saturday, when Lafayette played Lehigh at Bethlehem."

And football writer Walter Trumbull in the *New York Herald* offered his assessment on the top spot. "It begins to look as if Iowa and Lafayette would be in there claiming it."

As with most national contenders, Lafayette was not free from controversy. Brunner, the only player to star for both Lehigh and Lafayette, made Easton the fourth stop on his college football playing circuit. Having started his free agency in Bethlehem, the drifter made stops at Yale and Penn, before landing on College Hill.

Brunner's travels elicited a sharp response from Herbert Reed in the *New York Evening Post*. "The Eastern title is settled. Unless something unusual turns up, it will be won by the Lafayette Club. But it is about time that Bots Brunner either kick every goal he is at Lafayette for, or pass on to the next banner."

Brunner was the only player to tally points for Lehigh and Lafayette and record wins on both sides of The Rivalry.

Discussion did not end with Brunner, however. Maroon standout Joe Williams, the largest and perhaps most talented lineman, was banned on the eve of the Lehigh contest by the Lafayette Athletic Committee due to poor grades. Some argued Williams was a sacrificial lamb offered after Reed's comments hit the street.

The Easton Express provided this assessment. "The case of Williams should forever silence the rumors that floaters are harbored at Lafayette. A student enters college primarily for an education. Football is secondary consideration. It is the function of the Faculty Athletic Committee to guard against violations of this policy."

Bots' Bon Voyage

Brunner was back at Lafayette for one last season in 1922. It was this Benedict Arnold's drop-kick field goal with 45 seconds remaining that gave the Maroon a 3-0 victory over its rivals from Bethlehem. This game still holds The Series' record for the lowest point total in a game.

Bots led the East in scoring in 1922, with 12 touchdowns, 11 extra points, and one vital field goal for a total of 86 points.

With its 13-3 triumph in 1923, Lafayette was the first school to record five straight victories since The Game went to a once-a-year format in 1902. The 1923 game marked the swan song for coach Jock Sutherland, who accepted the head job at his alma mater Pitt. To greet its new coach, the University of Pittsburgh announced plans to build a 70,000 seat stadium.

Henry Levin tallied the only points for Lehigh on a 46-yard field goal, a Series' record for longest field goal which still stands.

Behind the blocking of All-American tackle and captain Arthur Deibel and the two touchdowns by halfback Frank Chicknoski, the Maroon out-gained its neighbors from Bethlehem on the ground 420-102 and in first downs 19-2. During its 6-1-2 season, Lafayette out-gained every opponent in total yards and first downs.

Diebel, who missed only seven minutes of play during his four seasons, was the first Lafayette person named to the East-West Shrine game. Unfortunately, a mail mix-up caused the invitation to arrive after the contest.

In game sidebars, Lehigh's Taylor Stadium, built less than 10 years before, was declared too small for the annual classic. And Lehigh fans paraded Lafayette's goat around the field — or

Multi-Sport Stars

Several members of the 1922 Lafayette football team set unique standards for other Maroon athletes to attain. They played on several varsity teams which were victorious over Lehigh squads.

Back Mike Gazella played on 12 Lafayette teams which bested their ancient rivals. Gazella and his team defeated Lehigh eight times in baseball and four times in football. Quarterback Matt Brennan followed with seven wins — four in basketball and three in football. Bots Brunner recorded six triumphs — three in baseball, two in football, and one in basketball. Brunner was the only man to play on varsity teams that defeated Lehigh in three different sports.

Lafayette's Finest Lineman

Frank "Dutch" Schwab captained the '20 and '22 Maroon squads and was named to the Walter Camp All-American team at guard for a second time in 1922, a rarity for a player from a small college. He also anchored the defensive line on the powerhouse 1921 National Championship team. In 1958, "Dutch" became the first Lafayette man inducted into the National Football Foundation's Hall of Fame. He was also named to two of the early "All-Time" college football teams by the Helms Athletic Foundation and the Eastern College Athletic Conference.

Doc Operates Elsewhere

During his five seasons, Sutherland restored the pride and prestige to the Lafayette football program. The Dentist led the Maroon to a National Championship, compiled a 33-8-2 record for a .791 winning percent, defeated Lehigh all five times, and shut-out 21 of 43 opponents. Sutherland would later coach the Brooklyn Dodgers and the Pittsburgh Steelers of the National Professional Football League, and was inducted into the National Football Foundation's Hall of Fame.

Ironically, it was pure chance that Sutherland landed as coach at Lafayette. In his first coaching job in 1918 at Camp Greenleaf, Fort Oglethorp, Georgia, Sutherland's team won the Cantonment Championship over undefeated Fort Dix. After the experience, Doc was unsure whether to turn to Dentistry or remain in coaching following his discharge from the military.

In his recollections to Francis March Jr., Sutherland reflected on discovering the Lafayette position.

"An accidental meeting with a friend decided me to go to Lafayette, I have never been sorry.

"Lafayette College, in my first impressions, presented many problems — the smallness of the squad, the difficult schedule, and the limited budget. I was green, I knew nothing about Lafayette or Lafayette traditions. But it wasn't long until I changed my mind, and it didn't take me the whole five years I was there to find out."

more appropriately, dragged the stubborn animal, causing Lehigh's faithful to wonder what was more stubborn, the Maroon's goat or its defense.

Lafayette Shatters Lehigh's Bid For An Undefeated Season

In his final season on South Mountain, coach Jim Baldwin brought Lehigh into the 1924 game with an unblemished record and its best shot at snapping a five-game skid against the kids from College Hill. Earlier in the season, Lehigh recorded its 200th career football victory by beating Gettysburg 12-0.

Leading the charges for Lafayette's 6-2 squad was first-year mentor, G. Herbert McCracken, who implemented the practice of taking his team to Stroudsburg on the eve of The Contest to escape the pregame madness.

The kick-off at March Field was delayed 30 minutes as groundskeepers tried to ready the pitch after 15 hours of rain. Sawdust was spread over the field in an attempt to turn the quagmire into playable terrain. Part-way through the process, Lafayette football authorities appeared on the field and ordered a halt to the spreading of the sawdust on the theory that the players could get better footing in the mud and water than in the slippery sawdust.

Lehigh faithful claimed the decision was an attempt to slow down its skilled people. Football critics said that the Brown and White had so many good athletes that Baldwin was at a loss to name starters.

Lafayette players were provided with temporary pockets sewn into their uniforms in which rosin was carried. The players were also equipped with new shoes with long, pointed mud cleats and a change of uniforms for halftime.

Even the officials were prepared for the monsoon-like conditions, donning sheepskin mackinaws instead of their customary white uniforms.

The inclement weather provided one advantage for Lehigh. It kept them *dry*.

The First Huddle

In his first season on College Hill, Herb McCracken earned a spot in football lore before a game against Penn in 1924. Aware that the Quakers had scouted his team 's previous five games and learned the Lafayette offensive signals, McCracken instructed his players to gather behind the line of scrimmage to learn the next play in secret. This was a dramatic change from the traditional method of starting each down by calling signals from the line. McCracken's new approach soon became known as the huddle.

The squad missed most of the rain-filled pregame warmup period, as the team bus got caught in a traffic jam. Instead of rolling in the muck and mire during calisthenics, the Brown and White players stayed protected from the elements in the warmth of the bus.

The Maroon recorded the contest's only score, as last year's star, Frank Chicknoski, blasted for an early first quarter touchdown. The Lithuanian Lord tallied game-winning scores in back-to-back Lafayette-Lehigh contests. All-American end Charlie "Chuck" Berry gave the Maroon's offense rhythm and gave Lehigh's defense the blues. Berry was named as a first team member of the Walter Camp All-American team and was inducted into the Hall of Fame of the National Football Foundation in 1980.

In the fourth quarter, the mud-covered Maroon twice denied the Brown and White in the red zone. First, Lehigh was halted at the Lafayette 20-yard line, and then again at the two in the game's closing moments.

Lucky Seven

Sevens were the lucky number for Lafayette in the 1925 contest. The Maroon's 14-0 whitewashing of Lehigh was its seventh straight victory in The Rivalry and capped coach McCracken's second straight seven-win season.

The Leopards — a nickname that an *Easton Express* sportswriter donned on the Lafayette squad during the 1924 season — won despite losing six of eight fumbles and three interceptions to the South Mountaineers.

Lafayette took full advantage of Lehigh's equally sloppy play. Both touchdowns tallied by the College Hill boys were the direct result of Brown and White miscues. The first score was recorded by Warren Brieg, who blocked a Lehigh punt from its own 15 and recovered in the end zone. The second was tallied by righthalf Bob Mittman, who pounced on a Walter Moore fumble in the end zone for the Leopards' last points.

The game was more notable for its sidelights.

Lehigh players donned white helmets for the first time and a LU cannon of centime-

Bring On The Irish!

After its successful 7-2 season in 1924, there were rumors that Lafayette would meet Notre Dame on a home-and-home basis. Plans called for the Fighting Irish to travel east in 1925 and face the Leopards at Franklin Field. The Eastonians would then face Notre Dame in South Bend the following year. The matches never materialized and Lafayette has yet to meet the Irish on the gridiron.

Lafayette's All-American back Mike Wilson rushed for 243 yards and three touchdowns against Lehigh in 1926.

ter caliber replaced the machine guns used in the last contest in Taylor Stadium. The machine guns were not used for crowd control, but for the "bang" effect after a Brown and White score.

Lafayette's band barely made it to the 1925 game. The bus broke down and the band members were forced to hitchhike to South Bethlehem. To compensate for its late arrival, the band didn't want to leave after the game. They had to be chased off the field by the Bethlehem police.

The Lehigh band never made it to the game and was conspicuously absent. Placed on double secret probation, the Leopard-followers claimed. Others said they were still stuck in the traffic jam from last year's game. They were replaced by the Bethlehem Steel Band.

Once again, fans, alumni, and media were screaming Taylor Stadium was too small.

Crowd control proved a problem, as the runways in front of the stadium's lower rows were clogged with humanity throughout the game, obstructing those who had thought they purchased prime seats.

The large contingent of word-painters taxed the pressbox facilities. The Bethlehem office of the Western Union did not complete the installation of all press wires until halftime.

And after the game, Lafayette players "broke training" and were seen puffing victory cigars.

Lafayette Wins Second National Championship

Lafayette completed another undefeated season in 1926 by beating Lehigh 35-0, and was proclaimed National Champions for a second time in a half dozen years. McCracken's "Parade of Sophomores" led the East in scoring, averaging 36 points per game, and established a single-season scoring record of 328 points. The defense was equally impressive, allowing a total of 37 points. The Leopards built a thirteen game unbeaten streak over two years. The 35-0 drubbing was the Brown and White's worst defeat in 20

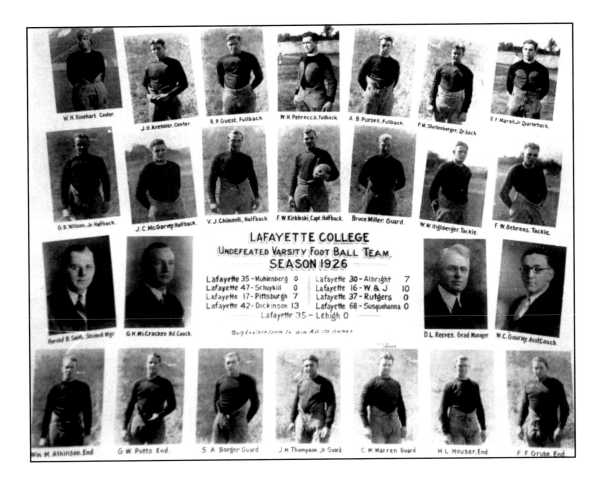

W. H. Rinehart, Center.
J. H. Kressler, Center.
R. P. Guest, Fullback.
W. H. Petrecca, Fullback.
A. B. Pursell, Fullback.
P. M. Shellenberger, Qr.back
R. F. Marsh, Jr Quarterback.

G. B. Wilson, Jr. Halfback.
J. C. McGarvey Halfback.
V. J. Chimenti, Halfback
F. W. Kirkleski, Capt. Halfback.
Bruce Miller. Guard.
W. W. Highberger. Tackle.
F. W. Behrens. Tackle.

LAFAYETTE COLLEGE
UNDEFEATED VARSITY FOOT BALL TEAM,
SEASON 1926

Lafayette 35 - Muhlenberg 0   Lafayette 30 - Albright   7
Lafayette 47 - Schuykill 0   Lafayette 16 - W. & J   10
Lafayette 17 - Pittsburgh 7   Lafayette 37 - Rutgers   0
Lafayette 42 - Dickinson 13   Lafayette 68 - Susquehanna 0
               Lafayette 35 - Lehigh 0

Only Eastern Team To Win All Its Games

Harold B. Smith, Second Mgr.
G. H. McCracken Hd Coach.
D. L. Reeves. Grad Manager
W. C. Gourley, Asst Coach.

Wm. M Atkinson. End
G. W. Potts End.
S. A. Berger Guard
J. H. Thompson Jr Guard
C. M Warren Guard
H. L. Houser, End
F. F. Grube End.

years at the hands of its ancient rival.

In The Game of 1926, All-American back Mike Wilson rushed for 243 yards and three touchdowns. At season's end, Wilson led the nation in scoring and accounted for 120 of Lafayette's 328 points. Fellow halfback Frank Kirkleski also received All-American accolades and played in the East-West Shrine Game in San Francisco. Tackle Bill Cothran joined his two teammates in earning *New York Telegraph* All-American honors despite being suspended from both the Lafayette grid squad and College prior to the Lehigh game.

Circumstances leading to his banishment were never made clear, except in Cothran's "Forgive and Forget" speech to his teammates after practice during preparation for the Lehigh game.

In his soliloquy, Cothran apologized for

1926 National Champions
Lafayette College (9-0)
Coach: G. Herbert McCracken

Muhlenberg	*35-0*
Schuylkill College	*47-0*
@ Pittsburgh	*17-7*
Dickinson	*42-13*
Albright	*30-7*
*vs Washington & Jefferson**	*16-10*
@ Rutgers	*37-0*
Susquehanna	*68-0*
Lehigh	*35-0*

* = at Philadelphia, PA

From March To Fisher

Lafayette's 1926 grid team was the first to play at newly constructed Fisher Field. With a capacity of 18,000, the structure replaced venerable March Field. The first contest was held September 25th, with the Leopards prevailing 35-0 over Muhlenberg College. The undefeated season concluded with the mauling of Lehigh. In all, Lafayette won its first ten games at its new ballyard, whose layout is oddly in a non-traditional east-west orientation. The preferred direction is north-south so that the sun never directly hits the players' eyes.

In 1973, to provide additional space for the construction of Kirby Fieldhouse, more than 4,500 seats were removed from the north stands. Fisher Field presently has a capacity of 13,750 (12,000 in the main south and 1,750 in the north).

To accommodate the overflow crowds for the Lehigh-Lafayette game every other year, more than 3,500 temporary seats are erected.

Initially called Lafayette Stadium, the field was soon renamed for Thomas Fisher, Lafayette College class of 1888, who almost single-handedly raised the $445,000 needed for construction through fund raising and a sizable personal contribution.

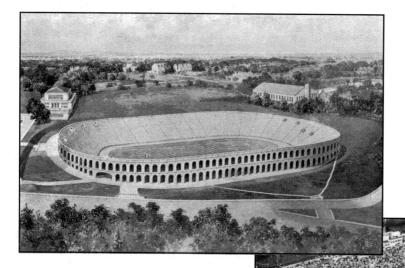

Fisher Field, shown below, replaced March Field as Lafayette's football stadium in 1926.

One of the design plans, shown above, proposed a bowl-shaped structure for Fisher Field.

his mistakes. "I am sorry to a degree that cannot be expressed in words. I have over-stepped the bounds and must pay the penalty. The strong arm of discipline has not only banished me from the squad and college, but has a more far-reaching effect. I will not be able to see Saturday's game. Instead, I will be many miles away. My heart will be bleeding in agony. All I ask is that you first forgive and then forget Bill Cothran. If you do these, you will be at your best Saturday to beat Lehigh."

With tears streaming down his cheeks, Cothran turned into the setting sun to begin his journey into exile.

Lehigh, coming off a big 14-0 win over Rutgers a week earlier for its only triumph of the season, also had a fire lit under its tail. On the eve of The Game, an unscheduled bonfire broke-out in the lower gymnasium on the south Bethlehem campus. The pre-game rally had ended earlier in the evening and students passing the building later in the evening noticed flames leaping from windows. Firefighters were summoned and prevented the "smoker" from spreading to the adjoining main athletic building.

Lafayette's Dominance Jeopardizes The Rivalry

The NCAA rules committee moved the goalposts from the goal line to the back of the end zone at the beginning of the 1927 season. The change had little impact on the outcome of The Game, as Lafayette topped its 1926 performance against Lehigh in 1927. The Maroon clobbered the undermanned Bethlehem rivals 43-0, before only 8,000 eye-witnesses in Taylor Stadium. With the Leopards recording their ninth straight victory in The Series and out-rushing Lehigh 506-127, serious questions were posed as to the competitiveness of The Rivalry.

Six different players scored touchdowns for the Maroon, including tackle Charles Burnett, who scored the only touchdown of his career on a blocked punt. Substitute halfback Jack O'Reilly, filling in for the injured All-American Mike Wilson, netted 256 yards rushing and scored one touchdown.

The 1927 contest was more notable for the no-shows and injuries than the play on the field. In addition to Wilson, absent from The Game was Lafayette captain Cothran, who was honeymooning. Two weeks earlier, after a game in Washington against Georgetown, Cothran married a D.C. coed from George Washington University.

Johnny Kressler, the Leopards' starting center, was carried from the field, suffering from acute appendicitis. He underwent surgery that evening in Easton Hospital.

Spectator Howard Juergens suffered a broken leg at the close of the annual contest. While celebrating Lafayette's victory, the Allentown resident was swept along in the wave of jubilant fans and fell, suffering a fracture of the lower left leg.

Allentown Hospital listed game official Charles McCarthy in unconscious condition Saturday night after The Game. He suffered from a severed artery over his left eye, a possible fracture of the skull, and body bruises. After the Lafayette-Lehigh contest, McCarthy took ill and fell down a flight of stone steps outside the waiting room of the Lehigh Valley Transit Company's ticket office. This was after discovering he had missed the last train of the evening to his residence in Philadelphia.

At the end of the 1927 season, Notre Dame announced the intention to build an $800,000 stadium for football. Lafayette fans were ecstatic, as they believed the two schools would eventually meet on the gridiron.

TIMEOUT

Editorial Comments

In 1927, *The Easton Express* headlines read "Play Lehigh First, Not Last Game of Season — Policy of Bethlehemites Is Wreaking Ruin On Traditional Rivalry of Over Forty Years Standing."

The Express continued, "Thousands of vacant seats at Saturday's game, mostly on the south side of the field, were a silent protest to Lehigh's poor teams.

"Saturday morning, an Associated Press dispatch from Bethlehem, dealing with the game, said: 'Both teams have had poor seasons.'

"All of which is true. Yet one team with a poor season was able to defeat the other by a margin of seven touchdowns.

"No, Lehigh teams are not poor, they're rotten.

"And the dear public was asked to part with $4 a ticket to see Saturday's game. Of course the public doesn't have to go. They can stay at home. That is what many did on Saturday. But there are thousands of Alumni of both institutions who deplore the situation and are crying for relief.

"Saturday's exhibition would have been justified on the other end of the schedule. Lafayette usually picks a setup for the opening game. If the Bethlehem authorities steadfastly refuse to strengthen their team, the Maroon schedule makers should give them the first game on the schedule at popular prices —not $4 per.

"Lehigh has adopted and is enforcing a policy that is bringing ruin to a traditional rivalry cherished in the Lehigh Valley for more than forty years; cherished by generations of Lafayette and Lehigh Alumni, but which is now in a decline, gradually becoming extinct.

"In short, Lehigh authorities have refused to permit Alumni to send boys through college; poor boys with athletic ability to play football. The policy is permitted at Lafayette and most other institutions in the land, including many that have considerably larger enrollments and are better known than the local institution.

"If Lehigh is right; then Lafayette and others are wrong. And if Lafayette is wrong, every victory won by the locals in the past 10 or 15 years is tainted.

"If Lehigh insists on her present policy, then the game should be played earlier, on the first date of the schedule. They should no longer ask for or expect the choice attraction on the end of the season's program."

Lafayette's Streak Continues ...

Lafayette completed the longest winning streak in The Series' history in 1928. Its 37-14 lynching of Lehigh made 10 victories in a row over its ancient rival, starting with 1919's 10-6 triumph.

Lafayette entered the season finale with a single loss at 5-1-2, including a 7-0 triumph over a Joe Paterno-less Penn State a week earlier.

Lehigh came into the 1928 version of The Classic with a new mentor, Austin Tate. Gone was Percy Wendell, who's three-year mark of 5-20-2 (.222 winning percent) was the second worst in South Bethlehem of all coaches who endured more than one year.

The Brown and White scored for the first time in five games against the Leopards, recording 14 points. Lafayette scored 38, rushed for 564 yards, and netted 22 first downs. Lehigh's ground attack totaled 163, and tallied but five first downs. It was coach Herb McCracken's fifth straight win in as many contests, matching Doc Sutherland's streak for most successive victories over a Lehigh team.

The scoreboard reflected a final margin of 37-14, when in fact it was 38. Some scribes in the press box, confused about the outcome, initially reported the incorrect score. Only correspondence between the media, McCracken, and referee Eckels settled the matter. Rumors spread that Lehigh engineers rigged the scoreboard but could not fully execute the score switch. To this day, a discrepancy remains on the final score. Lehigh's Sports Information reports the score as 37-14, while Lafayette's quotes 38-14.

The Narrowest of Margins

In a switch, Lafayette incurred a losing season in 1929, while Lehigh bounced above the .500 mark for the first time since 1924. In going 3-5, the Eastonians experienced their first losing season since 1918, which was also the last time the Bethlehemites were victorious in The Rivalry.

Not coincidentally, Lehigh triumphed in '29 by a narrow 13-12 tally, ending McCracken's bid to become the only Lafayette coach to top Lehigh six straight times.

Playing with an injured hand that was heavily taped, signal-caller Art Davidowitz orchestrated the Lehigh victory. In his farewell game, the quarterback rushed for an eight-yard touchdown around right end and kicked the extra point in the first quarter. Then in the second stanza, he connected with halfback Tom Nora for a 52-yard touchdown.

The Leopards matched the Brown and White's two touchdowns, but the defensive charges of Lehigh, led by captain Tubby Miller, blocked both point-after-touchdowns to preserve the win. At this time, college football rules had no provision for the two-point conversion.

Tate's Traditions

In 1929, Coach Austin Tate unveiled several new traditions for the Lehigh gridders. Tate instituted the ritual of spending the eve before The Game in Allentown at the Hotel Traylor, followed by a morning breakfast, then a pre-game relaxation period at the Saucon Valley Country Club before departing to the stadium. Then, during the game, Tate's men huddled in a double-rowed, choir boy formation instead of the traditional round table style.

> ## Close Call
>
> Lehigh's 13-12 victory over Lafayette in 1929 marks the closest margin of victory by either team in The Rivalry's history.

Flashbacks to a decade's-worth of Lehigh's losses in The Game occurred late in the fourth quarter, when an ill-advised Davidowitz pass was intercepted by a Lafayette defender and returned into Lehigh territory. But once again the defense rose to the occasion and squelched the Maroon's game-ending threat.

As usual, the postgame festivities were as heated as the play on the pitch. Immediately after the game, a fight broke out on the Taylor Stadium field that threatened to become a full-scale riot. It started when some over-zealous Lehigh students attempted to steal a Lafayette cheerleader's megaphone. The Leopard faithful defended their possession, exchanging several blows with their foes before the Bethlehem police dispersed the mob.

Record-Setting Crowd Fills Fisher

The 1930 teams were both anchored by Bethlehem boys. Joe McLernon secured the center of the Lehigh line, facing off against fellow neighbors Steve Edraney and Sonny Ellicott of the Lafayette front seven.

And on the eve of The Game, headlines proclaimed more trouble for legendary Notre Dame coach Knute Rockne. The Associated Press reported that Rockne had seen his Notre Dame team in action for the last time. An infection in the right leg, which forced the famous coach to direct his team from a wheel chair against Southern Cal a week earlier, had spread to his left leg. Complete rest was ordered by his physician.

The largest crowd in The Rivalry's history to date jammed Fisher Field for the 1930 edition. Fan interest was rekindled thanks to Lehigh's stunning victory from a year earlier. Ticket demand was so great in Bethlehem that Lafayette authorities were compelled to furnish additional seating in temporary bleachers to Lehigh boosters on the *Lafayette* side of the field. Included in the crowd of 20,000 people was Pennsylvania Governor John S. Fisher.

Lafayette overcame a veteran Lehigh team and avenged last year's defeat, 16-6.

For 52 minutes, the Brown and White made stand a first half touchdown by standout halfback Allen Ware. But a safety and two Bob Wilcox touchdowns in the contest's last eight minutes gave the game to the College Hill hosts.

Lafayette continued its hex over the Brown and White in Easton, despite Lehigh returning all starters except the ends from the team that vanquished the Leopards a year earlier. The Bethlehem school had not won on the forks of the Delaware since 1918, and had not yet been able to record a "W" on Fisher Field since the stadium was unveiled in 1926.

Forced to wear "unattractive" white jerseys trimmed in maroon because the regular maroon ones were ruined in the mud at the Temple contest a week earlier, the Leopards exhibited no superstitions in donning the old uniforms. Lafayette returned from a one-year victory hiatus to conquer the Brown and White, ensuring a winning season.

Heat Wave

A "Bust Lafayette" sign painted on the western slope of South Mountain greeted the Eastonians sitting in the visitors' bleachers for the 1931 game.

This 65th game in The Rivalry took place under a sun-splashed sky at Taylor Stadium. In what may have been the warmest third Saturday in November, ice cream took the place of hot dogs among vendors. Lafayette player Jack Kolasky was overcome by heat exhaustion and fell unconscious in the fourth period. The players from both squads sprawled to their backs during every time-out to recuperate from the sun's relentless pursuit.

Coach Tate prepared his troops for The Game by using the expertise of Cy Morgan, a former Lehigh stand-out and member of the University's Board of Strategy. Morgan scouted the Lafayette team all season, and devised ways to defense the Leopards' attack.

Tate also welcomed the try-out of star wrestler Phil Rauch, who despite playing his first season of varsity football, had won the starting right end spot from incumbent Warren Duke.

Rauch later became a benefactor of the University. The Field House located on the Saucon Valley Fields of the Murray Goodman Campus bears his name.

Coach McCracken countered by eliminating scrimmages during the Lehigh week. Citing a return to fundamentals, the Maroon's mentor brought the tackling dummies and bucking machine into action one last time.

Lehigh students were set to parade in an old-fashioned rally Friday night before The Game. A smoker, featuring corn cob pipes, tobacco, and "other incidentals" was planned. A parade followed across the New Street Bridge. It was the second successive year the police actually *led* the festivities instead of chasing the partying students.

And in a strange twist, Horace Booz, an alumni-trustee of Lafayette College was one of the keynote speakers at a *Lehigh* alumni rally at Bookbinder's restaurant in Philadelphia.

As in the previous year, Lehigh scored first. Captain Ware caught a ten-yard pass from left-half Chick Halstead, then rumbled 28 more yards with the reception for a first quarter touchdown. And as in the previous year, Lafayette punched in a pair of second half scores to top the Brown and White 13-7.

Phil Bugen, who would later be tossed from the game for "poking" a Lehigh gridder, punched the ball over from the two for the Leopards first score. Slippery Socolow crossed the chalk line for the game-winner in the fourth, capping a fine 7-2 season for McCracken's boys.

Two stats stood out in the ball game.

Lehigh's touchdown toss was the only pass completed by either team to one of its own players. Three were completed to members of the

Captain Ware

In addition to scoring both of Lehigh's touchdowns in the 1930 and 1931 Lafayette contests, halfback Allen Ware was a standout in basketball and baseball, captaining all three Brown and White teams. As a center in basketball and a rightfielder for baseball, he earned three varsity letters in each to go with his three from football. Ware was inducted into the Lehigh Athletic Hall of Fame in 1995.

opposition.

Lehigh quarterback and punter Paul Short booted one that lived up to his name. A punt by Short went straight up in the air, landed, and rolled backwards out of bounds for a net one-yard loss.

Monsoon Madness

Rain re-appeared for the 1932 contest and a fourteen-hour downpour continued until just after the opening whistle. Players from both sides took the field minus socks — a common practice thought to provide an advantage on wet playing surfaces during this era. And the poor weather was reflective of the poor seasons both were experiencing, as each team entered with two wins and five losses.

Dismayed with the kicking game, Lehigh's coach Tate held punting try-outs prior to the Lafayette contest, with Short drawing the short straw.

Total punts outscored points 35-31. Lafayette won on the scoreboard 25-6, but lost in punts 19-16. In swampy conditions with a water-logged ball, Lehigh's Paul Short managed to average 45 yards per boot, while Lafayette kickers averaged 42. Each team belted a seventy, sixty, and numerous fifty-yarders.

Lafayette's Frank Bialek landed face down in an end zone mud puddle after scoring a touchdown in the 1932 game. Bialek's power running under muddy track conditions made the difference for the Leopards.

With the kicking games neutralizing each other, Lafayette's Frank Bialek's power running on the muddy track made the difference. The Maroon fullback tallied two touchdowns, the second of which he landed face down in an end zone mud puddle and almost drowned.

The 1933 rendition of The Game was a repeat of the 1932 version as both teams entered The Game with the same records as in 1932, each at 2-5.

For the 14th time in 15 contests, the Leopards emerged victorious, 54-12.

By registering eight

touchdowns and six extra-points, Lafayette surpassed its previous Series' high-point total of 53 established in 1905. The Maroon kicked four field goals in a row establishing a new school record. Once again, Bialek made two visits to the end zone.

Mascot Change

During the 1933 contest at Taylor Stadium, Lehigh unveiled its first mascot since the goat of 1903. It was a burro, similar to the Army mule mascot.

50 Years of Football Tradition

Lafayette and Lehigh celebrated their first 50 years of football history in 1934. Lehigh and new coach Glen Harmeson celebrated by conquering its ancient rival 13-7. The win assured Lehigh of its first non-losing season in five years and was the Brown and White's first victory at Fisher Field.

The Lehigh backfield was comprised of four sophomores including Knox Peet at quarterback, Warren Fairbanks and Warren McCoy at halfbacks, and Log Pennauchi at fullback. The crowd in Easton was dazzled by the "Sophomore Sensations" and enjoyed an encore performance by a young Pat Pazzetti, III, off the bench.

The triumph represented the first opportunity for the Lehigh faithful to tear down the goalposts at Fisher Field. Reports of the day indicated that the posts were not only demolished in record time, but the Lafayette flag was also confiscated and paraded around the ball yard. A victory bonfire followed on Lehigh's Upper Field for the first

Players Suggest Grid Rule Changes

In a 1933 Associated Press poll of college players, numerous suggestions were made to improve the quality of the game.

Forty of seventy gridders surveyed said they would eliminate the rule which calls a ball carrier down without contact once any part of his body touches the ground other than the hands or feet.

Thirteen players suggested repealing the "dead ball" provision which prevents a defensive player from advancing a recovered fumble.

Nine athletes believed the offense should be allowed to pass from any point behind the line of scrimmage, instead of being restricted to passing from within five yards behind.

Four players advocated the return of the goalposts to its original position on the goal line.

Only 16 players expressed complete satisfaction with the present rules. Among other suggestions made:
- Resume play in the third quarter where it was left off at the end of the half.
- Allow the offense five downs when inside the opponents twenty.
- Eliminate the penalty for two incomplete passes in the same series of downs.
- Devise a way to credit a team for first downs.
- Limit the number of men the defensive team can put on the scrimmage line.
- Give the passer as much protection as the kicker.

College Football Probed For Professionalism

The Lafayette-Lehigh games scheduled in 1896 were cancelled because of a dispute over the eligibility of Lafayette halfback George Barclay, who Lehigh claimed was a professional athlete. Controversy regarding professionalism and eligibility of college athletes was not exclusive to The Rivalry.

In 1934, a number of university presidents urged the Carnegie Foundation for the Advancement of Teaching to investigate college athletics for professionalism and subsidization.

"We have found that college athletics are tainted with professionalism and that the situation is more reprehensible than ever before," commented Frank Vanderlip, treasurer of the executive committee of the Foundation in 1934.

He also recounted how a college president told of how more than $500,000 had been bet on a single college football game and that "one day, one of these games will be thrown."

In a similar study seven years earlier, the Foundation found that one in seven athletes in 130 colleges was subsidized. Officials declared the situation improved after the report's disclosure, only to become worse in 1935 and 1936. Eventually, the NCAA established strict guidelines to monitor and police recruiting activities and player eligibility in college athletics.

time since 1929.

The game was officiated by John R. Trimble, the first Bethlehemite to work the game in decades. Some complained that "hometown officiating" affected the game's outcome.

During the 1934 season, Lafayette commemorated its 300th football victory, a 19-0 whitewashing of Muhlenberg.

Snow Bowl II

Snow filled the air and covered Taylor Stadium for the 1935 game. Lehigh's 48-0 victory gave the hosts its first back-to-back wins against Lafayette since World War I. The Engineers, as a *Globe-Times* scribe christened the Bethlehem school, handed Lafayette its worst loss in The Rivalry since a 78-0 thrashing in 1917. It was a striking revenge for the Leopards' 54-12 mauling of the Brown and White only two years earlier.

Lafayette registered a dismal minus 28 yards rushing. But, if any consolation, they were penalized only a foot for the entire game. As it happened, Lehigh had less than a yard to go for the touchdown when Lafayette was whistled for its lone infraction.

Chat Bennett, playing his last game for Lehigh, bulled for two touchdowns from his fullback position. Halfback Ralph Heller, a Bethlehem boy who ran finer than a new set of snow tires on the frozen turf, broke open an 83-yard scoring run to start the third quarter. Tackle Howell Scobey, football captain and NCAA heavyweight wrestling champion, anchored the line and booted four extra points.

Lehigh turned four balls over to Lafayette. Unfortunately for the Maroon, it was prior to the opening kick-off, as Lafayette forgot its pregame practice balls in Easton.

End Of The McCracken Era

After 12 years on College Hill, Herb McCracken stepped down as head football coach after the 1935 season. As a 25-year old, he replaced the beloved Jock Sutherland. During Jock's reign, Lafayette had some of its most successful years on the gridiron, including a National Championship. McCracken took the helm in 1924, and two seasons later, crafted an undefeated team that was also declared National Champions.

McCracken compiled a record of 59-40-6 for a .590 winning percentage and 9-3 mark against Lehigh. McCracken's tenure in Easton was the second longest in the school's history.

The innovative coach's discoveries included the lateral-option forward pass behind the line of scrimmage, the use of the huddle, and a left-handed passing halfback.

McCracken was inducted into the National Football Foundation's Hall of Fame in 1973.

The Last Hurrah!

The "Sophomore Sensations" of Lehigh's 1934 squad completed their final season on the gridiron in 1936. The Brown and White, led by the senior leadership of the "Fab Four," whitewashed Lafayette for the second year in row, by an 18-0 margin. Pazzetti, Pennauchi, Heller, and Peet joined a select fraternity of Lehigh men who vanquished the Leopards three consecutive times. The last time the Engineers had such success against their ancient rivals was during the War years of 1916-1918. Under the tutelage of former Purdue stand-out Harmeson, the Brown and White compiled three successive non-losing seasons.

The 1936 Engineer team featured Fritz Bayer on a "guard-around." On the play, the guard received the ball from a back on an inside exchange, then swept around the far end much like a reverse.

After executing the "fumblerooski" successfully against Muhlenberg in the contest prior to the Lafayette game, Coach Harmeson crossed the Leopards by starting Bayer at the center position instead of his accustomed guard spot.

Lafayette suffered its worst season since the inception of college football on the Easton campus.

Remembering The First Win

Lehigh celebrated the "Golden Anniversary" of its initial intercollegiate football triumph during the 1935 Lafayette week. It was 50 years earlier in 1885 that the Brown and White bested Rutgers 10-5 on the Lehigh Athletic Grounds — the field where Taylor Stadium would eventually stand.

As part of the festivities, five local citizens were honored at halftime in recognition of 50 years of perfect Game attendance. The members of the exclusive club included Oliver Groman, E. L. Metzgar, John Miller, Charles Hafner, and Harry Ruthardt.

Star Player Nevers A Coach

Ernie Nevers, a former NFL, major league baseball, and pro basketball great, did not fare as well on the sidelines. As a football player for the Chicago Cardinals in 1929, he scored an NFL record 40 points in one game against Red Grange and the Chicago Bears. In 1927 as a baseball pitcher, he gave up two of Babe Ruth's 60 home runs. While at Stanford, Nevers was an All-American fullback and earned 11 varsity letters in four sports. In his only year as head coach at Lafayette, Nevers posted a 1-8 record in 1936.

Where's The Beef?

In 1936, the average team weight for each squad was 177 pounds. Lafayette's backfield average was 169 pounds and the line 182. Lehigh's backfield averaged 169 and the line 177.

Lehigh Defeats Penn State

Lehigh's 1936 football team stunned Penn State in mid-season by a 7-6 count, as Pat Pazzetti and Knox Peet teamed on a scoring pass. This was the last time Lehigh defeated Penn State. Lehigh's last game against Penn State was played in 1942. The Nittany Lions hold a 17-6-1 advantage in the series.

Olympian Grapplers

Success showed its face off the field for former Engineer gridder Howell Scobey, who qualified for the 1936 Olympic wrestling team, as did fellow team member and national champion Ben Bishop. The try-outs were held at Lehigh's Taylor Gymnasium complex.

Under first year coach Ernie Nevers, the Leopards finished 1-8, scoring only 26 points all season. The Maroon's lone triumph was 7-0 against Dickinson, which a few years earlier had considered dropping the sport because of its lack of competitiveness on the field.

At that time, the 1-8 mark was the worst in Lafayette history. Including modern times, only the 0-9 record of the 1952 squad and the 0-7-2 team of 1964 were more futile.

Lehigh students added insult to the inept '36 Lafayette team. Late in the night prior to The Game, a group of Bethlehem boys snuck into Fisher Field and began painting "Beat Lafayette" on the grass in the center of the gridiron. Apprehended in mid-sentence by Lafayette students, the graffiti artists received the expected punishment, but not before "Beat Laf" was etched into the stadium turf.

Lafayette Completes Fourth Undefeated Season

Lafayette entered the 1937 version of The Game with new head coach Edward "Hook" Mylin and an unblemished record of 7-0. Only Rutgers was able to penetrate the goal line against the stingy Leopard defense.

Lehigh, suffering from the graduation of the 1934 "Sophomore Sensations," sported a 1-7 mark. A unique opportunity for a four-year generation of Lehigh students in 1937 — graduating without losing to Lafayette — looked unlikely.

Despite being a prohibitive favorite, Lafayette was forced to rely on its special teams for the victory. The Leopards' lone touchdown was tallied after Ernie Kanzler blocked a Lehigh punt and recovered at the Engineer 20 yard-line. Associated Press All-American honorable mention halfback Tony Cavallo carried the ball on seven successive plays before bucking over for the game's lone score, as the Leopards clinched the perfect season with a 6-0 victory.

Lehigh scored an apparent equalizing touchdown by George Ellstrom in the second quarter. The play was disallowed after an official ruled that the Lehigh halfback stepped out of bounds during his 36-yard dash down the sideline.

A "Win one for the Gipper" approach motivated the Leopards, as they played without teammate Lester Walls, who was in a California sanitarium suffering from tuberculosis. After the game, a telegram left the Taylor Stadium press box to Walls. It read: "Lafayette 6; Lehigh 0. We did it for you. Coach Mylin and the Team."

Once again, postgame fights over the goalposts were long and brutal. Thirty minutes after the final gun, fans were still brawling. Somehow, the goalposts remained standing when the field was finally cleared by the local authorities. The Lehigh undergrads did admirable work protecting their prize possessions on the home turf.

1937 Undefeated Season	
Lafayette College (8-0)	
Coach: Edward " Hook" Mylin	
Upsala	*33-0*
@ Gettysburg	*2-0*
@ Georgetown	*6-0*
@ New York University	*13-0*
Franklin & Marshall	*14-0*
Rutgers	*13-6*
Washington & Jefferson	*16-0*
@ Lehigh	*6-0*

Little Brass Cannon

In 1937, Lafayette, Lehigh, and Rutgers began an annual competition for the Little Brass Cannon and Middle Three Championship. The winner of the annual round-robin series retained possession of the prize.

Deja Vu

"It's deja vu all over again!" is how New York Yankee Hall of Fame catcher Yogi Berra would have described the 1938 version of The Rivalry, as Lafayette bested Lehigh by the identical 6-0 score of a year earlier.

Forty-six punts were exchanged on a rain-filled, mud-splattered Fisher Field. The Leopards' Sammy Moyer kicked 22 times for a 48-yard average, including 72 and 54-yarders. Lehigh's Steve Smoke booted 24 times for a 46-yard average, including 70 and 69-yarders.

Pinned with poor field position early in the contest, Harmeson had Smoke punt immediately after receiv-

Early Tee Time

The 1938 Lafayette-Lehigh contest marked the first time kick-off commenced at 1:30 p.m. In seasons past, the opening whistle sounded at 2:00 or 2:30.

Lafayette and Penn State Conclude Rivalry

In addition to blanking Lehigh in 1938, the Leopards shut out Penn State 7-0 in the final contest between the two Pennsylvania schools. The Nittany Lions hold a 10-5-1 advantage in the series.

John Quigg, a Bethlehem native who played for Lafayette, was known for his unusual antics in the Lafayette-Lehigh games. In 1938, Quigg repeatedly wiped his muddy hands on the backs of Lehigh players and even the officials' knickers.

ing possession from Lafayette in hopes that the Maroon return men would bobble the wet pigskin. It was not until the end of the first period that Lehigh executed a rushing play from scrimmage.

Lehigh tallied only four first downs in the contest. Lafayette could muster only one.

Harold Simmons, once again captained the Leopards against Lehigh, becoming the first person to hold the distinction of captaining the Maroon to two successive wins over the South Mountaineers.

Assisting Simmons defensively in blanking the Engineers was Bethlehem native John Quigg. In 1937, the scrappy center drew jeers when he thumbed his nose at the Lehigh players at the conclusion of the contest. Quigg and numerous Lehigh linemen engaged in rough-house play throughout the day.

A year older and wiser in 1938, Quigg was never-the-less up to his usual antics, wiping his muddy hands on the backs of Lehigh players and even the officials' knickers.

It was also the second straight year the goalposts remained standing after the final whistle. The home-standing Lafayette students had no desire to trudge through the muck on the field and those from South Bethlehem were too sullen in defeat to mount an effort.

Only the Lehigh bench warmers had any desire to venture into the quagmire after the game. As the referee's pistol was fired for a final time, the white jerseys jumped off the pine and began to tackle each other in the puddles on the playing field, earning their "brown stripes" for The Game.

The skies cleared and the field remained dry for the 1939 contest. Lafayette's defense allowed a "Hail Mary" touchdown to Lehigh on the last play of the game, but still won by 16 after scoring 20 fourth quarter points. Northampton's Walt Zirinsky paced the Maroon, scoring 17, in the 29-13 triumph. Twice he plunged the line for scores, one of which was set-up when the Konkrete Kid intercepted a Lehigh aerial and returned it to the Brown and White 13. Four plays later, he carried the ball to pay-dirt. In addition, he knocked home a 20-yard field goal and converted two point-after-touchdowns.

Lehigh established a Rivalry record 178 yards passing in the '39 contest — a season's worth during that era. It was one mark that would be obliterated numerous times in future Lafayette-Lehigh games.

Leopard captain Quigg capped his career by venturing into Taylor Stadium's east stands for the game ball after Lehigh's "Hail Mary" point-after conversion kick. The Bethlehemite knew many in the crowd and was able to retrieve the football. Later, he was seen parading it through the streets of his hometown.

Quigg became the first Lafayette man to play for the Eastern Collegiate All-Stars in a game against the NFL's New York Giants. But like Art Diebel in 1923, Quigg's invitation to participate in the East-West Shrine Bowl arrived after the game was played.

Lafayette Posts Fifth Undefeated Season

Lafayette capped an unblemished 1940 season with a 46-0 thrashing of Lehigh at Fisher Field. Hook Mylin coached the Leopards to their second perfect record in four years and the fifth undefeated season in Lafayette history.

The Leopards pounded the Engineers for 545 total yards, 242 on the ground and 303 via the air, breaking the previous single-game record for The Rivalry. Offensive fireworks were led once again by Walter Zirinsky, who notched three touchdowns and three extra points. The 21

Smoking Those Kicks

With a 46.7-yard average, McKeesport native Steve Smoke is the all-time punting leader at Lehigh. In addition, he also holds the school record for longest fumble runback. Smoke returned a Penn State bobble 100 yards for a touchdown in 1938.

Sports Illustrated All-Americans

Four Lehigh linemen were honored as members of *Sports Illustrated's* Silver Anniversary All-Americans. Doug Reed, a stalwart on the '31 team, was honored as a Silver Anniversary All-American in 1956. Dean Stevenson from the '36 squad earned accolades in 1961. Frank Rabold of the '38 team, and Bob Good of the '39 squad were also named *Sports Illustrated* Silver Anniversary All-Americans in 1963 and 1964, respectively.

1940 Undefeated Season
Lafayette College (9-0)
Coach: Edward "Hook" Mylin

Ursinus	*20-0*
@ New York University	*9-7*
@ Muhlenberg	*26-7*
Gettysburg	*45-6*
@ Army	*19-0*
Washington & Jefferson	*25-0*
@ Rutgers	*7-6*
Western Maryland	*40-7*
Lehigh	*46-0*

points, when added to the 17 tallied from last season's game, established a new Rivalry record of 38 career points by one player.

Quarterback Charlie Nagle completed only seven passes for the Leopards, but gained 293 yards through the air, including two scoring strikes to Joe Condron.

Lafayette, on an 11-game winning streak over two seasons, finished third in the nation in scoring with 238 points on the season. Only Boston College's 313 and Tennessee's 299 ranked ahead of Lafayette.

The Leopards had two All-American halfbacks in 1940 — neither was Zirinsky. James Farrell and captain George Moyer both received Associated Press honorable mention.

Lafayette's 1940 Team

Front Row (Left to Right) — Condron, McKenna, Schultz, Allen, Martindale, Farrell, Pollschuk, McKnight, Thomas.
Second Row — Mitchell, Marsh, Alexander, W. Wermuth, Capt. Moyer, Tomczuk, Zirinsky, Laird, Giuoplo.
Third Row — Asst. Coach McGaughey, F. Wermuth, Marchetti, Smith, Morgan, Kirby, Meeker, Collins, Kresge, Williams, Coach Mylin.
Back Row — Mgr. Phelps, Nagle, Braldo, Svenson, Maddock, Curran, Casey, Graves, Baxter, Trainer Nagle.

Going Bowling?

At the conclusion of the 1940 Lehigh game, Lafayette Athletic Director Henry W. Clark announced that the school had received two feelers from New Year's Day Bowl committees. Both the Sun Bowl, in El Paso, Texas, and the Orange Bowl, in Miami, expressed interest in the untied, undefeated Leopards.

Clark said Lafayette would not consider a bid to the Sun Bowl but was interested in the Orange Bowl. Orange Bowl authorities in Miami said Lafayette would be considered along with three other Eastern teams.

Eventually, Georgetown received the Orange Bowl bid and lost to Mississippi State 14-7.

Lafayette Perfect In '40; Lehigh Perfect In '41

Lafayette completed a perfect season in 1940. Lehigh completed a perfect season in 1941, at least in the eyes of Lafayette fans. The Engineers went winless, finishing at 0-6-3, including a 47-7 thrashing at the hands of Hook Mylin's Leopards. It was Lehigh's first season without a win since the inaugural football team posted a 0-4 mark in 1884.

The Maroon steamrolled in the 75th renewal of The Rivalry behind 40 second-half points. Once again, Walt Zirinsky paved the way, crossing the goal line twice and booting five extra points. The 17 tallies gave the Leopard halfback 55 points scored in three Lehigh contests. Lehigh, *as a team*, managed to score only 20 points in those games.

The contest marked the final chapter for Lehigh coach Glen Harmeson, who became a commander in the United States Naval Reserve. As coach from 1934-1941, the former Purdue Boilermaker compiled a 23-42-5 record.

Zirinsky, "The Farmer," as Lehigh's Taylor Stadium faithful chanted throughout the game, admitted that he had received forms from six National Football League teams. These "forms" were data sheets completed by the player and used as part of the draft process. This was a legal contact under then-established college guidelines.

Teams showing interest and requesting information were the Brooklyn Dodgers (also then a football team), New York Giants, Philadelphia Eagles, Washington Redskins, Cleveland Rams and the Detroit Lions.

Free Substitution

The NCAA rules committee permitted free substitution beginning with the 1941 season. This rule was helpful during the war years when teams struggled with limited personnel. Before 1941, a player could not return in the same quarter he had departed. Free substitution ended in 1953, but was gradually restored in 1965.

In Remembrance

Halfback George Ellstrom, who recorded the controversial disallowed touchdown in the '36 contest, later became an Air Force pilot in World War II. On December 7, 1941, as the attack on Pearl Harbor began, Ellstrom's plane was shot down by the Japanese as it departed Clark Field in the Philippines.

The World War II Years

With the United States battling in World War II, both squads were decimated for the 1942 game, not only on the field, but in the stands and behind the bench.

Lafayette Athletic Director Henry Clark, assistant coach George McGaughey, and trainer John Nagle all entered the armed forces. On Lehigh's side, athletic business manager Paul Short and sports information director Charlie Moravee joined the service and were missing from The Rivalry. Lehigh had but two seniors starting against Lafayette.

An addition to the Lehigh staff was new head coach George Hoban, the former standout for the Tom Keady teams in the teens. Assisting Hoban as line coach was another past great, Leo Prendergast. Of course, Leo made his mark for *Lafayette* under Doc Sutherland.

Despite missing key players on both teams, the 1942 version had one of the most exciting finishes in The Series' history. With a deadlocked score of 7-7, Lafayette marched 78 yards to the Lehigh one-yard line as time wound down. The drive included an illegal substitution penalty against an injured Leopard player which moved the ball back from the Lehigh three-yard line to the eight.

Two plays later, Maroon halfback Henry Ciemniecki caught a swing pass from captain Nagle, but was brought down at the Lehigh one-yard line with two seconds remaining. Another Leopard player, Ramsey Maddock was "injured" on the play, stopping the clock and permitting the hosts one more opportunity to score the game-winner.

But as soon as Maddock was able to right himself and stepped off the playing field, the officials ordered play resumed and started the clock. In the confusion, Lafayette was unable to execute another play before time expired. The game went into the history books as a 7-7 tie, The Series' first in 53 years since the 6-6 draw in 1889.

Leading the Engineer team was captain and quarterback Bernie Deehan, who led the nation in punt returns handled, and Stanley Szymakowski, who was the first Lehigh University football player to win the Maxwell Club Award for his performance against Rutgers earlier in the season. Against the Scarlet Knights, Szymakowski rushed for a touchdown and kicked three field goals and an extra point.

New coaches stood on both sidelines the following season. Due to the War, both schools faced an abbreviated schedule in 1943 — including home and home games in The Rivalry for the first time since 1901.

Ben Wolfson's Leopards finished 4-1, including two victories over their arch rivals, while Leo Prendergast's Engineers were winless at 0-5-1.

The first contest was held in late October and was the second game of the season for each school. Because of the war, football practice did not commence until the semester began, and new candidates were welcomed every day and with open arms.

Season-Ender

The 1944 season was the last time The Game was not a season finale for both teams. Since 1916, only the contests of 1918, 1922, and 1931 were not season-enders. Due to a scheduling conflict, Lehigh played Rutgers after the Lafayette game in 1944. Since then, The Game has been the last regular season match-up for both schools.

Lafayette, behind two touchdowns apiece from Bill MaGee and Joe Marhefka, Jr., routed Lehigh 39-7 in front of 5,000 spectators — but no bands or cheerleaders — at Fisher Field.

In the rematch marking the traditional end-of-season game, the Leopards handed the boys from Lehigh their worst setback in series' history to date by a 58-0 count. That loss still stands as the seventh worst setback in Lehigh football annals.

A crowd of only 3,500 witnessed the slaughter in Taylor Stadium. Maroon backs Bill MaGee, Eddie Miersch, and captain Walter Sergy each visited the end zone twice. Sergy appeared in the East-West Shrine game, as his invitation arrived without any mail mix-ups and before the game was actually played.

By 1944, the War dramatically affected The Rivalry. In the season-opening contest, each team had ten freshmen in its starting line-up. Better than half of the Lafayette team was Lehigh Valley natives. The war years took its toll on Lehigh, as the Brown and White suffered its third winless season in the last four.

Once again, the Easton college took both games from its Bethlehem rival, by a combined 108-0 score. The 64-0 trouncing in the season finale marked the tenth consecutive Lafayette-Lehigh game in which the Maroon would celebrate afterwards. The score marked the first time the Maroon tallied more than 60 points against the Engineers. It was also Lehigh's worst defeat in The Rivalry.

In the first of the two contests, Lafayette blanked Lehigh 44-0 before only 300 fans in a rain-drenched Taylor Stadium. Leopard freshman halfback Fred Robbins notched three touchdowns running from the wing-T offense. Robbins, an Easton native who was raised just two blocks from Fisher Field, added five more six-pointers in the second contest — a single-game Series' record which still stands. The 48 points was the second best individual career performance in The Rivalry, behind Zirinsky's 55.

Underdog Prevails

The 1945 season finale once again featured a squad without a win. This time, the Leopards marched into The Game with an 0-7-1 mark, while Lehigh entered at 2-3.

In what became the swan song for both coaches, Wolfson's Lafayette squad — minus Wolfson, who was confined to an Easton Hospital bed suffering a severe case of the grip — squeaked-out a 7-0 triumph over Prendergast's Lehigh eleven. Like the 1942 classic, the '45 contest ended with one team knocking at the opponent's end zone door.

Crippled Players' Condition Upgraded to Injured

The 1945 season marked the first time journalists used the term "injured list" to report on the health conditions of football players. Prior to this, it was known as the "crippled list."

Under The Lights

Lehigh played its only home night game in the school's history in 1945. Temporary lights were installed in Taylor Stadium for a mid-season game against Connecticut. The Huskies used their superior night vision and emerged from the dark victorious by a 33-6 score.

Japan Bowl Forerunner

Former Lafayette Athletic Director Henry W. Clark became the United States 8th Army athletic officer for troops occupying Japan after the Japanese surrender in World War II.

He organized a New Year's Day 1946 exhibition pro football game on the main island for occupation troops. He also selected a group of college coaches to visit Japan and to set up divisional teams for G. I. competition. Among those coaches chosen was former Lafayette coach Hook Mylin.

After a fifteen-yard unsportsmanlike conduct penalty against the Leopards, Lehigh quarterback Al Wright eluded the Maroon rush and uncorked a 50-yard bomb. The pass was caught by Don Tarbell, who sprinted down the sideline before being bumped out of bounds by the Leopards' Dan Kovacs at the Maroon 14 as time expired.

Frustration filled the faces of Lehigh's players once again, as it was now ten years without a win against its venerable rival.

New Coaches ... Same Results

It was out with the old and in with the new, more or less, for the head coaches at both schools. The 1946 season saw the return of Hook Mylin to College Hill. Meanwhile, South Bethlehem welcomed former Brooklyn Dodger gridder Bill Leckonby as Lehigh's new mentor. Unfortunately for the two schools, they combined for only three wins prior to The Game.

Both teams had added motivation for winning The Game. Lehigh was gunning for its 250th all-time football victory. Lafayette wanted a victory over Lehigh to celebrate the 25-year anniversary of the Maroon's undefeated 1921 National Championship team.

Wining, dining, and tall tales filled the pregame reunion in Easton. The best of the bull involved former coach Jock Sutherland. Lafayette alumnus Bots Brunner was the keynote speaker.

During the 1921 pre-season training camp held in Delaware, New Jersey, the Maroon squad had to row boats to the practice field, which was located on an island in the middle of the Delaware River. On one such return trip to the mainland after practice, one of the players rocked the boat a bit too aggressively. All in the boat went overboard, including Dr. Sutherland. Fortunately, the water was shallow at this point and all were

Wearing Both Brown And Maroon

Leo Prendergast was the first and only Lafayette alumnus to coach Lehigh. A former stalwart under Jock Sutherland in the teens, his successes at Lehigh were appropriate for a Maroon double-agent manning the helm at the Bethlehem institution.

After two consecutive winless seasons, Prendergast finally recorded his first victory in his third year at Lehigh. Overall, Lehigh was 2-15-1 under Prendergast from 1943 to 1945.

S. B. Newton coached both Lehigh and Lafayette during the first decade of the century, but was not an alumnus of either school.

able to wade to shore. There was no mention of how skilled Sutherland was at the backstroke.

Lafayette blanked Lehigh for the fifth consecutive time. Parleying a blocked punt and a fumble recovery into 19 and six-yard scoring drives, the Leopards won 13-0 in the 1946 edition.

Little offense was generated by either side. The best play by the Lehigh contingent was when some Engineer undergrads made off with the pennants flying above Fisher Field, including a new Lafayette flag. Appropriately, Lehigh was billed for the mischief done by its students.

Liberty High School Hosts The Rivalry

Liberty High School Stadium hosted the 1947 contest, as Taylor Stadium was undergoing an expansion and renovation. This was only the second time The Game was not held on one of the school's campuses, as one other game was played in Wilkes-Barre during the 1891 season.

For the first time since 1924, both schools entered the season finale with winning records at 5-3. Like a broken record, Lafayette triumphed again. A fourth quarter flea-flicker call by new Lafayette coach Ivan Williamson netted the game's only touchdown.

On the game-winner, Frank Downing lateralled to Frank "Superman" Stanczak at the Lehigh 29. Stanczak then hurled a pass downfield to Sinbad Saylor, the captain and Bethlehem boy, who made the catch behind the Lehigh defense at the five-yard line and waltzed into the end zone.

Superman earned the name for his two-way, 60-minute performances in Lafayette's last four games.

For a change, the goalposts survived the game held at Liberty High School Stadium in Bethlehem. The posts were of steel construction and mounted and set in concrete casing.

Frank "Superman" Stanczak connected with Sinbad Saylor to score the game-winning touchdown for Lafayette in the 1947 game at Liberty Stadium.

UFO Sighting

Taylor Stadium played an integral part in the UFO paranoia in 1947.

The incident started when a former Lehigh professor of geophysics conceived a theory that sound waves caused by large explosions could be picked-up in the atmosphere much like sound waves could be monitored under water.

Using a kite-like structure of helium balloons to lift a sophisticated sensory-listening device to monitor Russian nuclear testing explosions, the idea was sold to the U.S. Army Air Force by former Lehigh professor Dr. W. Maurice Ewing.

Bethlehem was selected as the sight for the special mission codenamed Project Mogul because it was discrete and out of the way, not near a metropolitan area, and with no military installation nearby. The Taylor Stadium football field was spacious enough to launch the balloon structure, which when airborne would total 800 feet in length, and was located upwind from a Red Bank, New Jersey tracking headquarters. Besides, if any one asked about the events at the field, it was easy to write it off as part of the Lehigh-Lafayette football tradition or at least a wacky professor at work.

An April 3rd launch date was set to coincide with a British demolition explosion of the German island naval base Helgoland in the North Sea. The U.S. military wanted to see if Ewing's device could detect the blast.

After a successful launch, the device reached its desired height or 30,000 feet, then kept rising. Finally, at 50,000 feet the apparatus disintegrated and plummeted into the Atlantic Ocean.

As fate had it, the British also had to postpone its planned demolition of Helgoland, and another launch was set for April 18th. The result was not much different.

Unfortunately, the second launch was aborted due to high gusty winds at Taylor Stadium and a tracking device malfunction.

Project Mogul was then moved to Alamogordo Army Air Force Base in New Mexico. On a second test flight, the balloon structure fell to earth near Roswell, New Mexico. It was found by rancher W. W. "Mac" Brazel, who thought it to be the remnants of a crashed UFO. An Air Force official, not privy to the top secret Project Mogul, mistakenly identified the remains as that of a "flying disc." Hence the birth of the Roswell UFO incident. In later years, the story of the alleged crash and coverup would be retold in newspapers, books, movies, and the television show "Unsolved Mysteries."

In the 1970s, the U.S. government declassified Project Mogul, but the UFO tales continued. In July of 1994, the Air Force released all records on Roswell and Project Mogul, including Lehigh's role.

Lafayette Silences Lehigh's Cannon

For the second consecutive season, both schools entered The Game with more wins than losses. The 21,000-plus fans who jammed Fisher Field in 1948 saw Lehigh jump out to a quick 13-0 first quarter lead. Sophomore Dick Gabriel blasted over from the two. Dick Doyne broke-off a 71-yard dash on the next offensive series to quiet the throngs in Easton and helped sound a new brass cannon used to celebrate Lehigh scores.

The 70-pound brass cannon was a gift of James E. Hildebrand of Short Hills, New Jersey, an alumnus of the Lehigh fencing team. The cannon was once used to announce the safe arrival of whaling vessels at New Bedford, Massachusetts. It was fired every time Lehigh scored a touchdown, field goal, or safety.

But behind Gordon Fleming's two touchdowns, the Leopards outscored the Engineers 23-0 over the last three quarters. The 23-13 final kept Lehigh victory-less in the last 14 meetings.

In attendance at The Game was Penn's All-American lineman Chuck Bednarik. With an open date in the Quaker schedule, the Bethlehem native caught up with some friends on both sides. A day later, Iron Chuck would discover that he had been drafted by the Philadelphia Eagles of the National Football League.

While in the NFL, Bednarik was "The Last of the Sixty-Minute Men," playing every down on both offense and defense.

Lafayette Snubs Sun Bowl

Lafayette College rejected a 1948 post-season trip to the Sun Bowl in El Paso, citing Texas state laws which discriminated against its black halfback Dave Showell. Given the nation's position on racial tolerance, both the *New York Times* and the *Herald-Tribune* thought the event so newsworthy they treated it as a major news story.

Upset City, Baby!

The 1949 season gave Lehigh its best chance to snap the Leopard streak in The Rivalry. Leckonby's troops entered The Game sporting an outstanding 6-2 record, while new Lafayette coach Maurice "Clipper" Smith directed his men to a 1-6 mark.

Lehigh quickly jumped to a two-touchdown first quarter lead behind Gabriel and Doyne, with the former's touchdown giving him the Eastern college scoring lead. But once again, Lafayette rallied in the second half, outscoring its ancient rival 21-0, proving favorites carried no weight in this fall classic.

Lafayette took the second-half kick-off and drove 70 yards with Jack Savage scoring from the four. The Leopards took the lead 14-12 when George Cosgrove scored from the two. Defensive center Carl Potter intercepted a fourth quarter Lehigh pass and returned it 16 yards for the icing touchdown.

Gabriel finished the 1949 season with 1,023 yards and earned the "Beattie Feathers Award" as the first 1,000-yard rusher in Lehigh-Lafayette history.

Lafayette ended the 1949 season with a 21-12 victory over Gabriel and the Engineers.

Lafayette and Lehigh played The Game at Liberty High School Stadium for the second time. In the cramped quarters of the Liberty Stadium pressbox, two veteran Bethlehem newspapermen, Fred Nonnemacher and Frank Boyle, were heard reflecting on Lafayette's dominance in The Series, "Whereinhell is this thing going to stop!"

Lafayette completed its second longest winning streak against Lehigh in 1949, capturing the last nine games of The Series. Including the tie of 1942, the Leopards were undefeated in the last 15 contests against Lehigh — the longest streak in The Series. The win in 1949 set a record for the largest margin of victories (28) in Series' history. Heading into the second half of the 20th century, The Rivalry stood 55-27-3 in favor of Lafayette.

Second Quarter Wrap-Up (1906-1949)

The gun sounded and the teams trudged to the locker rooms, signaling the end of the second quarter of activity in College Football's Most Played Rivalry. As the players regrouped and the bands marched onto the field for the halftime show, the list of incidents and accidents grew along with the Lehigh-Lafayette football tradition.

Football rules changed over the years, but the heat of The Rivalry prevailed — on and off the field.

✔🖎 A cow greeted a President in a university's bell tower.

✔🖎 Two National Championships were claimed.

✔🖎 Ticket scalping charges tarnished the school administrations.

✔🖎 Undefeated teams and winless seasons.

✔🖎 Both schools christened new stadiums and soon each was too small to accommodate the overload of fans for The Game.

✔🖎 Caskets were paraded as part of a halftime show.

✔🖎 A wrong-way run somehow still turned into a touchdown after 115 yards of broken tackles, straight arms, and elusive cutbacks.

✔🖎 A halfback who played for both schools, and Penn and Yale too, and another back who bested the legendary Jim Thorpe in a track meet.

✔🖎 An expert used algebra to predict the outcome of The Game, while a calculator was needed to tally a record-setting 78-0 victory margin.

✔🖎 The traditional bonfire was lit prematurely, as Taylor Gym turned into a smoker.

✔🖎 Play signals were stolen, so an innovative, young Lafayette coach implemented the huddle.

✔🖎 Police actually lead a pregame rally instead of chasing party-goers, and an alumnus from one school was a keynote speaker at the other school's alumni rally.

✔🖎 A game featured only four completed passes, three to the opposition, the fourth for a touchdown. The same contest featured a backward punt.

✔🖎 Monsoon madness led to a near-drowning in an end zone mud puddle, players competed without socks, and a team bus docked late at the stadium because of severe currents crossing the roadway.

✔🖎 In one contest, punts outscored points 35-31. In another lopsided game, it was "Punts 46 - Points 6."

✔🖎 And in yet a third, one team was penalized only a foot for the entire game. Still, its penalty yardage out-gained its minus 28 yards rushing recorded for the contest.

✔🖎 An NFL record-holder, pro basketball star, and major league pitcher was a bust as a college head coach in The Rivalry, lasting only one season.

✔🖎 Cannons and guns became part of The Rivalry, and greeted traditional foes like Army, Navy, and the Marine Academy, but also the U.S. 7th Infantry, the Navy Yard, and the U.S. Ambulance.

✔🖎 Both teams were decimated by War-time restrictions, but the bands also suffered casualties as a bass drum and tuba took direct hits in one memorable postgame battle.

✔🖎 Two games a season, ten freshmen in each team's starting line-up, and a crowd of 300 for The Game highlighted the World War II years.

✔🖎 Coaches switching schools, Bethlehem boys on College Hill, and Easton kids at South Mountain.

✔🖎 Bowl considerations and bowl rejections.

✔🖎 One player outscoring the opposing team over three successive years.

✔🖎 Maxwell Club Award winners and beating a team coached by the Heisman Award namesake.

✔🖎 The Rivalry ended the second quarter with a pair of High School Homecoming games in '47 and '49.

Second Quarter (1906-1949)

Lafayette Coaches: Record vs Lehigh

Coach	Season	Wins	Losses	Ties
Dr. Alfred Bull	1906-07	2	0	0
George Barclay	1908	0	1	0
Bob Folwell	1909-11	3	0	0
George McCaa	1912-13	0	2	0
Wilmer Crowell	1914-16	1	2	0
Robert "Punk" Berryman	1917	0	1	0
Lt. L.A. Cobbett	1918	0	1	0
Dr. "Jock" Sutherland	1919-23	5	0	0
G. Herb McCracken	1924-35	9	3	0
Ernie Nevers	1936	0	1	0
Edward "Hook" Mylin	1937-42, '46	6	0	1
Ben Wolfson	1943-45	5	0	0
Ivan Williamson	1947-48	2	0	0
Maurice "Clipper" Smith	1949	1	0	0
Total		**34**	**11**	**1**

Lehigh Coaches: Record vs Lafayette

Coach	Season	Wins	Losses	Ties
Byron Dixon	1906-09	1	3	0
Howard "Bosey" Reiter	1910-11	0	2	0
Tom Keady	1912-20	6	3	0
Frank Glick	1921	0	1	0
Jim Baldwin	1922-24	0	3	0
Percy Wendell	1925-27	0	3	0
Austin Tate	1928-33	1	5	0
Glen Harmeson	1934-41	3	5	1
George Hoban	1942	0	0	0
Leo Prendergast	1943-45	0	5	0
Bill Leckonby	1946-49	0	4	0
Total		**11**	**34**	**1**

Second Quarter (1906-1949) Summary

Year	Where Played	Winner	Lafayette	Lehigh
			SCORE	
1906	Easton	Lafayette	33	0
1907	Bethlehem	Lafayette	22	5
1908	Easton	Lehigh	5	11
1909	Bethlehem	Lafayette	21	0
1910	Easton	Lafayette	14	0
1911	Bethlehem	Lafayette	11	0
1912	Easton	Lehigh	0	10
1913	Bethlehem	Lehigh	0	7
1914	Easton	Lehigh	7	17
1915	Bethlehem	Lafayette	35	6
1916	Easton	Lehigh	0	16
1917	Bethlehem	Lehigh	0	78
1918	Easton	Lehigh	0	17
1919	Bethlehem	Lafayette	10	6
1920	Easton	Lafayette	27	7
1921	Bethlehem	Lafayette	28	6
1922	Easton	Lafayette	3	0
1923	Bethlehem	Lafayette	13	3
1924	Easton	Lafayette	7	0
1925	Bethlehem	Lafayette	14	0
1926	Easton	Lafayette	35	0
1927	Bethlehem	Lafayette	43	0
1928	Easton	Lafayette	38	14
1929	Bethlehem	Lehigh	12	13
1930	Easton	Lafayette	16	6
1931	Bethlehem	Lafayette	13	7
1932	Easton	Lafayette	25	6
1933	Bethlehem	Lafayette	54	12
1934	Easton	Lehigh	7	13
1935	Bethlehem	Lehigh	0	48
1936	Easton	Lehigh	0	18
1937	Bethlehem	Lafayette	6	0
1938	Easton	Lafayette	6	0
1939	Bethlehem	Lafayette	29	13
1940	Easton	Lafayette	46	0
1941	Bethlehem	Lafayette	47	7
1942	Easton	Tie	7	7
1943	Easton	Lafayette	39	7
	Bethlehem	Lafayette	58	0
1944	Bethlehem	Lafayette	44	0
	Easton	Lafayette	64	0
1945	Bethlehem	Lafayette	7	0
1946	Easton	Lafayette	13	0
1947	Bethlehem	Lafayette	7	0
1948	Easton	Lafayette	23	13
1949	Bethlehem	Lafayette	21	12
			910	385

	Wins	Losses	Ties
Lafayette	34	11	1
Lehigh	11	34	1

Legends "All-Time" Team
First Half (1884-1949)

Lafayette	Position	Lehigh
Matt Brennan '23	QB/DB	Pat Pazzetti '11
George Barclay 1896	RB/DB	William Cahall '14
Mike Gazella '21	RB/DB	Allen Ware '32
Mike Wilson '26	RB/DB	Dick Gabriel '51
Bots Brunner '22	Line	Bots Brunner '16
Walter Bachman '02	Line	Howell Scobey '35
Babe Rinehart 1898	Line	C.E. Trafton 1893
John Quigg '40	Line	Robert Numbers '49
Frank Schwab '23	Line	Bob Good '39
Arthur Diebel '23	Line	Frank Rabold '38
Charles Berry '24	Line	D.M. Balliet 1882
Ed Bray 1898	P/K	Steve Smoke '38
Jock Sutherland (1919-23)	Coach	Tom Keady (1912-1920)

Honorable Mention:
— Lehigh: Doug Reed '31 Line; Dean Stevenson '36 Line; ; Dick Doyne '51 Back
— Lafayette: Bill Cothran '26 Line; Aaron Crane '09 Line; Joe Dumoe '19 Line; Harry Trout '00 Back; George McCaa '10 Back; Hooks Mylin (1937-42, '46) Coach; Herb McCracken (1924-35) Coach

HALFTIME:
The Traditions

The Bands

The Marching 97

Precision drills, snappy marching, and fight songs performed by the schools' bands are part of the pageantry of college football.

Lehigh's Marching 97 has charged the Engineer faithful into a football frenzy with "Rearing, Tearing, Down the Field" and its pre-game and halftime shows for decades. It's an outgrowth of the Lehigh University band which made its first appearance with 15 men during the 1908 football season.

The *Bethlehem Globe-Times* reported that "In October of 1973, after 67 years as an all-male band, a bastion of masculine tradition came tumbling down as seven members stepped forward, doffed their shakos, and let flow their long tresses to the tune of 'There's Nothing Like a Dame'."

The band got its name from the 97 members in the organization. It's capped at that number because most of its traditional drills are arranged for 12 ranks of eight led by one drum major.

Strike Up The Bands

Two schools, but three bands? The Lehigh and Lafayette bands, who performed as usual for the 1911 game at Taylor Field, welcomed a guest appearance by another local group of musicians — the Bethlehem Steel band. Allegedly comprised of numerous Lehigh Alumni, the 80-member Steel Band joined the Lehigh marchers in halftime revelry, forming the "Flying 'L'" and performing fight songs and the alma mater. This was the first of numerous appearances by the company's ensemble at The Game.

The Bands

War Casualties At Fisher Field

The two football teams weren't the only ones decimated by the War. Dr. T. Edgar Shields, professor of music at Lehigh, reported casualties due to the student warfare at Fisher Field after the 1942 game. The band director reported a smashed bass drum and crushed tuba as a result of the post-game battle.

Lafayette College Alma Mater

Words and Music by Walter C. Stier, Class of 1884

We'll gather by the twilight's glow
    In front of old Pardee
In all the world no other scene,
    So fair, so dear to me.
O Lafayette, O Lafayette,
    To thee our voices raise!
While loyal lips and loyal hearts
    Unite to sing thy praise.

(Chorus)
We'll gather by the twilight's glow
    In front of old Pardee
In all the world no other scene,
    So fair, so dear to me.

And future years shall not erase
    These gems of Mem'ry rare,
But oft we'll live the scenes again
    Impressed so firmly there.
O Lafayette, O Lafayette,
    O joyous college days!
E'er while these loyal hearts shall beat.
    We've loyal lips to praise.
(Repeat Chorus)

Lafayette Fight Song 1897

Tune — "There'll be a hot time in the old town to-night."

Oh! dear me what a cinch we're up against,
Poor Lehigh, we have smashed up your defense,
For we are here with a team from the top of Easton hill, and right here we give you the chill.
When you hear the chapel bell go ding-ling,
All join round and sweetly we will sing,
And when the game is through, the "peerade" all join in,
There will be a hoy time in the old town to-night.

We're out for blood,
We're out for gore, we're out for gore,
"Babe" Rinehart is the captain of the Lafayettes,
Let 'er go, let 'er go, let 'er go.

Dr. John Raymond
leads the Lafayette
band.

Lafayette Fight Song 1898

— from the scrapbook of Frank M. Scheibley, Class of 1898.

TUNE — "There is a tavern in the town."
1. There is a college called Lehigh, called Lehigh.
Whose boys think they are very spry, very spry,
But they can't beat Lafayette at foot-ball.
They'll never make a point at all.

CHORUS:
Fare thee well, for we must beat you,
Do not let this snow fall grieve you,
For remember that our boys have learned the game, the game;
Adieu, adieu, Lehigh, adieu, adieu, adieu,
There will be nothing left of you, left of you
For we must make just a few more touchdowns yet,
Shout, rah, rah, tiger, Lafayette.

2. Dig Lehigh's grave both wide and deep, wide and deep,
Put tombstones at her head and feet, head and feet,
And from each sweater take away the "L,"
Which Lafayette alone guards we. — CHORUS.

Halftime Entertainment

During halftime of the 1957 game, the Lehigh band, which received widespread attention from football enthusiasts during the past years, lived up to its reputation by performing difficult maneuvers on the snow-covered field without sacrificing sound musicianship. As a way of expressing thanks to alumni for their financial support, the band formed a test tube and beaker arrangement, symbolizing the pouring of money into the Lehigh University Treasury. The Lafayette band followed with a fine performance, but one Lehigh student was not in the mood to express praise. Instead, he swiped a Lafayette bandsman's straw hat and stomped on it at the sideline. A Bethlehem policeman immediately brought a halt to the action to avoid a possible confrontation.

Lehigh Fight Song — Rearing Tearing

Rearing, tearing down the field, down the field,
Lehigh's team will never yield, never yield,
Past the last white line that marks the goal,
And brings a victory again to old Lehigh,
And when the big Brown team
Goes crashing thru, crashing thru,
Rivals don't know what to do, what to do.
Rooters cheer another victory for old Lehigh.

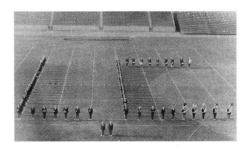

The Bands

Lehigh Fight Song — The Old Silver Goblet

Get out the old silver goblet,
With Lehigh upon it,
And we'll open another keg of
beer;
For we came to college
But we didn't come for knowl-
edge,
So we'll raise hell while we're
here.

Lehigh University Alma Mater

Where the Lehigh rocky rapids rush from
the West,
'Mid a grove of spreading chesnuts, wall in
ivy drest,
On the breast of old South Mountain,
reared against the sky,
Stands our noble Alma Mater, stands our
dear Lehigh.

Like a watchman on the mountain, stands
she grandly bold.
Earth and Heaven's secrets seeking, hoard-
ing them like gold.
All she wrests from Nature's storehouse —
naught escapes her eye
Gives she gladly to her dear ones, while we
bless Lehigh.

We will ever live to love her, live to praise
her name;
Live to make our lives add luster to her
glorious fame.
Let the glad news wake the echoes, joyfully
we cry,
Hail to thee, our Alma Mater hail! All hail!
Lehigh!

A Spirited Tradition

From before the turn of the century when Woodrow Wilson led the cheers in Wesleyan's conquest of Lehigh in the battle for entry rights to the Ivy League, cheerleaders have been an integral part of college football and The Rivalry.

The original "spirit boosters" of the 1880's were simply students who lined the field and led the crowd in cheers and songs. Donning straw hats and school sweaters, the early spirit teams' responsibilities included chasing fraternity dogs from the field in addition to the time-honored duties of leading pep rallies and victory parades.

The popularity of the squads evolved to the point where tryouts were conducted for the limited number of spots available.

Sometimes the cheerleaders became more involved in the action than they had planned. During the heat of The Rivalry, the group became targets for marauding students from the other school. Megaphones, hats, and sweaters from the opposing school's cheerleaders were valuable mementos at post-game fraternity parties.

The squads at both colleges faced a new set of problems when the two schools admitted women. Fighting for survival against the rival's storming students became a matter of protecting the female cheerleaders.

One approach involved "circling the wagons." The male cheerleaders would form a tight circle around their female counterparts and swing their megaphones to thwart attempts to kidnap the coed members.

The cheerleading highlights of the Lafayette-Lehigh game often featured "disconnections." This happened when a male squad member scored a direct hit with the megaphone to an attacking student's head, disconnecting the rival's mind from his body and feet from the ground — all in honor of saving the women.

The Cheerleaders

1993 Lehigh Cheerleaders

1994 Lafayette Cheerleaders

Nicknames and Mascots

Rent-A-Cat

In 1962, Lafayette's freshman class rented a six-month old Leopard for the Lafayette-Lehigh game. Each freshman paid one dollar to cover the rental fee. The class originally intended to rent a 300-pound leopard, but the administration nixed the idea after hearing of an incident at another college where a live bear mascot broke free and mauled several fans. The Eastonians paraded their mascot along the sidelines of Fisher Stadium.

The Leopards Unleashed

The 1924 season was the first time Lafayette's current nickname was used. A writer in the November 24th *Easton Express* used Leopards when referring to Lafayette's gridiron team in a story about The Rivalry. Prior to this time, the college had been called "The Maroon" based on its school colors, maroon and white.

The first sighting of Leopards on campus appeared in the October 7th, 1927 edition of *The Lafayette*. George Parkman, who then served as the sports editor for the student paper, recalled that "a number of our opponents had animal nicknames and someone decided Lafayette should also have one."

There is no known explanation as to why the nickname appeared at that time or why Leopards was chosen.

Nicknames and Mascots

The Brown and White

The Lehigh Engineer nickname has a long and storied history. Its origins fill one long story in the history of The Rivalry.

It seems that the Engineer moniker was tagged by a *Globe-Times* sportswriter on the Lehigh football team in the 1930's. Until that time, the South Mountain school was known as the Brown and White, after its school colors.

Despite being an all-male school for more than its first one hundred years, a woman ironically played a prominent role in the choice of Lehigh's colors and first nickname.

According to an exchange of letters in the 1918 Alumni Bulletin, students from the Class of 1876 were responsible for "discovering" the brown and white color scheme.

One autumn day, a group of the undergrads were sitting outside Christmas Hall trying to agree upon suitable school colors when a stunning young lady passed before them. As she crossed the street, the girl raised her skirt slightly to keep it out of the mud, and provided the college boys with a glimpse of brown stockings and white petticoats.

Impressed with her beauty, the students took the flash of color as a sign from above, and immediately decided that both the woman and brown and white were a special combination and just what Lehigh needed.

Thus, they adopted the official school colors, though the University did not adopt women until 1971.

Another letter writer in the Bulletin had a slightly different recollection, claiming that it was simply a young lady wearing brown and white stockings that caught the men's fancy.

Either way, Brown and White became both the school colors and the original nickname.

The Engineer nickname was coined in 1935 in honor of the predominance of the students pursuing engineering degrees. As the University evolved and the Arts and Business Colleges grew, the Engineer nickname became identified with the school's founder, industrialist Asa Packer, who was also the founder of the Lehigh Valley Railroad.

In 1948, a motion was made to change the nickname to Packers by those students and alumni who were not mechanical, industrial, or train engineers. The name never caught on with the sportswriters who penned the game stories.

The 1980's saw another movement to scrap the Engineer nickname, as a University effort to change the name to Brown and White quickly blended into obscurity.

Today, the Engineers live, as reflected in the old locomotive steaming through a letter "L" in the sports logo. Others refer to the teams as the South Mountaineers after the geological name where the University stands. And some still use the Brown and White.

Bonfires

Bonfire Security

The woodpile for the traditional Lehigh bonfire was well-guarded from Lafayette arsonists in 1964. The Lehigh freshmen set up a campus-wide security network, complete with walkie-talkie radios, to protect the towering pile of wood. An abundant supply of wood was available thanks to the demolition of Lehigh's education department building. The white, wooden structure, considered an eyesore by many, provided more than enough wood to fuel the inferno to a height of 68 feet, signifying the graduation year of the freshmen class. The pile came up one two-by-four short when Dr. John S. Cartwright, a member of Lehigh's education department, confiscated a piece of the building's remains as a memento.

Bonfires

Mission Impossible

In 1953, an enthusiastic Lafayette student attempted the near-impossible task of lighting the Lehigh bonfire. The fleet-footed frosh somehow maneuvered his way around the Lehigh security guards and penetrated deep into enemy territory. The student was only a few feet from his destination when an alert Lehigh man tripped him. The guards quickly grabbed the torch and gasoline can and sent him back to College Hill with a South Mountain haircut.

Woke Up Without Wood

Lehigh's traditional bonfire, held on the eve of the Great Battle, was short on wood in 1961. A group of enthusiastic Lafayette students raided the South Mountain campus and set fire to the kindling gathered by the Lehigh freshmen. The ever-resourceful Lehigh student body hastily replenished the woodpile, and with the help of a stiff breeze, the bonfire reached a height of 65 feet, keeping in tact the tradition of having a bonfire as tall as the year of the freshmen graduating class.

Gotta Light?

The bonfires at the pep rallies offered a test of bravery for the students. To prove manhood, students attempted to light their cigarette or cigar using the bonfire flame. To pass the test, the cigarette or cigar had to be lit while in the student's mouth. Few passed the test and most retreated from the flame with singed hair, eyelashes, and eyebrows.

Be Prepared!

In 1967, the Lafayette and Lehigh campuses were filled with pregame festivities for the 103rd meeting. The schools scheduled pep rallies and bonfires to prepare for The Game. Lehigh students raided the Lafayette campus the morning before the game and set fire to the Leopard woodpile. Anticipating a Lehigh raid, the battle-tested Eastonians had practiced the Boy Scout motto "Be Prepared" by flanking a makeshift woodpile as a decoy; the real woodpile was untouched.

Goalposts

Golden Goalpost Award

The winners of the Golden Goalpost Award for the longest continuous piece of goalpost from a Lafayette-Lehigh game:

Lehigh - Alpha Tau Omega Fraternity (10' 1" section of crossbar from the 1987 game).

Lafayette - Chi Phi Fraternity (entire cross bar measuring 23' 4" from the1964 game).

Lehigh Alpha Tau Omega brothers (Scott Kim, Garry Foltz, Brett Almassy, Alex Cottrill, Michael Diedrichs, Nate Farmer, and Fritz Lloyd) display a section of the crossbar from the 1987 Lehigh-Lafayette game at Taylor Stadium.

Premature Goalpost Destruction

In 1968 on the eve of the Great Battle, a group of Lehigh marauders, whose calendars were freed up by the cancellation of the bonfire and pajama parade, raided the Lafayette campus and uprooted the goalposts at Fisher Field. The goalpost pieces were reassembled in the form of "LU" at midfield.

Goalposts

Memorabilia

After the victory in the 1956 game, the Lehigh fans, not content with only bringing the Brass Cannon back to Bethlehem, stormed Fisher Field to capture the goalposts. Little resistance was provided by the Lafayette students and Easton police, and the students returned to campus with the posts and one minor casualty. Lehigh's Douglas Sommerville was treated at St. Luke's Hospital to remove a splinter (of the goalpost variety) from his arm. Not to be denied his souvenir, Douglas requested that the doctor return the splinter to its rightful owner after it was removed.

Men Of Steal Meet Goalposts Of Steel

A favorite pastime of the students at The Game was securing a piece of the wooden goalposts as a badge of courage for their fraternity. That practice came to an abrupt end in 1991 at Goodman Stadium, as the traditional wooden posts were replaced by a specially-engineered tubular steel version.

The "H-shaped" posts were "made of a steel alloy able to withstand the force of thousands of goalpost crashers and are virtually indestructible," as one administrator described them.

Sunk four feet into subterranean concrete encasements, the goalposts survived the post-game attack and have been used at The Game in both Bethlehem and Easton since.

Auxiliary Posts

In the early 1970's, the NCAA passed a rule that required the home team to provide an auxiliary set of goalposts in case the original posts were torn down or damaged before the end of regulation. The tradition of goalpost destruction at Lafayette-Lehigh games undoubtedly influenced the NCAA's ruling, but the Rutgers-Princeton rivalry was also a big factor. After the goalposts were torn down prematurely in a Rutgers-Princeton game in the early '70's, a spare set of goalposts from a nearby high school were hurriedly transported to the stadium so that Rutgers could kick the tying extra point at the end of the game.

Plan B

The Lehigh administration started a new tradition when it outlawed goalpost destruction for the 1991 Lehigh-Lafayette game at Goodman Stadium. Steel goalposts encased in concrete and beefed up police protection curtailed the destructive efforts of the students — at least on the Goodman Stadium field.

A renegade group of students improvised after the 1991 game by partaking in extracurricular activities on the practice field. One Lafayette alumnus jokingly coined a new saying aimed at the Lehigh administration and Bethlehem police, "If you can't beat 'em, tear down their practice field goalposts."

Goalposts

More of a Good Thing

In 1959, the NCAA changed the width of the goalposts from 18' 6" to 23' 4" in an effort to increase the scoring in college football. The NFL goalposts remained at 18' 6".

How was The Rivalry affected by the change in dimensions? Lafayette was thankful that the rule change wasn't implemented until 1959, when Lehigh's game-winning extra-point attempt missed by a Leopard's whisker in the 1958 game.

In 1961, Andy Larko and Lehigh needed every inch of the widened cross-bar to convert the game-winning field goal.

For Lafayette and Lehigh students, the change meant an extra 4' 10" of goalpost memorabilia was available for the postgame battle.

The impact was dramatic in college football. In 1959, there were 103 successful field goal attempts; in 1975, there were 1,164.

A Lasting First Impression

Senior defensive tackle and Lafayette co-captain Rich Doverspike relished the tradition of The Rivalry. As a freshman in 1980, the Pittsburgh native was initiated into The Game when Lehigh walloped Lafayette 32-0 in Neil Putnam's last game as Lafayette head coach.

Doverspike's first impression was a lasting one: "We were getting blown out so I got to play almost the entire fourth quarter. There were five minutes left and as we broke the huddle I looked over my shoulder. I saw all these people up on the goalposts. I was amazed. The fans were going nuts. All the students were in the end zone. That's when I found out what the Lehigh-Lafayette game is all about."

An official watches the ball sail through a primitive set of wooden goalposts at Fisher Field.

Police Stories

In The Beginning ...

The police have been as much a part of the Lehigh-Lafayette tradition as smokers, parades, and pep rallies. In the first Lehigh-Lafayette game played at Easton, the police made a lasting impression on Richard Harding Davis, the Father of Lehigh Football, who wrote, "My chief recollections of it consist of personal encounters with the spectators and Easton policemen, who had an instinctive prejudice to Lehigh men, which they expressed by kicking them in the head, whenever one of them went under the ropes for the ball."

The Missing Hat File

During Lafayette-Lehigh week on College Hill in 1961, several mischievous Lafayette students jumped an Easton policeman and made off with his hat. The officer did not take kindly to the shenanigans and used his night stick in an attempt to regain his cap. The policeman was still hatless the next day, and a Lafayette student, along with a pair of sore shins, had a prize for his trophy case.

Bethlehem police officer John Pulley, who had his hat stolen during the 1959 Lehigh-Lafayette game, sympathized with the Easton lawman, as yet another incident report was added to the "missing hat" file for Lafayette-Lehigh week.

Hats Off To The Police

The tradition of "hat stealing" has long been a part of The Rivalry. A policeman's hat was considered a trophy to the students, but the penalty for getting caught was a stiff fine and possible jail time. After the 1959 game, Bethlehem policeman John Pulley's hat was knocked off by what was identified in the police report as a hard green pear. Before Pulley could recover his cap, an unidentified Lafayette student abducted the hat and fled.

Police Payback!

Outside Taylor Stadium after the 1973 Lehigh-Lafayette game, Bethlehem patrolman John Ladics caught up with a group of hat-thieving students and arrested one of the slower gang members for disorderly conduct. Detective Charles Donchez suffered a dislocated wrist while helping Ladics pursue the gang. Later the same day, Ted Kukawski, a Lehigh student from Drinker House, returned the hat to Ladics saying he found the cap on campus.

Parades, Smokers, and Pep Rallies

Friday nights before The Game were reserved for the smoker and pajama parade in Bethlehem. The smoker in Taylor Gym featured pep talks by coaches, senior players, administrators, and faculty. Bosey Reiter, professor of phys ed and former head football coach, often led the inspirational speeches to fire-up the student body and team.

Bosey was so revered by the student body, that in 1922, each contributed one dollar to purchase a new Ford automobile which would replace his old bike. Not content to just turn over the keys to the car, the students dismantled the car and reassembled it in the gym.

"It wasn't the gift, but when and how I got it," said Reiter about receiving the vehicle in its surprising location.

Following the smoker, the Lehigh marching band led the parade down New Street and across the toll bridge to the north side of town. Pajama-clad freshmen followed, singing "We pay no tolls tonight." This in reference to the penny toll for walkers across the bridge, a nickel for cars.

The march continued to Broad Street and traversed to Main Street and the Moravian Seminary's dormitory. The frosh then serenaded the girls of Moravian before returning to the south side across the Hill-to-Hill Bridge. The more adventuresome climbed drain pipes and trellis to gain access to the women who were securely locked in the Seminary's dorms.

One year, three freshmen scaled a balcony to talk to the Moravian coeds. Later, using the more conventional stairway to exit rather than climb back out the window, they were confronted by the housemother. Although upset, she let them pass.

Almost out the door, the three were met by the college president, who did not take a favorable view of the escapades. He locked the Lehigh men in a room, interrogated them, and called police. Moments later, while the president was distracted by another disturbance, the three broke through the window and "ran like hell because we were scared as hell."

For those not spending time in the girls' dormitories at Moravian, "sit-ins" on the bridges became the "in-thing." After tying up traffic for hours, police would eventually intervene and disperse the crowd of freshmen. The morning after, the sanitation department hired extra help to dispose of the confetti, beer cans, and other party favors from the bridges.

Parade Mania in Easton

In 1961, Lafayette students, numbering in the hundreds, engaged in pregame festivities that included a parade and "sit down" on downtown Easton's Northampton Street that halted traffic for over an hour.

Finding the street cold and unstimulating, the parade members took to the air and climbed to the top of Easton's Center Square monument. The age-old saying, "What goes up, must come down," held true, but in this case, not without police intervention. Once the climbers were "helped" down by Easton police officers, the student mob invaded local radio station WEST to get a different kind of "air" time.

Unhappy with the radio station's reception, the disgruntled mass proceeded to toss eggs, water balloons, overly-ripened fruit, and homemade bombs around town until the Easton police once again "helped" the students to their dormitories.

ECO 1 — LU's Best Pep Rally

Lehigh-Lafayette game week held many special memories. For those attending Lehigh after the mid-1960's, the Friday morning ECO 1 lecture during Lehigh-Lafayette week meant cocktails and an impromptu pep rally complete with the Marching 97, cheerleaders, noisemakers, fight songs, and fraternity dogs.

On the Friday morning of Lehigh-Lafayette week, Professor Richard Aronson found himself delivering his lecture to a standing-room only crowd, which included students from other courses and sometimes other schools who were interested in the fun and frivolity.

The tradition started innocently enough when Aronson made a comment during a lecture about not being able to understand what the band was yelling across the field to the visiting fans and band.

"From my seats, it always sounded like 'Hey! Gettysburg!' — or whatever team we were playing that week, 'You %$Kgh&#)!'" recounted Aronson. "It was always so badly mumbled I had no idea what was being said. Evidently, my comments got around and that Friday morning, the band showed-up and serenaded the lecture hall with music and a special greeting for me. In perfectly clear harmony, the band shouted, 'Hey! Aronson! You %$Kgh&#)!' It brought the house down, and started a Lehigh-Lafayette tradition."

Mr. Lafayette

In 1953, the Lafayette campus experienced a changing of the guard in the spirit department. Dr. Samuel Pascal, head of the Department of Romantic Languages, replaced Professor Danny Hatch as Mr. Lafayette for the pep rallies. Hatch had been a College Hill icon for the past 53 Lafayette-Lehigh games.

The Media

Television

Television became a household item in 1951 with approximately 10 million Americans owning sets. The Rivalry became a household item in 1981 when The Game was broadcast live from Taylor Stadium on WLVT-TV Channel 39 of the Lehigh Valley.

The first national television broadcast of the Lafayette-Lehigh game was in 1993 from Murray Goodman Stadium on ESPN2. The Game was also the first collegiate football telecast on ESPN2.

WFMZ-TV, Channel 69 of Allentown, PA, has been broadcasting the Lafayette-Lehigh game live since 1989.

You Asked For It!

The 1967 Lehigh-Lafayette game action was heard coast-to-coast by alumni who tuned into a special radio broadcast by Lehigh student radio station WLRN. Utilizing a switchboard at the Bethlehem Steel offices, the game was transmitted via telephone lines from the Taylor Stadium pressbox to the Steel offices, then reconnected to a network of other phone lines to remote broadcast sights around the nation.

For the first time in series' history, the Lafayette-Lehigh game was shown on television — WLVT-TV Channel 39 televised The Game locally via a one-day delayed broadcast.

Live from Taylor Stadium ... It's Lehigh-Lafayette!

The early sellout of the 1981 game prompted Lehigh to seek permission from the NCAA and ABC-TV to air the first live television broadcast of the historic rivalry. The NCAA and ABC-TV waived their rights, and WLVT-TV, Channel 39 of the Lehigh Valley, televised the 117th Lehigh-Lafayette game live from Taylor Stadium.

Local radio stations WJRH of Lafayette College, WGPA of Bethlehem, WEST of Easton, and WLVR of Lehigh University also covered the play-by-play action. A telephone hotline, set up in the pressbox, provided periodic updates and a postgame summary of the day's events.

The Lafayette

The Oldest College Newspaper in Pennsylvania

VOL. 120, NO. 12   LAFAYETTE COLLEGE   DECEMBER 10, 1993

School Newspapers

The Lafayette. Lafayette's school newspaper —the oldest college newspaper in Pennsylvania — was founded 1870 and covered The Game since its inception.

The Brown & White. The Lehigh student-run newspaper celebrated its 100th-year of Game coverage in 1994.

Radio

WEST	Easton, PA
WIPI	Easton, PA
WJRH	Lafayette College
WKAP	Allentown, PA
WLVR	Lehigh University
WGPA	Bethlehem, PA

Toll-Free Play-By-Play

Keeping pace with the 1990's, a 1-800 phone line was made available so that fans could hear the live play-by-play broadcast of the Lehigh-Lafayette football game from anywhere in the United States.

Football Stats Hit The Newspapers

The 1913 contest was the first Lehigh-Lafayette game in which statistics were published in *The Lafayette*.

THE Brown and White

Lehigh University's Student Newspaper Founded in 1894

Vol. 101 No. 46   Tuesday, May 3, 1994   'All the Lehigh News First'

Haircuts

The Barber Shop

Haircuts became so widespread during Lafayette-Lehigh week that Lafayette Dean Charles Cole issued a statement in 1957 urging that no headshaving or physical harm be administered to Lehigh students during the guarding of the bonfire. A group of conscientious Lafayette students, taking heed to the Dean's request, visited Lehigh's campus instead to sharpen their barber skills. The barber shop trainees gave buzz cuts to several unsuspecting Lehigh students sleeping in Richards House.

Goodwill Games

Tired, weary Lehigh students were easy victims for a group of College Hill men in the 1950's. Masquerading as goodwill ambassadors from Lehigh, the Lafayette undergrads would drive to the train station and greet students returning to Bethlehem from breaks via the railroad. Offering food, drink, and transportation up South Mountain, the Eastonians would hijack the now-slightly tipsy Lehigh students and shave "LC" on the unsuspecting victims' heads.

American Graffiti

On the eve of the 1963 game, three Lafayette freshmen were "cruising" the Lehigh campus when their car was stopped outside Taylor Stadium by a large group of South Mountain students. The Lehigh gang proceeded to deflate the tires, rewire the ignition system, and give the coupe a Brown and White paint job. The Lafayette freshmen returned to College Hill carless and with "LU" haircuts.

Lafayette students give free haircuts to two Lehigh students after the vandals were caught trying to prematurely light the Lafayette bonfire.

Tailgating

Tailgating is a Lehigh-Lafayette tradition that has withstood the test of time. Throughout the years, changes in the rules and by-laws have altered the habits of tailgaters. But, the resourceful pregame partiers have always found a way to adapt.

When the kickoff time was moved to 10:45 a.m. for the game at Fisher Field in 1988, one student responded, "What a great concept! Now I don't have to go to bed before I start tailgating."

Another avid tailgater stressed the improvement in tailgating conditions with the move from Taylor to Goodman Stadium. "I enjoy the games at Goodman much more. With the larger scoreboard at Goodman, I can still see the numbers from the back of my pickup truck after four quarters of tailgating."

Campus Raids and Pregame Mischief

Peace Treaty

Campus raids, a tradition dating back to the late 1800's, wreaked havoc on both campuses during the 1940's. The unruliness became so widespread that in 1951, the Lafayette and Lehigh student governments agreed to a pact to protect both campuses from vandalism during Lafayette-Lehigh week. The student presidents signed the historic document that started by proclaiming, "We the undersigned do hereby agree to uphold to the best of the following codes of rivalry..."

Just A Reminder

The Lafayette freshmen raided South Mountain the night before the 100th game, leaving behind a reminder of who Lehigh's opponent was the next afternoon. The freshmen painted one letter on each of the steps leading to the library and University Center spelling "L-A-F-A-Y-E-T-T-E."

Preventive Maintenance

Before the 100th game, Lehigh students raided the Lafayette campus and doused the Leopard statue with Brown and White paint. After cleaning up the statue, the Lafayette students covered their mascot with a plastic shield to prevent future dousings.

Post-War Bombing Of Lehigh

An air raid occurred on the South Mountain campus three days before The Game of '47. No one was injured, as the yellow plane miscalculated its target. Believed to be piloted by a Lafayette student, the "bomber" swooped in from the east and dropped "Beat Lehigh" pamphlets in the campus  vicinity. No leaflets were found on the University's South Bethlehem land. Bad wind conditions and poor aim by the triggerman accounted for the failed sortie.

Campus Raids and Pregame Mischief

The Banner Heist And Break-In Of '33

Two Lehigh freshmen incited riots at each campus on successive nights during the week of the 1933 Lehigh-Lafayette game and were later charged with burglarizing the Lehigh administrative building.

The incident started Wednesday before The Game, when the two frosh placed calls to Lafayette dormitories and fraternity houses, challenging the College Hill students to come to Lehigh and take the "Beat Lafayette" banner which had been hung between two dorms on the South Mountain campus.

After scouting the scene, a group of Lafayette students returned at 2:30 a.m., entered the residence halls, cut the ropes, and hauled in the banner.

Before they were able to escape the enemy's building, the Lafayette students were trapped by a group of Lehigh men. A brawl ensued, during which fire hoses doused the invaders and the dormitories. Considerable damage was done to the building and two Lafayette intruders were captured.

One hostage was released Thursday morning. The other was released after negotiations established a William Penn highway drop point.

While the battle was waging on the hill, the two Lehigh freshmen broke into the administration building. They rifled through a cash draw in the bursar's office, but found only loose change. They then attempted to break into the supply room when they were apprehended by university police.

After interrogation, the two freshmen admitted to instigating the brawl over the banner by placing calls to Lafayette. It was their intention to use the disturbance as a smoke screen to divert the police to the dormitories, while they burglarized the office.

Late Thursday night, about 300 Lehigh students returned the favor and retaliated for the assault on the school's banner. A small group of Lafayette men stood guard at the entrance to the college grounds at the east end of Pardee Hall. Underestimating the size of the Lehigh army, the College Hill contingent retreated to defend the Lafayette statue in front of Colon Memorial Chapel, which was believed to be the target of the Lehigh mission.

For nearly an hour, a battle waged. Rotten eggs, potatoes, artichoke hearts, and other vegetables were launched back and forth. Eventually, the Easton police entered the fracas and dragged 29 Lehigh combatants to cells at the central station. Bail was set at $7.50 for some, $12.50 for others.

Meanwhile, in South Bethlehem, the police arrested 27 more Lehigh students near the South Mountain campus. One group of 17 students was arrested as they were boarding a truck for Easton. Another gang of 10 was nailed as they returned from the war front. Many wore nothing more than shreds of clothing because their garments had been torn off during the battle.

The "Beat Lafayette" banner re-appeared behind the Lafayette bench during the game.

The Fans

Lehigh students join in the revelry that makes Lehigh-Lafayette one of the most spirited rivalries in college football.

Two youngsters enjoy a Lafayette-Lehigh game at Fisher Field.

Fans endure the cold at the 1987 Lehigh-Lafayette game at Taylor Stadium.

"Beat Lafayette" and "Beat Lehigh" Display Contests

The "Beat Lehigh" display at Lafayette's Phi Kappa Psi fraternity house delivers a subliminal message during the '60's. The first letter of each word in the "Lehigh Shall Die" message were lighted at night spelling "LSD."

A Tradition is Born

The "Beat Lafayette" display tradition started in 1947 as an event sponsored by the Lehigh Interfraternity Council. Displays were erected by fraternities and living groups and were judged in three categories: 1) originality of theme, 2) inventive use of mechanical devices, and 3) artistic qualities. A possible five points was awarded in each category. The contest was judged the night before The Game by a panel of Lehigh professors, and the winner was announced at halftime. Plaques were awarded to the top three.

Lafayette followed the tradition in the 1950's with "Beat Lehigh" display contests during Lafayette-Lehigh week. The College Hill event was sponsored by Lafayette's Interfraternity Council.

"Beat Lafayette" and "Beat Lehigh" Display Contests

"Beat Lafayette" Display Woes

In 1950, the annual "Beat Lafayette" display contest for Lehigh students became a self-fulfilling prophecy after the Engineers whitewashed the Leopards, 38-0 before 20,000 spectators at Fisher Field. Phi Sigma Kappa's winning banner illustrated the Lafayette Leopard being dunked into a large beer mug, washing the spots off the mascot.

The brothers of Delta Phi fraternity were not as fortunate as Phi Sigma Kappa with their "Beat Lafayette" display. Delta Phi's banner — a map of the world with historical events including a prediction of Lehigh's victory over Lafayette in 1950 — collapsed the night before the contest. Before the judges arrived, some of the more innovative Delta Phi brothers improvised with a hurriedly-painted sign proclaiming, "Honest, We Tried!"

A different kind of Lehigh-Lafayette display is shown in the photo above. Located at an intersection in Boulder, Colorado, the street signs are a reminder that college football's most played rivalry is alive and well, even in the Rocky Mountains.

The Taverns

Bethlehem's Tally Ho Tavern and Easton's College Hill Tavern have been a part of the Lehigh-Lafayette tradition for many years. The festivities at the establishments are nonstop while classes are in session during the fall and spring semesters. On Lehigh-Lafayette game day, the taverns provide a forum for pregame luncheons, halftime refreshments, and postgame celebrations.

The College Hill Tavern

The Tally Ho Tavern

THIRD QUARTER
The Modern Era
(1950-1983)

After four decades of dominance, Lafayette firmly established itself as the leader in The Rivalry. Entering the second half of the 20th Century, Lafayette held an impressive 55-27-3 mark against Lehigh, won three National Championships, and recorded six undefeated seasons. A strong Lafayette coaching regime, led by Jock Sutherland, Herbert McCracken and Hook Mylin, instilled a winning spirit on College Hill.

Lafayette sought to continue the success over its arch-rival, which included a 14-0-1 record since 1936, the longest streak in The Series without a loss. Lehigh struggled to find a way to defeat its formidable foe. The Engineers had not defeated the Leopards in 13 years. A 7-7 tie in 1942 was the only feather in the Engineers' cap since 1936.

The Rivalry experienced dramatic changes during the Modern Era. College football implemented free substitution and the two-point conversion and featured the advent of modern day equipment. During the next three decades off the field, new traditions and campus activities developed and intensified the already heated rivalry to a fever pitch unknown to any other college football match-up.

Lehigh's First Undefeated Season

Lehigh entered the 1950 Lafayette game with an 8-0 record and arguably the strongest team in the school's 67-year football history. The Lafayette squad had managed only one victory in eight games before the traditional showdown with Lehigh. As the United States was preparing for its police action in Korea, the football squads prepared for their 85th gridiron battle in 1950.

In 1950, the annual "Beat Lafayette" display contest for Lehigh students became a self-fulfilling prophecy after the Engineers whitewashed the Leopards, 38-0 before 20,000 spectators at Fisher Field. Phi Sigma Kappa's winning banner illustrated the Lafayette Leopard being dunked into a large beer mug, washing the spots off the mascot.

Lehigh was guided to victory by co-captains Dick Gabriel and Dick Doyne. The Dazzlin' Dicks closed their careers in spectacular fashion, combining for 310 yards and 18 points. The duo outgained the entire Lafayette team which was held to just 90 yards.

With a 38-0 score, the football game was a contest in name only, but Doyne and Gabriel had their own score to settle. Gabriel had established a new

Lehigh's Undefeated 1950 Season (9-0)	
Delaware	21-0
Case	21-20
Bucknell	27-6
Gettysburg	49-6
Dartmouth	16-14
Rutgers	21-18
Muhlenberg	42-13
Carnegie Tech	66-0
Lafayette	38-0
	301-77

Old-Timers Day

Lehigh held all the cards in 1950. Just in case the "pair of Richards" couldn't beat Lafayette, Justice C. Cornelius was in attendance and sitting in his usual front-row, 50-yard line seat. Cornelius, a Phillipsburg, New Jersey native and member of the Lehigh Class of 1889, was Lehigh's first quarterback on Richard Harding Davis' inaugural 1884 squad. When asked about the game at halftime, Lehigh's first field general responded, "I'll be right on hand if necessary to keep Lafayette from scoring in the second half, but I expect Lehigh to win anyhow."

Plenty of Postseason Activity

Although Lehigh's 1950 undefeated football team did not participate in a bowl game, the University was adequately represented in postseason action. The Sun Bowl matched the University of Cincinnati against West Texas State. Dr. Raymond Walters, a Lehigh graduate and former faculty member and administrator, was President of Cincinnati. Also, Lehigh's Dick Doyne became the first Lehigh player to participate in a postseason All-Star game by playing in the East-West Shrine Bowl in San Francisco.

Eastern Intercollegiate Football Association single-season rushing record of 1,023 yards in 1949. Entering the Lehigh-Lafayette game, the other Richard needed 175 yards to break Gabriel's record. Late in the fourth quarter, Doyne had rushed for 145 yards against Lafayette , but the record fell out of reach when Doyne was sidelined with an ankle injury with 2:10 remaining. After losing hard-fought battles against the 'Pards in 1948 and 1949, the victory over Lafayette was enough to ease Doyne's ankle pain.

Lehigh's victory over Lafayette was its first since 1936 and the little town of Bethlehem staged a victory celebration that unleashed 13 years of frustration.

By defeating Rutgers and Lafayette in the same season, Lehigh won its first Little Brass Cannon and Middle Three Championship. Along with the Cannon came the Fisher Field goalposts, which the fans tore down before the final whistle. Unlike previous years, little resistance was offered by the Lafayette students and Easton police, who seemed content watching the Bethlehemites celebrate the successful completion of Lehigh's first undefeated season.

Several bowl representatives attended the 1950 Lehigh-Lafayette game. After the game, representatives from the Sun Bowl (El Paso, Texas), Tangerine Bowl (Orlando, Florida), President's Bowl (Washington, DC), Salad Bowl (Phoenix, Arizona), and Cigar Bowl (Tampa, Florida) extended postseason bowl bids to Lehigh. But there would be no cigar, no visit to the White House, and no Florida sunshine for Lehigh as President Martin Whitaker, citing academic reasons, announced that Lehigh would not participate in postseason play. With Lehigh's bowl opportunities flushed, the student body petitioned the school for an extra day of vacation during Thanksgiving break to celebrate Lehigh's undefeated season. The administration accepted the students' version of a bowl bid and an extra day of celebration was granted.

Dick Gabriel

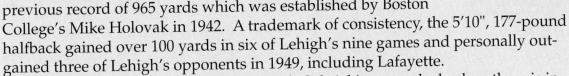

Combining a rare blend of speed and power, Lehigh's Dick Gabriel established the standard by which future backs would be judged after his record-setting 1949 season.

The Associated Press First Team All-American was the leading scorer in the East with 96 points on 16 touchdowns. Gabriel became the first player in Eastern Intercollegiate Football Conference history to exceed the 1,000 yard rushing mark when he tallied 1,023 in nine games. His 1949 performance broke the previous record of 965 yards which was established by Boston College's Mike Holovak in 1942. A trademark of consistency, the 5'10", 177-pound halfback gained over 100 yards in six of Lehigh's nine games and personally outgained three of Lehigh's opponents in 1949, including Lafayette.

Coach Bill Leckonby on Gabriel: "Dick Gabriel is as good a back as there is in the East. He is hard running and fast ... not only has speed but is a power runner. Some people compare him to Steve Van Buren of the Philadelphia Eagles — that is to style not size. His long stride makes his speed deceptive, and when he gets in a jam, he powers through instead of dancing. In 1948, he was known for his outside speed. In 1949, he developed considerably in faking. Needless to say, he is the fastest man on the Lehigh squad."

Along with fellow back Dick Doyne, Gabriel anchored the undefeated 1950 team. Gabriel held the Lehigh career rushing mark of 2,506 yards for 25 years, and was inducted into the Lehigh Hall of Fame in 1994.

A Farewell to Liberty Stadium

With the renovations to Taylor Stadium not yet complete, a crowd of 12,000 watched Lehigh and Lafayette play for the third and final time at Bethlehem's Liberty Stadium in 1951.

Lehigh held Lafayette scoreless for the second consecutive year. The Engineer offense was driven by sophomore running back Joe Kryla, who rushed for 127 yards in 14 carries in Lehigh's 32-0 victory.

Lehigh's next home game against Lafayette was played in the newly-renovated Taylor Stadium in 1953. The Engineers hoped the new and improved Taylor Stadium would end a Lafayette jinx. The last time the Brown and White defeated Lafayette at Taylor Stadium was in 1935.

Coach Hokuf's Initiation

In 1952, The Game matched Lehigh's seven-year veteran coach, Bill Leckonby, against Lafayette's rookie coach, Steve Hokuf. The first season was not kind to Hokuf, whose team was winless in eight games. Lehigh brought into The Game a mediocre 4-4

All-American Selection

Often, the only two people who recognize an offensive lineman in a crowd are his quarterback and his mother. Standing only 5'8" and 190 pounds, it was easy to overlook Lehigh tackle Bill Ciaravino. However, the *International News Service* did not, as they made Ciaravino a first team All-American selection in 1950.

Ciaravino became only the seventh Lehigh football player honored with All-American status. Ciaravino joined the elite group which included Associated Press All-Americans Dick Gabriel at halfback and center Bob Numbers (both 1949), and Walter Camp All-Americans D.M. Balliet (1891) at center, guard C.E. Trafton (1893), quarterback Pat Pazzetti (1912), and halfback Billy Cahall (1914).

Expanded Guest List

In addition to the expansion of Taylor Stadium in 1953, the Lehigh Home Club expanded its guest list. For the first time, the Lehigh Home Club added women to the guest list for its annual Lafayette smoker held at Bethlehem's Beethoven Maennerchor.

record but a defense that was tops in the Eastern Intercollegiate Football Association.

In an attempt to revamp the offense for the Lehigh game, coach Hokuf switched to an "A" formation, used by the NFL's New York Giants. The "A" formation received an "F" on the post-game report card. Lehigh's defense held the Leopards to minus one yard rushing in a 14-7 Brown and White victory.

With three minutes remaining in the game and the score deadlocked at 7-7, Leckonby replaced starting quarterback Tom Gloede with sophomore backup Jack Conti to divert attention from the Lehigh passing game. In the midst of a torrential downpour, Conti, a Bethlehem High School product who had played only 20 minutes all season, was about to engage in the most important three minutes of his Lehigh football career.

With the ball on the Lafayette 45-yard line and 1:30 remaining, Conti connected with Bobby Clark for a spectacular, diving pass reception at the Lafayette 23-yard line. On the next play, Conti heaved a cross-field wounded duck to Tommy Gunn. Gunn was double-covered but managed to pull in the pass with a head-first dive into the end zone mud for the winning tally.

Lafayette's 1952 squad became only the second team in the school's 71-year football history to finish a season without a victory. In 1882, Lafayette's first football team posted a 0-2 record.

Taylor Stadium Gets a Facelift

A refurbished Taylor Stadium was the site for the 1953 game. The Bethlehem stadium boasted an upper deck grandstand and press box above the south stands for The Game. The official seating capacity of Taylor Stadium increased to 15,000 with the addition.

The outcome of the 1953 game meant the difference between a winning and losing season. Both teams entered the contest with 4-4 records. The game pitted Ground Lafayette against Air Lehigh. Lafayette led the East Coast Athletic

Conference in rushing, averaging 255 yards per game. The Lehigh aerial attack was led by junior quarterback Tom Gloede, who completed 35 passes in 98 attempts for 522 yards in eight games. Although not impressive by modern-day standards, Gloede's statistics were outstanding during an era when the forward pass was still a mystery to most college football teams and the rules committee had yet to change the color of the penalty flags from red to yellow.

The Leopards dusted-off some mystery plays in The Game and spooked Lehigh 33-13. Assistant coach Jim McConlogue pulled the "sleeper" play out of his old Allentown Central Catholic High School playbook and defensive coach George McGaughey unveiled an eight man front that shut down the Engineer offense.

The surprised Brown and White never adjusted. Leopard halfback Bryan Satterlee accounted for 212 yards and three touchdowns on just four plays in one of the most spectacular individual performances in The Game's history.

The sophomore's banner day started on the first play from scrimmage with the "sleeper." Lafayette lined-up without a huddle and without flanker Tom McGrail, who was standing just in-bounds and apart from his teammates. Satterlee took the opening snap, and heaved a 74-yard strike to McGrail, who was sneaking down the sideline. Moments later, Satterlee hit John Burcin for a touchdown.

Taylor Stadium received a facelift for the 1953 game complete with an upper deck grandstand and pressbox.

Super Janitor

Dutch Rahn, nicknamed "super janitor" for his perennial cleaning of the Fisher Field press box windows, visited Lehigh's new press box during the 1953 game. According to others in the press box, Rahn was spotted crossing the field from the north stands during pre-game. After taking some oxygen on the Lehigh sideline, Rahn started his ascent to the press box. Finally, at halftime, Rahn completed his climb and visited with colleagues at the summit.

Later in the first quarter, Satterlee performed his version of M.C. Hammer's *"Can't Touch This"* when he dashed 87 yards, untouched, on a quick opener for a touchdown.

A 34-yard Satterlee touchdown pass off a reverse to Burcin capped the halfback's four-play extravaganza.

In the second half, Joe O'Lenic nearly duplicated Satterlee's long run, as the Leopard captain exploded 73 yards for a score — dragging several Lehigh defenders the last three yards across the goal line.

Lehigh's lone highlight came after the final whistle when the students successfully defended the goalposts in their newly-renovated stadium. The postgame scrum did not seem to matter to one Maroon grad who responded, "Let them have the posts, we'll take The Game."

As the Korean Conflict ended in 1953, so did Lehigh's three game win streak over the Leopards. The victory preserved a 70-year old football tradition of never having a class at Lafayette graduate without a win over Lehigh.

A Lafayette Laugher

"If you see a defensive team with dirt and mud on their backs, they've had a bad day."

— *John Madden*

Both Lafayette and Lehigh struggled during the 1954 season. Lafayette entered the final game with a 3-5 record while Lehigh was 2-4-2. The poor records did not keep 16,000 diehard fans from attending the 90th game at Fisher Field. The game was more of a test for the scoreboard operator than for Lafayette. The Leopards beat Lehigh like a rented mule, 46-0. The 46 points were the most scored in The Rivalry since Lafayette defeated Lehigh 64-0 in 1944.

The Lafayette offense was fueled by junior fullback Dan McCarthy, who rushed 19 times for 72 yards and three touchdowns. The 'Pards intercepted six passes and recovered three fumbles.

The Bethlehemites had little to cheer about during the game. The Engineer defense left Fisher Field with dirt and mud on their backs after surrendering 46 unanswered points. Lehigh's performance on the field was critiqued by one disgruntled fan who exclaimed, "The best thing I saw in Lehigh was her marching band."

Lehigh's senior quarterback Tom Gloede ended his career at Lehigh on a losing note, but managed to tie Lehigh's total offense record of 1,045 yards, while falling two yards short of the single-season passing mark of 791 yards.

═══════════════════

"Gloede is the nearest thing to Sammy Baugh the Lehigh Valley ever saw, despite his poor performance Saturday (against Lafayette)."

— *Parnell Lewis, <u>Express</u> Sportswriter*

═══════════════════

Dog Day Afternoon

Two rushing touchdowns by the deceptive quarterback Joe Bozik helped Lafayette plow the Engineers 35-6 on a snow-covered Taylor Stadium field in 1955.

Both schools entered The Game with strong teams. Lehigh, with its 7-1 record, was favored for the third consecutive year. After upsetting heavily favored Lehigh teams in 1953 and '54, Lafayette willingly accepted its underdog role.

The 1955 Lafayette squad was well-prepared for The Game, boasting a 5-2 record, including victories over Dartmouth and Rutgers. The victory over Dartmouth marked the first Lafayette defeat of an Ivy League school in 22 seasons and the win over Rutgers was the first in 11 years. Since Lehigh also defeated Rutgers, the winner of The Game would own the Little Brass Cannon and Middle Three Championship, which Lehigh held since 1950.

The Leopard offense was led by the sophomore Bozik, who dazzled fans with deceptive ballhandling maneuvers. In the Dartmouth game, Bozik's sleight of hand fooled everyone in the stadium, including the officials. With hand speed quicker than a one-armed juggler, Bozik faked a hand-off to his fullback, then scampered down the sideline unmolested with the ball tucked at his side like a holstered Colt .45 pistol. Meanwhile, the officials blew their whistles after an empty-handed fullback was apparently stopped for no gain. "Sorry son" was the only explanation the referee could offer to Bozik after the would-be touchdown run was called back.

The Game had its share of unusual events. After the opening kickoff, a lengthy delay was required to remove a fraternity dog that made her way into the Lehigh backfield during the Engineers' first play from scrimmage. The collie was finally

Clarence The Wonder Dog

Dogs have long been a part of college life. Fraternity dogs, mooching dogs, dogs that ride the school shuttle bus, and even dogs that attend class.

Lehigh had a special canine Engineer named Clarence, who was decorated with paint and a special wardrobe for Lafayette weekend each year. And proving that he wasn't afraid of cats, even if they were bigger, Clarence made a bi-annual appearance on the Taylor Stadium field every Lafayette game.

Upon his death, there was discussion as to burying the noble warrior under the fifty yard-line. Eventually, he was interred in the Taylor Hall quad.

For The Record!

Lafayette's defeat of Lehigh in 1955 tied the record for the largest margin of victories (28) in The Rivalry. After the 1955 game, the series stood 58-30-3 in favor of Lafayette. Only one other time in history did a team lead the series by 28 victories — Lafayette held a 55-27-3 advantage in 1949. The last time Lehigh enjoyed the lead was in 1892 with a 8-5-2 record. Lehigh held a slight edge until 1899, when Lafayette recaptured bragging rights. Going into the 1995 game, Lafayette owns a commanding 71-54-5 advantage.

Coach Hokuf and his players celebrate Lafayette's victory over Lehigh in 1955.

Lafayette Dominates the Bottom Line

A quick glance at the football balance sheet summed up Lafayette's domination of Lehigh from 1953 to 1955. In the offense department, the Leopards compiled 1,214 yards to Lehigh's 390. In the turnover column, Lafayette tallied 18 assets (takeaways) against only four liabilities (giveaways). In the subtotal column, the scoreboard flashed in favor of Lafayette, 114-19. The healthy bottom line of Lafayette College read three assets (victories) and zero liabilities (defeats).

caught by a Lehigh cheerleader, who carried the intruder from the field. "Lassie" wasn't the only one to visit the Lehigh backfield; the Lafayette defense hounded sophomore quarterback Dan Nolan all afternoon during its frequent visits to the Lehigh backfield.

Future Lafayette Hall of Famer Joe Bozik plowed his way down the snow-covered Taylor Stadium field, rushing for two touchdowns enroute to the 'Pards 35-6 victory.

The Lafayette triumph returned the Little Brass Cannon to Easton after a 10-year hiatus.

Since taking over in 1952, Lafayette's top dog Steve Hokuf, often in an underdog role, enjoyed three years of success against his cross-town competitor Bill Leckonby. When an ex-Lafayette player was asked to reveal the secret to Hokuf's success against Lehigh, he responded, "Never underestimate the heart of a champion."

Bozik-Nolan II

In 1956, Lehigh's Dan Nolan and Lafayette's Joe Bozik squared off on the gridiron for the second matchup of their best of three series. This time, the Engineer quarterback led his team to a 27-10 victory.

The Brown and White signal-caller scored three second-quarter touchdowns, including an eight-yarder around right end where he twice faked laterals before diving between two Leopards and across the goal line. He also set-up the Engineers' first score by intercepting a Bozik pass.

"Now we're even," joked Nolan after the game, reflecting on his rivalry with Bozik. "Next year we'll have the rubber match."

Trailing 20-3 at half, Lafayette fought to cut into Lehigh's 17-point margin in the third quarter. The 'Pards were stopped short on a fourth-and-goal situation when Pete Williams dropped halfback Jack Slotter like a bad habit for a one-yard loss.

Bozik, returning from an earlier injury, rallied Lafayette with an eight-play, 48-yard scoring drive that closed the gap to 20-10 with 12:45 remaining. Lafayette's fourth quarter comeback fell short when Lehigh's Austin Short blocked a Gordi Brown punt. The Engineers' star wingman grabbed the pigskin and headed for the end zone. With the Leopards in hot pursuit, Short lateralled the ball at the 10-yard line to Lehigh's 225-pound guard Williams, who finished the touchdown run.

The win enabled the Engineers to reclaim the Little Brass Cannon and the Middle Three Championship which Lafayette had held.

Coach Bill Leckonby described the win over Lafayette as "the most satisfying victory during 11 years of coaching football at Lehigh University. In those years (1950 and '51), we held all the big cards. It was just a matter of turning the boys loose. This year was different. This year's game was won by the team with the greatest desire. It was a great accomplishment for the seniors to come back from 46-0 and 35-6 defeats in 1954 and 1955."

Equipment Change

In the early fifties, the first helmets with facemasks were unveiled in Lafayette-Lehigh action. Along with the advent of facemasks came the "grabbing the facemask" penalty instituted in 1956.

Lehigh's Winningest Coach

The week before the 1957 Lafayette game, Bill Leckonby became the "winningest" coach in Lehigh history, surpassing Tom Keady. Lehigh's 27-7 victory over Buffalo in week eight gave Leckonby a 56-38-2 record in his 12th year as head Engineer. During the World War I era, Tom Keady compiled a 55-22-3 record from 1912 to 1920. Keady was on hand for the 1957 Lehigh-Lafayette game to congratulate Leckonby on his accomplishment.

Lehigh quarterback Dan Nolan became a priest after his gridiron career.

The Bozik-Nolan Rubber Match

The 1957 Lehigh-Lafayette game loomed big for the Engineers. Lehigh was in the running for the first Lambert Cup, awarded to the best small college football team in the East. Lehigh and Williams College of Massachusetts were extremely close in the balloting all year, with Lehigh dropping slightly after a loss to Virginia Military Institute in week seven. Lehigh entered the Lafayette game with a 7-1 record. An impressive victory over Lafayette was critical for Lehigh to remain in the hunt. Lafayette, at 4-3, could spoil Lehigh's Lambert Cup chances with a win at Taylor Stadium.

The 1957 game set the stage for the final Nolan-Bozik matchup. The senior quarterbacks, each owning one victory in The Rivalry, matched wits in the tiebreaker.

Bozik fractured his leg during a pre-season scrimmage and had the option to redshirt his

Lafayette's Joe Bozik runs for a touchdown against Lehigh in 1955.

senior year. Instead of redshirting, Bozik decided to play one last time against Nolan. "Besides," Bozik recalled, "before the 1955 game, coach Bill Leckonby said he had two quarterbacks at Lehigh that were better than Lafayette's, and I wanted to prove him wrong."

A capacity crowd of 17,000 braved a first quarter snowstorm during the 93rd renewal of College Football's Most-Played Rivalry. The crowd was the largest ever to witness a football game at Taylor Stadium at the time.

Lehigh freshman football coach Frank Maze had a tough time gaining entry into the Lehigh locker room before the 1957 Lehigh-Lafayette game. The custodians would not admit Maze, even after he identified himself. Eventually, Maze flagged the attention of the press box attendant, who immediately recognized him. Armed with a fistful of passes from the attendant, Maze finally gained admission to the stadium in time for the kickoff.

The Home of Champions!

Joe Bozik's career at Lafayette ended after the 1957 Lafayette-Lehigh game. The Maroon Hall of Famer, who turned down scholarship offers from West Point and Syracuse to attend Lafayette, grew-up in the small Western Pennsylvania community of Denora. Known as "The Home of Champions," Denora is also the home town of baseball great Stan Musial and heavyweight boxer Lee Sala.

Tough "D"

Only three teams — Lafayette, Delaware and VMI — scored more than seven points against the Engineer defense during the 1957 season. Lafayette was the only team to score two rushing touchdowns against Lehigh in 1957.

Plowing was more appropriate than passing, as the Lehigh trio of Walt Pijawaka, Dick Pennell, and Charley Burger combined for three touchdowns and 199 yards rushing in Lehigh's 26-13 victory. In addition, the Engineers skated away with the inaugural Lambert Cup.

Nolan, who managed five completions under difficult weather conditions, broke Tom Gloede's record of 56 set in 1954. Nolan kept the crowd in suspense, waiting until midway through a frigid fourth quarter before completing his 57th pass. Earlier in the contest, the veteran quarterback surpassed Gloede's passing yardage record of 1,056, finishing with 1,140.

Don Nikles and Joe Bozik led Lafayette's ground assault across Taylor Stadium's frozen tundra. The duo provided Lafayette's scoring punch, twice blazing a trail to the snow-covered end zone.

Steve Hokuf ended his coaching career at Lafayette after the 1957 game. The fiery Hokuf coached Lafayette for six seasons, compiling an overall record of 25-27-0, splitting six games against his Lehigh rival Bill Leckonby. Jim McConlogue, Lafayette's backfield coach for several years, took over as head coach in 1958.

The Final Score: 9.50 - 9.41

Lehigh's victory over Lafayette earned the Engineers the 1957 Lambert Cup in the closest vote in the award's 38-year history. Lehigh (8-1) edged Williams College (6-0-1) by nine one-hundredths of a point. When the final votes were tallied, Lehigh averaged a score of 9.50 to Williams' 9.41. The selection committee agreed that Lehigh's tougher schedule was the deciding factor. In addition to the Lambert Cup, Lehigh successfully retained the Middle Three Championship and the Little Brass Cannon by defeating Rutgers and Lafayette.

TIMEOUT

Lambert Cup History

Lehigh won the inaugural Lambert Cup in 1957, and would proceed to win five more. Lafayette, having never won the Cup, came close to securing the second Lambert Trophy in 1937. The trophy, which was awarded to the best major college football team in the East, was the forerunner to the Cup and among the oldest and most coveted awards in all of college athletics.

During the inaugural year of the trophy, Fordham University, located in the Bronx, New York, was among the nation's elite football teams and favored to win the first Lambert Trophy. Two New York City brothers, Victor and Henry Lambert, established the award in memory of their father, August. The brothers, a pair of well-known college football supporters and principal owners of a distinguished Madison Avenue jewelry house, hoped to present the award to the hometown Rams.

As the season ended, the brothers found themselves aboard a train to Pittsburgh and traveling through a snowstorm to present the award to Jock Sutherland's Panthers. This was the same Sutherland who guided Lafayette College to a National Championship in 1921 and a 33-6-2 record from 1919 to 1923. Sutherland's Pitt Panthers repeated as Lambert Trophy winners in 1937. Lafayette College completed undefeated seasons in 1937 (8-0) and 1940 (9-0) under Coach "Hook" Mylin, but was handicapped by its strength of schedule in the Lambert Trophy polls.

The Lamberts finally got the chance to present the trophy to James Crowley's Fordham Rams in 1941.

After World War II, the return of college-aged GI's to the United States created a dramatic increase in enrollment at universities and colleges. In addition, schools developed different recruiting policies, academic standards, and athletic commitment levels. To accommodate the changes, the Lambert Cup was created in 1957 to recognize non-Division I football programs. Coach Bill Leckonby's Lehigh squad won the first Lambert Cup award in 1957. The Engineers also won the Lambert Cup in 1961 under Leckonby, in 1973 and 1975 under Fred Dunlap, and in 1977 and 1980 under John Whitehead.

In 1966, the Lamberts added the Lambert Bowl

Coach "Hook" Mylin, despite leading his Lafayette team to an undefeated record in 1937 and 1940, could not capture the elusive Lambert Trophy.

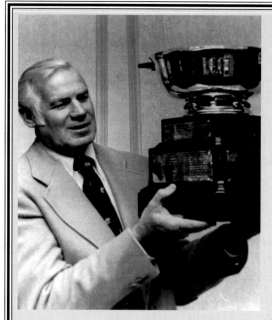

Lehigh coach Bill Leckonby with the Lambert Cup.

for Division III schools. The reclassification of many Eastern college teams into Division I-AA in 1982 created the need to separate Division I-AA from Division II schools resulting in a fourth Lambert award.

An unprecedented 159 schools were eligible for Lambert/Meadowlands Awards in 1994. The breakout includes Division I-A (11 schools), Division I-AA (40 schools), Division II (27 schools), and Division III (81 schools).

In the early 1980's, the Lamberts searched for a sports organization with a sincere interest in college athletics that could sponsor and manage the awards. The Meadowlands Sports Complex was chosen as the organization that best represented the tradition of college football and the Lambert trophies. Since 1983, the awards have been consolidated under the name Lambert/Meadowlands Awards and are presented to the best Eastern college football team in Divisions I-A, I-AA, II, and III.

"We feel by sponsoring the Lambert/Meadowlands Awards, we make a major contribution towards the growth of Eastern college football at all levels, and we're proud to do it."

— Robert E. Mulcahy III, President and Chief Executive Officer of the Meadowlands Sports Complex

Schools from New England and the Middle Atlantic states, and their rivals who play at least half of their games against schools from these regions are eligible for the awards. Weekly polls are conducted in each division by a separate panel of media members. At the end of the season, a final poll determines the winner. The Lambert Trophy (Division I-A) and Lambert Cup (Division I-AA) are rotating awards remaining in the winning schools' possession until the following year. Each year, the division winners receive plaques for permanent possession.

Since 1936, the Lambert Trophy has been won by 13 different teams. No other team has come close to matching Penn State, who has won the trophy 21 times.

Delaware has won or shared the Lambert Cup 14 times including an unprecedented seven in a row from 1968 to 1974 under head coach Tubby Raymond. During Delaware's 1970 Lambert Cup season, Lehigh upset the Blue Hens, 36-13. In 1973, Lehigh shared the Lambert Cup with Delaware, despite losing to the Hens, 21-9.

Howard "Bosey" Reiter

Howard "Bosey" Reiter, known as "The Spirit of Lehigh" during the first half of the 20th century, passed away in 1957. His legacy lives on in the Alumni Memorial Building, where a conference room and oil portrait, painted by James Arnold Todd '23, were dedicated in his remembrance. During the dedication ceremony, Lehigh Vice President Dr. E. Kenneth Smiley professed, "Lehigh University has had a gallery of faculty men. In such a gallery, no face has persisted longer than Howard Roland Reiter. We deem it appropriate that this conference room be dedicated for use to the welfare of the University in tribute of 'Bosey' Reiter."

After graduating from Princeton and coaching football for five years at Wesleyan, Reiter came to Lehigh as a coach and professor. Vincent Pazzetti, who was a star player under Reiter at Wesleyan, transferred to Lehigh along with his coach in 1910. Bosey coached the Lehigh football team during the 1910 and 1911 seasons and compiled a 7-11-2 record before becoming the school's first Director of Athletics in 1911. On the Lehigh campus, Bosey was a colorful and inspirational leader of many Lehigh smokers and pep rallies.

Always an avid supporter of Bethlehem's youth, Reiter founded the Bethlehem's Boys Club and organized the Lehigh Booster Club, which issued special passes to youngsters so they could attend Lehigh athletic contests, including the Lehigh-Lafayette football games.

In football history books, Reiter is credited as one of the founding fathers of the forward pass. In Lehigh history books, Reiter is characterized as the epitome of honor, wisdom, and the preservation of youth.

A Dead Heat

Jim McConlogue brought an unpredictable Lafayette team into the 1958 Lehigh contest with a 5-3 record. McConlogue, although in his rookie season as head coach, was a veteran to The Game. As backfield coach, McConlogue masterminded Lafayette's "sleeper" play in the 1953 game against Lehigh. Throughout the 1958 season, McConlogue surprised opponents with unorthodox formations and maneuvers, from the "lonesome end" to the "fast start" play.

Leckonby's team struggled during the 1958 season, bringing a 3-3-2 record into the grand finale.

Using its trickery, Lafayette jumped to a two-touchdown lead. Lehigh fought back to tie the score at 14-14. Then both squads squandered late game-winning opportunities for the first tie in The Series since 1942.

Before a capacity crowd of 20,000 fans at Fisher Field, the Leopards scored quickly on a Charley Bartos seven-yard run. Then another Lehigh-Lafayette history-maker

1958 Game at a Glance

The 1958 game was one of The Series' most evenly-matched contests. Lafayette outgained the Engineers by one yard, 255 to 254. The 14-14 stalemate was the fourth in Game history. The 1942 contest at Fisher Field ended in a 7-7 deadlock. Earlier ties occurred in 1885 (6-6) and 1889 (6-6).

	Lehigh	Lafayette
First Downs	14	14
Yards Rushing	229	216
Yards Passing	25	39
Total Yards	254	255
Punts	5	4
Average Distance	35	36
Turnovers by	2	3
Yards Penalized	30	30
SCORE	**14**	**14**

Going For Two

The NCAA implemented the two-point conversion in 1958. Lehigh wasted no time in taking advantage of the newly-established rule. In its first game of the 1958 season, the Engineers used the two-point conversion to defeat the Delaware Blue Hens, 8-7. The two-point conversion was a critical factor in the 1958 Lehigh-Lafayette game. Both Lafayette and Lehigh converted a deuce in the game which ended in a 14-14 deadlock.

occurred, as quarterback Wayne Cipriani fired a pass to Don Nikles to tally The Game's first two-point conversion. Later in the first quarter, Nikles banged three yards over right tackle for Lafayette's second touchdown. This time, the Leopards opted for the traditional extra-point-kick attempt which failed and Lafayette settled for a 14-0 halftime lead.

The momentum changed to Lehigh in the second half. Backup quarterback George Theiss tossed a touchdown pass to Joe Wenzel and then dove over right tackle for Lehigh's first two-point conversion in The Series.

In the fourth quarter, Lehigh drove 65 yards in 12 plays to patdirt. Charley Lull played a key role, converting a first down on a fourth-and-one situation at midfield. Lull's number was called once again when Lehigh faced a fourth-and-goal situation at the Lafayette one-yard line. The sophomore fullback crashed over the goal line to knot the score 14-14.

With the capacity crowd on its feet, Lehigh kicker Frank Koziol ran onto the field to attempt the decisive extra point. The kick missed by a margin that could only be determined by the referee standing under the left upright. After the game, Leckonby said, "I thought the kick was good. It looked okay from the bench."

Lehigh continued its comeback. Al Richmond broke a big gainer to the Lafayette five-yard line, but the play was nullified by a clipping penalty. Later, Leckonby said, "It didn't look like a clip to me on the films. Movies show Nevil's initial contact was legal, although the defender — Don Dilley — turned and a clip resulted before the action was completed." The penalty pushed Lehigh back to the 23-yard line. Don Westmaas abruptly ended Lehigh's late-game rally with an interception on third down.

Lafayette had its chances to break the tie, but missed two 29-yard field goals in the second half. The game ended in a 14-14 deadlock. Lehigh finished with 3-3-3 record — the first time in 74 years that the Engineers recorded three ties in a season. Under the clever leadership of McConlogue, Lafayette overwhelmed five, underwhelmed three, and whelmed one opponent to post a 5-3-1 record.

Little Brass Cannon Update

In 1958, Rutgers won the Little Brass Cannon and Middle Three Championship previously held by Lehigh in 1956 and 1957. The Scarlet Knights would hold the honors for 11 years until Lehigh recaptured the trophies in 1969.

75 Years of Lafayette-Lehigh Football

"No other college teams have met more times on the football field than Lehigh and Lafayette. The rivalry has been intense, sometimes bitter, but always one of good, hard football."

— *New York Times*, November 22, 1959

Lafayette and Lehigh celebrated 75 years and 95 games of football tradition in 1959. With both teams entering with 4-4 records, the outcome of The Game again meant the difference between a winning and losing season.

The game featured two rugged fullbacks, Lafayette's battering ram Don Nikles and Lehigh's Boyd "The Crasher" Taylor. Nikles was a big part of Lafayette's offense in the 1958 game, carrying the ball 28 times for 108 yards and a touchdown. Nikles was appearing in his third contest, while Taylor was making his Lehigh-Lafayette debut.

Nikles was a little nicked-up for The Game — the usual bumps, bruises, knots, aches, and pains that came along with playing fullback and linebacker for Lafayette. When Leckonby found out about Nikles condition, he replied, "Sure, he'll probably only be able to play 58 or 59 minutes (instead of his usual 60 minutes) against us."

Nikles starred for Lafayette, setting up two touchdowns and scoring on a 23-yard run in the Leopards 28-6 triumph.

Nikles closed out his brilliant career at Lafayette with 191 yards rushing on 22 carries, exceeding Lehigh's team total by 67 yards. The Nazareth native won the Middle Atlantic Conference rushing title in 1958 and 1959 and was a first team Middle Atlantic Conference selection both years. The Maxwell Club Award winner set school records

Don Nikles — Lafayette Hall of Famer and Two-Time All-MAC Selection.

for career carries and yardage that stood for 13 seasons. Nikles was the workhorse during his three years of varsity action at Lafayette. A rival coach once said, "For offense, Lafayette throws once a week and gives it to Nikles the rest of the time."

The Lafayette defense played superbly, limiting the Engineers to one first down until late in the third quarter. Charley Lull found the end zone in the fourth quarter for Lehigh's only score of the day.

Tug-of-War

The emotional buildup during Lehigh-Lafayette week became as much a part of The Rivalry as the football game itself. Traditionally, the players released their emotions during the game, while the students had their chance to unwind during the postgame battle for the goalposts. In 1959, the emotional buildup was vented prematurely as tempers flared at the halftime Tug-of-War competition during the freshmen version of The Game.

The freshmen match was played at Easton's Fisher Field the Friday before the varsity contest. The first half ended with Lafayette leading 15-6. During the intermission, the traditional freshmen Lehigh-Lafayette Tug-of-War contest took place.

The Lehigh freshmen, after gaining an early advantage in the strength test, secured a stronghold by tying their end of the rope to the goalpost. The post was no match for the infuriated Eastonians. The Lafayette freshmen dragged the Lehigh team and post to the other end of the field and secured their end of the rope to the other post, which was eventually uprooted. The situation escalated as the "Masters of Disaster" proceeded to pull down the scoreboard and a pair of flagpoles during the quest to find a formidable anchor for the tug-of-war rope.

The premature goalpost destruction during the halftime tug-of-war contest in 1959 made for an uneventful second half for the placekickers.

With no more inanimate objects to tear down, the freshmen continued the frenzy by throwing crabapples and punches at each other. Eventually, order was restored and the remainder of the football game was played without goalposts, flagpoles, or a scoreboard. The second half was scoreless and extremely unexciting for the goalpost-less placement kickers. Lafayette emerged from the tainted event victorious, 15-6.

The Lafayette administration sent a bill to Lehigh for the cost of two goalposts. Reportedly, it went unpaid. The other damage expenses were absorbed by Lafayette.

A Pear of a Game

"Football is, after all, a wonderful way to get rid of aggression without going to jail for it."

— Heywood Hale Brown

The fever pitch of the 1959 Lafayette-Lehigh freshmen game continued into the varsity contest. At a pregame luncheon in Lehigh's University Center, hard green pears, not fit for human consumption, were part of the buffet spread. One anonymous Lehigh student, upset with the menu selection, placed a sign next to the pear tray reading, "Take One for Lafayette!"

Armed with projectiles, the Lehigh students marched to Taylor Stadium, prepared for battle. Since the Lehigh football players didn't have much to throw at Lafayette on the field, the students began launching pears at the Lafayette student section. The situation deteriorated when Engineer fans tossed pears at the players and officials on the field after a long run by a Lafayette player. A referee unknowingly screened several potential Engineer tacklers from the ballcarrier. The offficial was then forced to block numerous pears tossed by irate Lehigh fans.

With the game out of reach, the Lehigh students became restless and mounted a final

Preserving A Tradition

Lafayette's victory over Lehigh in 1959 preserved a 75-year old tradition of not having a Lafayette class graduate without a victory over Lehigh. As of 1959, Lehigh's longest win streak in the series occurred in the late 1800's when Lehigh completed a five-game sweep, which included two victories in 1890 and three in 1891. Lafayette owns the longest win streak in The Rivalry, winning 10 in a row from 1919 to 1928.

Double Secret Probation

In an attempt to curb the rowdy and damaging misbehavior of the students in 1959, Lafayette's Dean Cole and Lehigh's Dean of Students J. D. Leith discontinued the tug-of-war. After the varsity melee, Leith placed the entire Lehigh student body on special disciplinary probation. Taking a page from Dean Warmer's double-secret probation at Faber College, Leith banned alcoholic beverages at all social functions for an indefinite period. Lehigh students, whose ability to consume large quantities of alcoholic beverages was legendary, reacted negatively to the prohibition effort. Their withdrawal symptoms were short-lived as the ban was lifted three days later due to pressures from the student governing bodies, particularly the Interfraternity Fraternity Council.

attack against their rivals. The Lehigh air strike was not taken kindly by the Lafayette students, who retaliated by giving the Bethlehem boys a taste of their own pears.

With 1:10 remaining in the game, a massive riot broke out involving approximately 700 students. The players, shielding themselves from the pears with their helmets, headed for the locker room. After a lengthy delay, the 21-man Bethlehem police force, accompanied by University police, cleared the field so the game could be completed.

The aftermath of the battle included one of the most extensive injury reports in the rivalry's long-lived history.

One *New York Times* reporter described the postgame scene as "a contest between gladiators in the Roman coliseum."

The police report filed by Assistant Chief of Police Melvin Packard stated the entire incident was incited by the Lehigh students who threw pears on the field and into the stands. Packard stated, "I guess those pears were harder than bullets."

Individual accounts by police officers in the pits revealed the severity of the situation.

Policeman 1: "It was the worst I've ever seen."
Policeman 2: "I saw a student with five teeth hanging loose."
Policeman 3: "At one point, I saw quart beer bottles and cider jugs (used to concoct cider and vodka mix — the drink of choice for the 1959 Lehigh-Lafayette game)

being hurled into the crowd."

Policeman 4: "One student stood his ground by swinging a two-by-four at anyone that came near him. Another student hurled his crutch into the stands."

Policeman 5: "It was the toughest ten dollars I ever earned."

During the aftermath, groups of opportunistic students made a quick buck by selling "I Survived the 1959 Lehigh-Lafayette Game" memorabilia on the street corners of Bethlehem and Easton.

The Year After

After a year of recuperation from the 1959 fracas, the students' bruises, cuts, and hangovers healed and missing teeth were replaced. The bands pounded the dents out of the instruments and the Lafayette musicians replenished their stock of straw hats, which had become a trademark of the Leopard band. The Leopard cheerleaders purchased new megaphones. Officer John Pulley was back patrolling the streets of Bethlehem, donning a new police cap and searching for the elusive thief who escaped the 1959 game with his old one. Hard green pears were hard to find in area supermarkets and disappeared from the Lehigh

1959 Injury Report

Lafayette Student Injuries

Dr. Kenneth Kressler of the Lafayette infirmary had a busy postgame. Twenty-two Lafayette students were treated, the most serious being Robert Lewis, who suffered a concussion from a bottle broken over his head. Rounding out the injury report: four broken noses, assorted black eyes, bumps, bruises, and several severe cuts about the knees (a prime target zone for police billy clubs).

Lehigh Student Injuries

Five Lehigh students were treated by Dr. George McCoy, Jr. of Lehigh Health Services. The most serious was Frank Kear, Jr. who received 11 stitches in his upper lip from a misguided beer can. Although Lafayette beat Lehigh on the scoreboard 28-6, Lehigh won the riot — five reported casualties to Lafayette's 22.

Lafayette Band Casualties

Several missing straw hats, two instruments — a trumpet and a coronet — smashed.

Cheerleader Casualties

Outside the stadium, a youth, clad in a Lehigh jacket, swiped two megaphones from the Lafayette cheerleaders and raced down the street. Another youth, wearing Maroon and White, nonchalantly stuck his leg out and tripped the Lehigh student. Punches were exchanged until an adult man intervened and put a stop to the shenanigans. The megaphones were added to the final casualty list.

Hats Off to The Police

One police casualty was reported — a lost hat. Bethlehem Policeman John Pulley's hat was knocked off by what was identified in the police report as a hard green pear. Before Pulley could recover his cap, an unidentified Lafayette student abducted the hat and fled.

Craig Anderson

Craig Anderson's right arm was accustomed to workouts while pitching for the Lehigh baseball team. Anderson recorded 228 strikeouts and a 1.94 ERA during his three years of varsity competition from 1957-59. In the fall of 1959, Anderson decided to give his right leg a workout as punter for the Lehigh football team.

After watching weak punting performances in Lehigh's first three games of the 1959 season, the former Washington, D.C., Anacostia High School punter approached assistant football coach Tony Packer, who was also the baseball coach, to offer his punting services.

Packer consulted with Leckonby and set a tryout for Anderson, who took over punting duties for the remaining six games of the season and averaged 37 yards per punt.

On the diamond, Anderson applied Ben-Gay to his pitching arm to endure the rigors of a NCAA season. After putting in an extra-inning performance on the gridiron in the 1959 Lehigh-Lafayette football game, Anderson needed Ben-Gay for his right leg. The senior hurler-turned-punter kicked nine times and was seemingly on the field almost as often as the Lehigh offense, which tallied only one first down through the third quarter.

After graduating from Lehigh in 1959, Anderson played professional baseball for the St. Louis Cardinals and the original New York Mets in 1962. Anderson owns the distinction of being the winning pitcher for both games of the first doubleheader ever won by the Mets. After the sweep, Anderson ran into some hard luck. During the next three years, the former Lehigh punter lost his next 19 appearances as a Met pitcher, a team record until Anthony Young dropped 27 in a row for the Mets during the 1992-1993 seasons.

Anderson completed his baseball career in 1966 and returned to his Alma Mater as Assistant Baseball Coach and Assistant Director of Development. From 1969 to 1982, the ex-Met sold thousands of Lehigh-Lafayette game tickets as the Business and Ticket Manager of Athletics at Lehigh before directing Lehigh's Athletics Partnership.

and Lafayette cafeteria menus. Somehow, the Lehigh and Lafayette students survived the aftermath of the 1959 brawl, and the campuses returned to normal — just in time for the 1960 Game.

Lehigh traveled to Fisher Field with a veteran line-up of eight seniors looking to avenge a 28-6 battering by Lafayette in 1959 and a 14-14 tie in 1958. Lafayette had a less experienced team, starting only four seniors, but was armed with a secret weapon — placekicker Walt Doleschal — who could put three points on the scoreboard almost everywhere inside the 50-yard line.

Lehigh dominated the game from the opening coin toss and won 28-6. The Engineers scored a touchdown in every quarter without completing a single pass. Lehigh ended the day 0-6 in the passing category, but gained 283 yards on the ground, behind Al Richmond's 108 yards and two touchdowns. Charley Wentz and Charley Lull scored Lehigh's other touchdowns. Richmond's rushing performance earned him the first Most Valuable Player award in Lehigh - Lafayette history.

Lehigh Captures Its Second Lambert Cup ... Just Barely

"This week's game against Lafayette is going to be as tough as any other. They've won only two games this year, and they can make a respectable season by beating us. Lafayette says they've been getting ready for us for the last four weeks. Well, we've been preparing for them since the first day of the season."

— Lehigh coach Bill Leckonby's pregame comment (1961)

Lafayette entered the 1961 game against Lehigh with a disappointing 2-5-1 record. Coach Jim McConlogue, a Moravian College grad in his fourth season at Lafayette, fielded a small and injury-laden team all year. The Leopards were limited by an injury to their star halfback Walt Doleschal — a converted soccer player from Germany — who also handled the punting and placekicking chores.

Lehigh started the season with an inexperienced squad but avoided serious injuries. Improving with each game, Leckonby developed his boys into contenders for the Lambert Cup. The Engineers entered the Lafayette contest with a surprising 6-2 record.

The Most Valuable Player and Winning Team Trophies

For many years, press box veterans informally picked "Players of The Game" for Lehigh-Lafayette football games. In 1960, the schools' student governing bodies officially instituted the Most Valuable Player award along with a trophy to be presented to the winning team.

Selected by a vote of the media members covering the game, the Most Valuable Player award, along with the team trophy, have become part of the deep-rooted tradition of college football's most played rivalry.

Lehigh received the first winning team trophy with its 26-3 victory.

The inaugural Most Valuable Player award was presented to Lehigh's senior halfback Al Richmond, all 160 pounds of him, for his fine rushing performance.

The MVP Trophy

The Game Trophy

A Real Bronx Cheer

The *New York Times* sent a reporter to cover the pageantry of the 1961 game. During The Game, the writer witnessed an unusual performance in the stands when a Lehigh student vomited into a grinder noisemaker. Then moments later, the unsuspecting grinder operator cranked the noise device, inadvertently showering the crowd with chunks of spew. Instead of reporting on the color of the Lehigh-Lafayette rivalry, the scribe wrote an article featuring the antics and color of the inebriated crowd.

Vincent J. "Pat" Pazzetti

The game program and halftime ceremony of the 1961 Lehigh-Bucknell game were dedicated to Vincent J. "Pat" Pazzetti in honor of his selection to the National Football Hall of Fame. Pazzetti, inducted into the Lehigh Hall of Fame in 1993, was presented with the game ball and later described the ceremony as one his greatest thrills.

Lehigh President Harvey Neville spoke at halftime, praising Pazzetti's accomplishments on and off the field. Among the milestones, in 1912 Pazzetti became the first Lehigh player to throw a touchdown pass in a Lehigh-Lafayette game. Harvey Harmon of the Hall of Fame presented the award to Pazzetti. Lehigh's Marching 97 honored the All-American quarterback during halftime, spelling "P-A-T" at midfield. The Lehigh football team responded by giving Pazzetti a 12-7 victory over the Bisons.

The game started as if the Engineers would steamroll the Leopards. It ended with what many described as the most exciting 15 minutes in The Game's history.

Tied at 14, the teams turned the pigskin over six times in the dramatic fourth quarter, setting a new Lehigh-Lafayette record for self-destruction. Lafayette's Gene Denahan intercepted two passes and Lehigh's Jim Minnich recovered two Leopard fumbles in the final frame. Excited by the rollercoaster of turnovers, the 15,000 fans at Taylor Stadium held tightly to their seats as the ride approached the last turn.

The ball rested at midfield with 40 seconds remaining. The Engineers had one final chance to break the deadlock. Coach Leckonby stayed with long-ball threat Denoia, even though he had completed more passes to the Lafayette secondary than to Lehigh receivers. The strong-armed Denoia met the challenge by threading the needle through double coverage with a perfect pass to the outstretched fingers of Pat Clark at the Leopard three.

With 25 seconds remaining, Lehigh sent Taylor up the middle twice, netting only one yard. Just six ticks remained on the scoreboard clock when Leckonby sent in Andy Larko, listed as QB/FB/E/LB/P/K on the Lehigh roster, to attempt the game-deciding field goal. The pressure hung over Larko's head like a hangman's noose.

Larko's kick from the right hash mark sailed left and low, and barely cleared the outstretched arms of the Lafayette defensemen. The kick spun sideways, like a flying saucer, instead of end-over-end. Floating as if in suspended animation, the ball eventually snuck through the lower-left corner of the uprights, giving Lehigh a 17-14 advantage.

Jubilant Lehigh students rushed the field and tore down the goalposts. A few seconds remained on the clock, and the police restored order and cleared the field so the game could be completed.

Lafayette returned Lehigh's squib kick to midfield and had time for one last "Hail Mary" pass attempt, which was intercepted by Clark. The speedy Clark ran out the clock in his typical crackerjack fashion, frantically running circles around the Lafayette players.

After six turnovers, two penalties, a "Hail Mary" pass, and a UFO sighting, the fourth quarter came to an end with Lehigh capturing a thrilling 17-14 victory.

When asked about the game-winning field goal, Larko responded, "I knew it was good the minute it left my toe. I was never in doubt!" The field goal was Larko's first successful attempt during his two years of kicking at Lehigh. Larko dismissed the questions from the press about the peculiar trajectory and rotation of the kick by responding, "Aw, I kick a lot of them like that in practice." Larko's teammates remember the kick a little differently.

Andy Larko's game-winning field goal in the 1961 Lehigh-Lafayette game.

"Wild Card" Substitution Rule Change

In 1960, the NCAA Rules Committee introduced the "Wild Card," a significant reform to college football's substitution rule. The new rule relaxed the stringent substitution guidelines, allowing a designated "Wild Card" player, regardless of previous appearances, to re-enter the game at any time between downs. Other substitutes could enter the game along with the "Wild Card" twice in the same quarter without drawing a 15-yard "Illegal Return" penalty. Before the new rule, a player could not re-enter during the same quarter he exited.

Initially, the Committee modified the "Wild Card" rule to prevent injuries and to allow more players to participate in the game. If a player was shaken-up, a coach could take him out of the game, check his condition, and if the injury was not serious, allow him to return to the action without being charged an official time out.

But, opportunistic coaches, always looking for the decisive edge, used the relaxed substitution rule as a way of conveying information to their teams on the field between every play.

On a positive note, the rule changes started the evolution of multiple defense and offensive sets and specialty players which dramatically impacted the game in later years. Free substitution, permitted from 1941 to 1953, was gradually restored in college football after 1965.

How did the rule change affect The Game? Much to the delight of coach McConlogue and the dismay of coach Leckonby, the "Wild Card" rule did not deter Lafayette from executing the "sleeper" play to perfection in the 1961 Lafayette-Lehigh game.

Mike Austrian '63: "Did it really hit both the crossbar and the upright?"
Coach George Halfacre '50: "Ugly!"
Chuck Gibson '63: "It looked like a wounded duck... It had to be the worst looking kick ever. The ball defied the laws of gravity (but that is possible because Larko never understood them)."

The Engineers controlled the early action. Touchdowns by Walt King and fullback Boyd "The Crasher" Taylor capped first-half Lehigh scoring drives.

After narrowing the gap to 14-6 behind Charles Zarelli's one-yard sneak, Lafayette coach McConlogue reached into his bag of tricks and pulled out his patented "sleeper" play.

Faced with a second-and-20 situation in the third quarter, halfback Ray Moyer got himself "lost" among his Lafayette teammates on the sideline. Overlooked by the Lehigh defenders, Moyer streaked down the sideline uncovered and hauled in a 41-yard pass from Mike Dill. The surprise play put Lafayette in excellent field position at the Lehigh 27.

Three plays later, the Leopards were faced with a crucial fourth-and-goal at the Lehigh one-yard line. Zarelli handed off to John Contarino, who apparently forgot to check the Bethlehem traffic report. Someone had parked a semi across the Lehigh goal line. The senior halfback, attempting to move one yard forward, was met head on by Lehigh captain Mike "Semi" Semcheski, who knocked Contarino two yards backwards. Lehigh's defense trucked off the field and its offense was bussed in on downs.

Lafayette was knocked back but not out. Two possessions later, the Leopards threatened again; this time sparked by John Brown's punt return to the Lehigh 34-yard line. Shedding two tacklers, Doleschal found paydirt three plays later with a brilliant 22-yard scamper which was his only rushing attempt of the game.

Fullback Boyd Taylor won Most Valuable Player honors. The Crasher rushed for 75 yards and a touchdown and blocked a field goal. Although Taylor received the Most Valuable Player trophy, Lehigh had many heroes in the game. Mike Semcheski's goal line stand, Denoia's long-bomb, Clark's spectacular catch, and Larko's dramatic field goal were all deserving of Most Valuable Player honors.

Had the final score gone the other way, both Walt Doleschal and the diminutive Charlie Zarelli (5' 6" and 151 pounds) had MVP performances for Lafayette. After the game, several Lehigh running backs told Doleschal, "That's the hardest we've been hit all year." Lehigh's four fumbles were a direct result of bone-crushing hits from the 'Pard defense.

The 17-14 victory earned Lehigh its second Lambert Cup in five years. This was accomplished with a team which graduated 16 seniors from a year earlier.

Leckonby was promoted to Athletic Director after the 1961 season leaving behind one of the greatest coaching legacies in Lehigh football history.

Going to the Go-Go

Michael Cooley succeeded Bill Leckonby as the Engineer coach in 1962. Since graduating from the University of Georgia, Cooley had been Leckonby's line coach and right-hand man for twelve years.

Cooley experienced hard luck during his debut season, managing only two victories against six defeats going into the Lafayette game. With secret code names for his platoons, Cooley had his squad in the hunt for The Game.

"I hope we'll be like a hound dog smellin' out a bone ... gettin' downfield and across that goal line," replied Cooley in his down-home style when asked about The Game.

His Lehigh team was divided into three units tagged "GO," "GO-GO," and "STOP." The "GO" crew was Lehigh's ball-control offensive unit. The "GO-GO" lineup was used when Lehigh wanted to score quickly. "STOP" was designated for the Lehigh defense.

Lafayette struggled through the 1962 season, losing five of eight games prior to the Lehigh finale. Despite a subpar record, the Leopards had their share of offensive weapons, including senior halfback Ray Moyer and sophomore quarterback George Hossenlopp.

"Our biggest problem will be containing this Hossenlooper (Hossenlopp), because he's a real good one who can throw on the run. Give him a little daylight, and he goes around you. Play him tight, and he pitches that ball over your head."

— Lehigh coach Mike Cooley, 1962

William B. Leckonby

Bill Leckonby coached the Lehigh football team to new heights during his 16 seasons on South Mountain. In building the Engineers into an Eastern powerhouse, the Lehigh Hall of Famer led Lehigh to its first and only undefeated and untied season in 1950 and captured the Lambert Cup trophy in 1957 and 1961.

A star halfback and punter for the NFL's Brooklyn Dodgers, Leckonby played his last pro contest on December 7, 1941. Following the attack on Pearl Harbor, Leckonby accepted an officer's commission in the United States Navy, continuing to play and coach football in the service.

After the war, Leckonby, just 28 years old, took over as Lehigh's head football coach in 1946, making him the youngest coach in the school's history.

Leckonby came to South Bethlehem when the football program was struggling. Lehigh had managed only two winning seasons in the past ten years and had not beaten Lafayette in eight years. With the assistance of a young coaching staff, Leckonby tallied 10 winning seasons and a 85-35-5 record - including seven over the Leopards, making him the winningest coach in Lehigh's history.

The 1950 and 1957 Coach of the Year was a master of fundamentals. Leckonby's teams were always well-coached and well-conditioned. The coach was a soft-spoken man of few words, except when it came to commenting on the officiating in Lehigh-Lafayette games. The games against Lafayette were always emotional, and Leckonby's teams, at least in the coach's opinion, often came out on the short end of the close calls.

On and off the field, Leckonby was a true leader by example. During a practice session in 1961, the Lehigh punters were kicking at Taylor Stadium from sideline to sideline when coach Leckonby strolled over to check on their progress. Their performance was not meeting the coach's expectations and Leckonby quickly reviewed with them the fundamentals of kicking a football. The former Brooklyn Dodger star proceeded to teach by example and booted the ball into the cheap seats of Taylor's south stands. According to safety James Wilson's calculations, Leckonby's punt traveled over 80 yards before landing in the bleachers. As his players stood in disbelief, Leckonby mumbled a few inaudible phrases and continued with his stroll.

Hossenlopp wasted no time in making Cooley's concerns a reality, directing Lafayette's first scoring drive late in the first quarter. Unfortunately for the Maroon, it would be their only scoring drive of the day, as Lehigh bested its long-time rival 13-6.

Lehigh had a tough time getting its "GO" offense started, but finally shifted into "GO-GO" in the fourth quarter.

After a short punt, the Engineers took possession at Lafayette's 15-yard line. Lehigh quarterback Walt King rolled right then rifled a pass to Chuck Ortlam on the one-yard line. The sophomore wingman made a dazzling catch, stepped across the goal line, and then dropped the ball as he crossed the plane. A lengthy meeting ensued, with the officials ruling that Ortlam was safely across the goal line before losing possession. Joe Walton kicked the point-after and Lehigh took the lead, 7-6, with 10:22 remaining.

Late in the game, the difference appeared to be the blocked extra point by Lehigh's 1961 hero Andy Larko. After Lester White capped Hossenlopp's first quarter drive with a one-yard scoring plunge for the Leopards, Larko deflected the point-after kick.

With Lehigh's touchdown and conversion kick early in the fourth stanza standing as the margin of victory, Larko — who seemingly blocked as many kicks as he made — was a candidate for the MVP trophy.

The award ended in the hands of QB Walt King, behind a two-of-seven day passing for 25 yards and one touchdown. Although King did not finish with impressive statistics, his scrambling ability and veteran leadership during Lehigh's comeback impressed MVP balloters. One pollster summarized the MVP's performance, "When Lehigh needed cash, King took them to the bank."

Lehigh running back Pat Clark grossed 70 yards rushing, but was thrown for 21 yards in losses. After receiving several stitches in his upper lip, Clark returned to the game to score Lehigh's second touchdown with 17 seconds remaining. Clark's teammates awarded him the game ball in recognition of his hard play, determination, and stiff upper lip.

The Game Postponed!

Following the assassination of President John F. Kennedy on Friday, November 22, 1963, The Game was postponed for only the second time in its history. The tragic event led to the rescheduling of the Lafayette-Lehigh football game to the

Scrambled Eggs

Utilizing their engineering course work, students from both schools often designed special weapons to use in the heat of the Lehigh-Lafayette battle. One such contraption was an egg launcher built by the students on College Hill in the early 60's.

The device, much like an oversized sling shot customized for egg launching, was unveiled once a year for The Game. Although designed by engineering students, the accuracy of the launcher was random and sporatic.

Except one year, when the Lafayette students scored a direct hit from across the gridiron on an assistant Lehigh dean . The egg splattered on the lapel on the dean's brand new blazer, which some say was an appropriate indicator of Lehigh's rotten play that day.

The following Monday morning, the dean marched into the athletic department and demanded that the jacket be cleaned. Craig Anderson, an Associate Athletic Director, had just started in an entry level position at Lehigh. Anderson, who was not particularly fond of the assistant dean's shallow sense of humor, was given the responsibility of dealing with the dean's demands.

"I politely took the sport coat and told him that we would take care of it," recounted Anderson. The sport coat reportedly never made it to the dry cleaners. In fact, one staff member attests the jacket is still tucked away in a closet in Taylor Gym.

Presidential Woes

The Game's post-ponement in '63 was the second in The Series' 80-year history. The first occurred in 1904 after the death of another President — Lehigh's Dr. Henry S. Drown.

following weekend.

The postponement resulted in one of the smallest turnouts in modern Lehigh-Lafayette history. The sparse crowd of 7,000 at Taylor Stadium was attributed to several factors: (1) the poor records of both teams — Lafayette was 1-7 and Lehigh was 0-8 entering The Game, (2) the absence of students who were home for Thanksgiving break, (3) a cold, windy, snowy afternoon, and (4) many football fans still mourning the death of President Kennedy.

Kenneth Bunn, who replaced Jim McConlogue after the 1962 season, was coaching his first Lafayette-Lehigh game. Bunn, who compiled a 41-10-1 mark at Juniata (Pa.) including a 27-game winning streak, recorded only one victory, a 14-13 triumph over Bucknell during his first season on College Hill.

Lafayette's single victory was one more than Lehigh had posted. Cooley, plagued by a small, slow group of inexperienced players and a brutal schedule, was winless in eight tries.

With two of the most inept squads in The Game's history, a 0-0 tie would be a fitting conclusion.

Scoreless into the second quarter, then knotted at eight in the fourth, both teams appeared destined to tie.

A late touchdown by Lehigh captain Jake LaMotta gave the Engineers a 15-8 lead, but Lafayette did its best to assure the game ended in a deadlock.

Starting at their own three behind a poised George Hossenlopp, the Leopards marched deep into Lehigh territory against a "prevent" defense.

The Class of '64

The 1963 Lehigh squad avoided a winless season and a line in the record books as the worst team in Lehigh football history by defeating Lafayette in the final game of the season. The victory was Lehigh's fourth in a row over Lafayette, breaking a 79-year old tradition on College Hill. For the first time in The Series' history, Lafayette graduated a class ('64) without recording a victory over Lehigh.

With one second remaining and the ball on the Lehigh 33-yard line, Hossenlopp connected with John Brown at the 15. The two Lehigh defenders collided, knocking themselves out of the play and leaving Brown with an open angle to the end zone. Lehigh's LaMotta, the only player between Brown and paydirt, closed the gap and wrestled the ball carrier to the ground at the 10-yard line as time expired. Lehigh narrowly escaped through the Taylor Stadium tunnel with a 15-8 victory.

After Lafayette drew first blood driving 68 yards for a touchdown and an 8-0 lead, Lehigh moved 78 yards in 13 plays to tie the game in the third quarter. Sophomore quarterback Les Kish scored on a bootleg left, then rifled the two-point conversion to Chuck Ortlam, who caught the ball deep in the end zone. Apparent to most, but not the referee, Ortlam did not have both feet in-bounds for a legal catch as was required by 1963 NCAA rules. The controversial end zone grab tied the game at 8-8. As photos confirmed after the game, Ortlam's left foot was clearly over the end line when he caught the pass.

Lehigh's Kish won Most Valuable Player honors, becoming the first sophomore to win the award since its inception in 1960. Kish rushed for 103 yards in 16 attempts and a touchdown. The lad from across the Delaware River in Phillipsburg, New Jersey completed four passes for 37 yards including a two-point conversion. On defense, Kish recovered the fumble that set up Lehigh's winning touchdown.

Introducing new offensive formations he developed at Juniata, coach Bunn gained the attention of the football world in his first Lafayette-Lehigh game. Lafayette caught Lehigh offside on several occasions by shifting from a "T" to a single-wing formation.

Lehigh coach Mike Cooley did not take kindly to Bunn's deceptive tactics. "It's a sucker shift," Cooley said, "but we were too good a team to be beaten by it. It's legal enough, but of no value except to pull a team offside. I feel it's kind of a rinky-dink thing in a game such as Lehigh-Lafayette, with its fine history and tradition. Maybe it was helpful at Juniata."

The 100th Game

"When it's Lehigh vs. Lafayette, it matters not how you play the game, but how many times you play it."

— excerpt from November 22, 1964 New York Times article by Steve Cady.

Coaches Mike Cooley and Kenneth Bunn prepared their teams for the 100th Lehigh-Lafayette game after struggling through nightmarish 1964 seasons. Cooley's Engineers were 1-7 and Bunn's Leopards 0-7-1. With only one victory between the teams, the Fisher Field stands were absent of bowl scouts. Instead, 19,000 devoted fans packed the bleachers to watch the 100th game of the nation's most-played football rivalry.

The 1964 contest received national media coverage for its centennial game milestone. Pregame press conferences were held in Bethlehem, Easton, New York, and Philadelphia. Special publicity efforts catered to national television broadcasts and media outlets. Included in the promotional activities was the distribution of one million commemorative matchbooks, souvenir glasses, and game programs. On NBC's "Today Show," Jack Lescoulie boldly predicted a Lehigh victory.

Much to the chagrin of both schools, the NCAA did not include the 100th Lehigh-Lafayette game in its approved NBC telecast

Death Wish

The Lafayette students paraded a coffin, with "L-E-H-I-G-H" written on the sides, through the streets of Easton the night before the 100th game.

100th Game Nightmare

The extensive preparation for the 100th Lehigh-Lafayette game took its toll on Lehigh public information director Sam Connor. On the eve of the centennial game, Connor was awakened by a nightmare during which he thought the game was only the 99th. The scare was short-lived as Lafayette and Lehigh did indeed line up for the 100th game the following afternoon.

schedule. Lehigh public information director Sam Connor proclaimed "taxation without representation," since all member colleges paid annual dues to the NCAA.

Connor contended, "It's time that universities and colleges which maintain football in the proper perspective such as Lehigh, Lafayette, Moravian, Muhlenberg, Swarthmore, Johns Hopkins, RPI and the like, have a chance for regional television exposure." Connor eventually got his wish in 1993, when the 129th Lehigh-Lafayette game was nationally televised on ESPN2.

The absence of national television coverage did not stop the 100th game celebration from reaching a fever pitch.

During the pregame festivities, The Marching 97, under the direction of Jonathan Elkus, spelled out "L-E-H-I-G-H" without missing a step or a beat. John Raymond's Lafayette band, sporting blazers and straw hats, brought an end to the pregame show with a Leopard rendition of the National Anthem. The only thing missing was the Olympic torch as the chant of, "Let THE GAME begin!" bellowed from the crowd in Greco-Roman fashion.

"This rivalry has produced not only the heat of the battle, but the warmth of friendship."

— Dr. W. Deming Lewis, 1964

The heat of the battle prevailed on the field and in the bleachers as the teams fought for victory in the landmark game. In the stands, the emotions of the fans flared. Play was stopped several times because the combatants could not hear the signals due to the crowd noise, complete with horns, bells, buzzers, and whistles.

When the final gun was sounded by the referee, the Fisher Field scoreboard — a gift from the Class of '56 — flashed the score 6-6, which was entered into the history books as the fifth deadlock in the 100-game series.

The noisemakers left with a subdued feeling and the gridders experienced a hollow sensation in the hallowed rivalry.

With offenses that resembled a Rockettes' stage show — one, two, three, kick — and punts filling the air, each team was forced to relish its opponent's miscues to tally points.

Lehigh scored first, capitalizing on a first-quarter fumble by Leopard halfback Bill Horvath. The Engineers' Big Jim McCleery recovered at the Lehigh 45, giving the offense a shortened field to reach paydirt.

Lehigh's field general Les Kish marched the team downfield with a 31-yard aerial strike to Joe Weiss at the Lafayette 12-yard line. Halfback Hal Yeich plowed three times to the five-yard line before Kish plunged for a six-pointer. Joseph V. Walton, whose father Joseph L. scored a Lehigh touchdown in the 1936 game, missed wide on the extra-point attempt.

In the second quarter, Lafayette blocked an Ed Peck punt at the Lehigh four. Three plays later, George Hossenlopp bucked the line to even the score. Horvath's extra-point attempt sliced wide-right and the half ended in a 6-6 deadlock.

After intermission, the intensity built to a crescendo, both on and off the field.

Returning from the locker room, the Leopards defense pounced on their prey. The home team forced two Lehigh fumbles in Leopard territory, but failed to capitalize on the Engineer miscues. After a Lehigh punt, Hossenlopp called a mix of running and passing plays to move his team into scoring position.

A Lehigh penalty gave Hoss and company a first down at the Lehigh five. Fullback Bernie Carlson surged for two yards. Bill Horvath was stopped on second down for no gain. Lafayette tried the middle a third time, with Carlson crashing to the one-foot line.

The sound of the horns in the stands was

A Taste of The Past

During the 1964 pregame press conference, Lehigh co-captain Chuck Ortlam wore a replica of Lehigh's 1884 uniform, complete with a brown and white striped shirt and stocking cap. The old-time uniform also sported a belt with handles which were used by teammates to help pull the ball-carrier downfield during a pileup.

100th Game Recognized by Hall of Fame

Immediately after Lafayette received the opening kickoff, an officials' time out was called for a brief ceremony to commemorate the start of the centennial game. Harvey Harmon, Director of the National Football Hall of Fame, accepted the game ball from the co-captains, Lafayette's Doug Dill and George Hossenlopp and Lehigh's Chuck Ortlam and Joe Weiss. The football used for the opening kickoff was retired to the Hall of Fame in New Brunswick, New Jersey.

100th Halftime

The 1964 halftime ceremony was highlighted by speeches from Lafayette President Dr. K. Roald Bergethon and Lehigh President Dr. W. Deming Lewis. Bergethon reflected on the tradition of the rivalry and stressed how relations between the schools had improved through the years while Lewis captured the competitive spirit of the matchup.

Lafayette's George Hossenlopp accepts the 1964 MVP trophy.

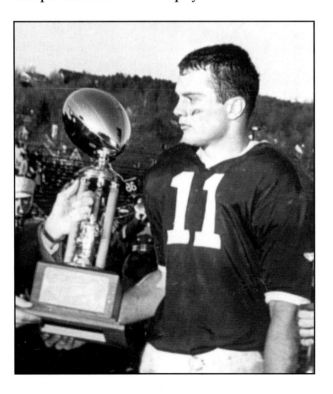

muffled by the cheers of 19,000 fans on their feet to watch THE play of The Game. Carlson got the call on fourth down, only to be dumped short of the goal line by veteran tackle Tony Hrincevich and John Bissett.

Lehigh took over on downs, but the fired-up Leopard defense did not allow the Brown and White any breathing room. The Engineers couldn't gain an inch, forcing Peck to punt on third down with his back at the end line. Aided by a favorable wind and a good roll, Peck got off the punt of a lifetime, netting 64 yards. With 3:45 remaining in the game, Lehigh escaped from the jaws of the Leopards without serious injury.

The Lehigh defense held, giving the offense one last chance to break the tie. Starting from their own 46-yard line, the Engineers drove downfield under the leadership of Bob Draucker, who took over for Kish in the second half. On fourth-and-three with 1:55 remaining, Draucker delivered a 23-yard strike to Walton at the Lafayette 24. On the next play, hard-running fullback Hal Yeich crashed over right tackle for seven yards before losing a fumble, his third of the afternoon. The Leopards recovered, killing Lehigh's belated scoring effort.

George Hossenlopp won Most Valuable Player honors, making him the first Lafayette player to receive the award since its inception in 1960. Hoss ended his brilliant career at Lafayette by connecting on eight-of-17 passes for 79 yards, rushing for 28 more, and scoring the Leopards' lone touchdown.

Sports Illustrated

Since 1884, 100 games of football have been played between Lafayette College and Lehigh University, which is the most times two colleges have met on the grid-iron. (In the old days they used to play two and three times a season.) The game played last Saturday, which ended in a 6-6 tie, was memorable only because it was the 100th, but there were old grads in the stands who recalled not the Game of '98 but the Riot of '02, the Pregame Riot of '33, the Brawl of '48, and the Snowball Fight of '55. The 1964 game was pretty quiet - Lehigh's flagpole was painted a Lafayette maroon and the Lafayette leopard statue was painted a Lehigh brown, but not much else of interest happened.

Pish-tush. One year, they say, Lehigh students burned down the Lafayette library. And there was another year that Sam Harleman, Lehigh '01, remembered, "We played two games at Lafayette," he said. "That meant two fights. It got kind of rough." Just how rough may be judged by the legend of Tom Keady, who coached Lehigh from 1912 to 1920. A big man, he was a quiet one, too, and therefore considered weak on the pep talks that preceded each game. Ah, but before one game, the story goes, he evoked the proper mental attitude by silently choking a leopard to death and throwing the carcass of the beast at the feet of his players.

He did it, a Lafayette follower said, to "appeal to their intelligence."

— *Sports Illustrated* Scoreboard Section (11/30/64)

Winless Season Avoided

"One loss is good for the soul. Too many losses are not good for the coach,"
— Knute Rockne

In his third year as Lafayette coach, Kenneth Bunn enjoyed one of his more successful seasons with a 3-6 record including victories over Columbia, Rutgers, and Bucknell. A victory over Lehigh would give the Leopards their best record in five years.

Fred Dunlap, who succeeded Mike Cooley as Lehigh head coach in 1965, had yet to record a victory in eight games prior to the season finale against Lafayette. A win over Lafayette would save the humiliation of posting one of the worst records in Lehigh history. To date, Lehigh recorded winless seasons in 1884 (0-4), 1941 (0-6-3), 1943 (0-5-1), and 1944 (0-6).

Anticipating a triumph over the Leopards, Dunlap supporters sent the coach an eight-week old bottle of champagne carried with them through the winless season.

With only seconds left on the third quarter clock and holding a 20-0 lead, the Engineers and Dunlap prepared to toast the town.

But seasoned observers of The Rivalry weren't as quick to pop the cork. Neither was the Lafayette team.

Shocking the crowd of 13,000 at Taylor Stadium, the Leopards used two big plays

The Keystone State

The 101st Lehigh-Lafayette game revisited the roots of The Rivalry — the Keystone State. The three Lafayette captains and two Lehigh captains for the 1965 game were Pennsylvania natives as were two of the four officials. In the spirit of The Rivalry, the Lehigh and Lafayette bands considered playing the Quaker State Polka in addition to the National Anthem during the pregame at Taylor Stadium.

Maroon & Brown?

Lafayette wide receiver David Brown set new single-season school records for pass receptions and yards receiving in 1965. The standout receiver was later inducted into the Maroon Club Hall of Fame in 1991.

late in the game to keep the bubbly bottled and the fans on the edge of their seats.

An 84-yard kick-off runback for a touchdown by Bill Vonroth and a 47-yard interception return by Dave Weaver late in the game pulled the 'Pards to within six with 2:15 remaining. But the Maroon's onside kick attempt failed to travel the required ten yards. Lehigh took over at the Lafayette 43 and killed the clock and the Leopards for a 20-14 victory.

The winless Engineers jumped to a 14-0 first-half lead on touchdown runs by Jon Rushatz and Hal Yeich. Lehigh padded its lead with a 26-yard touchdown pass from Bob Draucker to Dick Pochman with two seconds remaining in the third quarter.

In the fourth quarter, with the Engineers still in command, coach Dunlap went for the record books and inserted quarterback Bill Semko. The sophomore needed four completions to break Lehigh's season pass completion record held by Dan Nolan (1957) and Walt King (1962).

Semko quickly completed three passes in two offensive series and aimed to tie the record on his next attempt when Lafayette's Weaver picked-off Semko's record-tying pass attempt and returned it for the Leopards' second TD.

After the game, Lehigh's mentor celebrated with his eight-week old bottle of champagne while acknowledging his rookie coaching mistake: "I never should have done it (allow Semko to pass) because there was too much at stake," said Dunlap. "The kids worked too hard and took too many lumps this season to lose a game that was all sewed up."

Lehigh's Yeich won Most Valuable Player honors with a career high 174 yards rushing, a touchdown, and no fumbles. Yeich set up Lehigh's second touchdown with a 75-yard run off left guard. The Lehigh workhorse redeemed himself after fumbling three times in the 1964 Game.

Sophomore receiver Rich Miller padded his Lehigh season pass reception record, adding seven catches to bring the total to 36.

Although not apparent from the 20-14 score, Lehigh dominated the 101st meeting statistically and outgained the Leopards 421 to 159 in total yards.

Lafayette's First Game Trophy

Lehigh made a habit of entering the Lafayette game winless and leaving with its first victory of the season. In 1963 and 1965, the Engineers entered the Lafayette game with an 0-8 record, but saved their best for last, emerging victorious both years.

The 1966 season was no exception, as Lehigh once again brought its 0-8 record to Fisher Field. Lafayette, which had not defeated Lehigh in Easton since 1954, hoped to change the recent trend.

Much to the delight of the partisan crowd of 14,000, Lafayette blanked Lehigh 16-0.

Rick Craw, Bill Messick, Gary Marshall, Dave Robertshaw, and Bill Vonroth provided the offensive punch for Lafayette. In the first period, Marshall connected with Robertshaw on a six-yard pass for the Leopards' first touchdown. Robertshaw's touchdown catch set a new Leopard record for touchdown receptions in a season (five) and established a new single-season receiving mark of 515 yards. Messick booted the extra point and added a field goal in the second quarter. Vonroth finished the Lafayette scoring with a 70-yard punt return for a touchdown in the fourth quarter.

Lafayette's Craw earned Most Valuable Player honors as the game's leading rusher with 121 yards. Craw became only the second Lafayette player to win the award since its inception in 1960.

Kenneth Bunn ended his coaching career at Lafayette on a winning note and gave Lafayette possession of its first Lafayette-Lehigh game trophy. Bunn compiled a 7-28-2 record during his four years on College Hill. Harry Gamble took over as head coach in 1967.

In defeat, Lehigh's Rick Laubach, who completed 11-of-25 pass attempts for 136 yards, established a new Lehigh single-season passing record which was previously held by Dan Nolan. Laubach finished the season with 869 yards passing, outdistancing Nolan's 1956 total by one

Aerospace Engineering

As part of the antics of Lafayette weekend, Lehigh students held a unique contest in the 1950's and 60's. Led by the Pi Lams, students would take turns riding inside the local laundromat's dryers.

The ride was called "orbiting," and the record number of orbits was reportedly 35. The "astronauts" would board the craft, insert the fare, input the cycle type and time, and off they'd go. The orbiting continued until the occupant submitted to the heat and rotations or the timer reached zero.

yard.

Lafayette handed Lehigh its ninth loss of the season and the worst record (0-9) in the school's history.

The Grim Reaper

First-year Lafayette coach Harry Gamble brought the Leopards into the 1967 game with a mediocre 3-5 record.

Fred Dunlap struggled through his third season as Lehigh coach with a 1-7 record. The 1967 season brought several unexpected setbacks for Lehigh, including the tragic death of backfield coach Jim McConlogue, who joined the Lehigh staff after holding the head spot at Lafayette from 1958 to 1962. McConlogue died of a heart attack after Lehigh's midseason game with Furman. Adding to Dunlap's dismay, two senior offensive starters decided not to play in their final year and Lehigh's top two running backs were lost to injury during the season.

Lafayette had not defeated Lehigh at Taylor Stadium since 1959 when McConlogue was head coach of the Leopards. The 'Pards were looking to break the Taylor Stadium jinx as a tribute to its deceased ex-coach.

In a battle of attrition, the game's highlight reel featured 25 punts. During the scoreless first half, the Leopard offense mustered one first down, netted minus six yards on the ground, and 16 yards passing. Lehigh's first-half performance consisted of seven first downs, 36 yards rushing, and 87 yards passing. The Engineers had several scoring opportunities in the first half, but walked away empty-handed as a result of turnovers and missed field goal attempts.

A fumbled punt in the third quarter gave Lehigh its best scoring opportunity of the day at the Leopard 13-yard line. Two plays later, Engineer quarterback Rick Laubach fumbled and Ed Kercher recovered for the Leopards. Later in the same quarter, Lehigh snowballed downfield again, only to melt in the hot glare of the red zone when a 28-yard chip shot sailed wide.

Lafayette was in a position to win the game late

Parade Cancellation

In 1967, Lehigh's traditional pajama parade was canceled due to inclement weather, but the "Beat Lafayette" display contest proceeded as planned with Sigma Phi Epsilon's "Mr. Easton and the Spider" taking first place.

In Remembrance

Tragically, two spectators, not involved in the goalpost melee, died of natural causes at Taylor Stadium during the 1967 Lafayette-Lehigh game. The 1967 game was dedicated in memory of Rush Lerch, 81-years old, from Easton and Edward Craft, 61, from Belle Mead, N.J.

Lehigh's 50-Game Club

In 1967, Lehigh officially established the 50-Game Club, an elite group of Lehigh Alumni who witnessed 50 or more Lehigh-Lafayette games. The club consisted of six charter members, led by Howard A. Foering, Lehigh Class of 1890 and the University's oldest living alumnus.

Foering, who celebrated his 100th birthday on November 24, 1967, witnessed his 94th Lehigh-Lafayette contest that year. The ageless Foering attended his first game in 1886 as a freshman. The thrill of the previous 93 games had taken its toll on the devoted fan, turning his mustache white during the course of The Rivalry.

Three of the 50-plus club members were Bethlehem residents including Dr. W. L. Estes Jr. (58th game), Hall of Famer V. J. Pat Pazzetti (58th game), and A. W. Chenoweth (56th game). Completing the venerable group was Harry Yeide of Washington D.C. (51st game in a row) and Laurence Kingham of Verona, N.J. (50th game in a row).

in the final period. With just over three minutes remaining, linebacker Gene Weidemeyer blocked Laubach's punt on the Engineer 21-yard line. Three plays later, Leopard quarterback Ed Baker swept around left end for the game's only score. On an afternoon filled with bad luck, Bill Messick's extra point attempt hit the crossbar and bounced back.

Lehigh made a late charge with 2:48 left in the contest, reaching the Lafayette 24-yard line before Don Hughes intercepted a Laubach pass at the goal line. After the interception, a large crowd of Lehigh freshmen, conceding defeat, rushed onto the field and tore down the goalposts to prevent Lafayette from taking the prize back to Easton. The Lafayette students wanted a piece of the treasure and a melee ensued. Two Lehigh students were treated for contusions, the result of some of the best blocking, tackling, and hitting on the field that day. After order was restored, Lafayette ran out the clock to preserve the 6-0 victory.

Unlike the students, the Lehigh kickers, who missed four field goals on the afternoon, had trouble finding the uprights.

The Lafayette defense forced five Lehigh turnovers and deserved the game ball in a contest that coach Harry Gamble described as "one of the hardest hitting games I've ever been associated with."

The fine punting of Bob Zimmers kept Lafayette out of the hole throughout the afternoon. Zimmers' 14-punt performance was highlighted by a 72-yard quick kick in the first half.

In a game that lacked offensive punch but was a defensive hit , the Most Valuable Player trophy was appropriately awarded to a defensive player. Lehigh's All-Middle Atlantic Conference linebacker Art Renfro was named MVP, making him the first defensive player and the first player on the losing team to win the award.

Lafayette's Lambert Cup Bid Spoiled

"Whoever said one game does not tarnish a season never lost a Lafayette-Lehigh football game."

— *Unknown*

The 1968 game loomed large for the Leopards. Lafayette, 7-2, was leading a close race for the Lambert Cup. A decisive victory over Lehigh would give Lafayette a boost in the final Lambert Cup balloting.

Harry Gamble's team was tough at the Leopards' Lair during the '68 season. Lafayette was undefeated and unscored upon at Fisher Field, blanking Hofstra 7-0, Drexel 27-0, Gettysburg 37-0, and King's Point 7-0. The Leopards hoped to add to their 78-0 scoring advantage and 4-0 record on home turf when Lehigh visited Easton for the 104th meeting.

Lafayette's "BEAT LEHIGH" uniforms unveiled a new fashion statement in the 1968 game.

Lehigh, with a 2-7 record, was looking to spoil Lafayette's Lambert Cup bid and home winning streak.

The Brown and White wasted little time in ending Lafayette's bid for a fifth straight shutout at Fisher Field. Much to the surprise of the 16,000 fans, Lehigh took the opening kickoff and mounted a 14-play scoring drive. The Engineer drive was directed by sophomore quarterback Jerry Berger, who took the starting role from co-captain Rick Laubach at mid-season. Fullback Justin Plummer, sporting a Larry Csonka-type bull ring nose guard, scored from the one-yard line to snap Lafayette's home shutout streak.

Late in the second period, Dunlap inserted the more experienced Laubach for Berger hoping to tally a quick score before halftime. Laubach responded with a touchdown strike to speedster Mike Leib for a 14-0 Lehigh lead.

Lafayette mounted a comeback effort early in the fourth quarter on a 30-yard romp by tailback Bob Zimmers, cutting the lead to 14-6.

Lafayette's quest for its first Lambert Cup was squelched midway through the fourth quarter when Jack Paget crossed the goal line for Lehigh's third touchdown. Paget's touchdown upped his season total to 68 points, the highest for a Lehigh player since the legendary Dick Gabriel scored 96 in 1950. Schattenberg kicked his third extra point of the game and completed the season with a perfect 11-for-11 extra points, establishing a new Lehigh record.

Lehigh's Jim Petrillo, the game's leading ground gainer, was awarded the Most Valuable Player trophy.

Despite the 21-6 loss, the 1968 Lafayette squad posted an impressive 7-3 record — the best on College Hill since the 1948 Leopards finished 7-2.

Old Traditions Die Hard

Much like the 1968 Democratic National Convention in Chicago months earlier, authorities cracked-down on college-aged radicals. Bethlehem was no different. A new 1968 ordinance banned the bonfire and marches across the New Street and Hill-to-Hill bridges.

For the first time in many years, the traditional bonfire and pajama parade were not part of the Lehigh-Lafayette pregame festivities on the South Mountain campus. The familiar cry of "We Pay No Toll Tonight" by the Lehigh freshmen was painfully erased from the New Street Bridge on the eve of The Game. The women's dormitories at Moravian College were surprisingly calm — absent of Lehigh serenaders. The bonfire was missing from Upper Taylor Field, leaving the night sky free of smoke and flames.

Approximately 450 freshmen, protesting the cancellation of the events, held a spontaneous rally on the Lehigh campus. The Class of '72 was greatly disappointed about not being able to build a 72-foot bonfire. Some freshmen had suggested building a 72-foot beer can to replace the bonfire, but consensus on a suitable substitute was not reached. John Steckbeck, Director of Intramural Athletics and leader of the pajama parade in previous years, rushed to the protest rally to make sure the situation did not get out of hand.

University officials expressed the need to fill the void and find alternative events for the bonfire and pajama parade. One school official suggested that the University send a delegation to talk to Bethlehem Mayor Gordon Payrow about allowing the bonfire. The idea was nixed when the University found out that the Mayor was in on the original decision.

The cancellation of the bonfire and pajama parade aside, the pep rally and "Beat Lafayette" display contest went on as planned. The pregame activities on the College Hill campus were unaffected by the ordinance.

Unlucky 19!

Lafayette's 36-19 loss to Lehigh in 1969 put the Leopards in the record book as the first team to finish The Game with 19 points. Lafayette's 19 points were tallied on three touchdowns and an extra point kick. The Leopards were unsuccessful on both of their two-point conversion attempts in the fourth quarter.

50-Game Club

In 1969, the 50-game club became the "Magnificent 11" as five new members were added to the original six. Robert Dynan, Robert Watson, Roy Coffin, Jamieson Kennedy, and Lathrop Bevan joined the six charter members of the elite club who witnessed 50 or more games in The Rivalry.

The Chill of Victory

The Lehigh pajama parade was reinstituted as part of the pregame celebration for the 1969 Game. Several hundred freshmen, led by the oldest freshman of all, John Steckbeck, braved record-low temperatures as they paraded from South Bethlehem to Moravian's Church Street campus. The students were accompanied by The Marching 97 and cheerleaders. The Lehigh entourage serenaded the coeds and shouted support for the Moravian football team which was scheduled to play rival Muhlenberg the following afternoon.

On the coldest night of the year, the Lehigh students desperately needed a bonfire to heat South Mountain on the eve of the Lafayette game. No such luck. For the second year in a row, the bonfire was doused by the Bethlehem ordinance. Instead, candles replaced the ritualistic fire during the pep rally which was moved to Grace Hall. A group of spirited students was unsuccessful in an attempt to build a candle that was 73-feet tall to replace the tradition of building a bonfire as tall as the graduation year of the freshmen class.

The Engineers dazzled the crowd of 16,000 at Taylor Stadium in 1969 with a balanced display of offense and defense that proved to be too much for the Leopards. The Lehigh defense limited Lafayette to 149 yards on the ground and pressured the Maroon quarterbacks into throwing four interceptions. Against a Lafayette defense that was designed to stop the run, the Lehigh running backs combined for 304 yards. The result was a 36-19 Engineer victory.

Lehigh's Don Diorio, a Bangor native who played his high school ball at Pius X of Roseto, scored twice on runs of 46 and 10 yards and finished the day with 166 yards on 26 carries. The sophomore running back also punted six times for a 33-yard average, returned kicks, and caught one pass for 20 yards. Diorio was named Most Valuable Player for his all-purpose performance.

The victory concluded Lehigh's best season (4-5-1) since 1961 when the 7-2 Engineers won the Lambert Cup. The 36 points were the most scored against Lafayette since 1950, when an undefeated Lehigh team

"Chuck" Berry Rocks The Baseball World

In 1969, former Lafayette football star Charles Berry was inducted into the Pennsylvania Sports Hall of Fame in Pittsburgh. The Maroon Club Hall of Famer was selected to Walter Camp's All-American first team as an end in 1924. The grid star also captained the Leopard baseball teams and chose baseball over football after graduating from College Hill. Berry played professional baseball for the Philadelphia A's (1925), Boston Red Sox (1928-31), and Chicago White Sox (1932-33). After his playing career, Berry became one of the major leagues' most respected umpires and served as a special aide to Joe Cronin, then President of the American League.

beat the Leopards 38-0.

Despite the season-ending loss to Lehigh, the Maroon gridders shattered 22 school records with eight individual marks going to quarterback Ed Baker and five to split end Mike Miller.

The Brown and White, who upset Rutgers 17-7 earlier in the season, captured the Middle Three Championship with its victory over Lafayette in 1969. The crowning of Lehigh ended an 11-year Rutgers Little Brass Cannon dynasty that spanned from 1958 to 1968.

Lafayette Foils Lehigh's Trickery

The 1970 Game brought the "foot" back into football, as a "shoelace" play netted a big gain for Lehigh, but it was Lafayette that untied the score to win by a toe.

Rich Nowell kicked the winning field goal with 1:10 left in the contest to give the Leopards a 31-28 victory in the 106th renewal of College Football's Most-Played Rivalry.

The game-winner came after the Maroon defense halted a Lehigh drive that featured a 26-yard run by Don Diorio on a trick "shoelace" play.

With quarterback Jerry Berger busy tying his shoelace in the backfield, John Aylsworth side-snapped the ball to Diorio who darted around left end for the big gain. Coach Fred Dunlap revived the play from his days at Cornell and had the Engineers practice the play especially for the

College football celebrated its 100 year anniversary in 1969. Princeton and Rutgers played the first collegiate football game on November 6, 1869 at New Brunswick, N.J. Rutgers defeated Princeton 6 goals to 4.

Record-Breakers!

Rich Nowell's game-winning field goal against Lehigh in 1970 was his fourth of the season and sixth of his career, tying a Leopard record set by Walt Doleschal. The Leopards' team total of five field goals for the year established a new school record. In later years, Lafayette's Jim Hodson twice approached the season mark in a single game. Hodson booted four field goals against both Fordham ('89) and Kutztown ('90) and holds the school record with 40 successful career field goals.

During the 1970 Lehigh game, Lafayette set a school record for most offensive plays in a season (782). For the Leopards, the most important was number 782 — the final play of Lafayette's victory over Lehigh in 1970.

Co-eds on College Hill

Lafayette College started a new tradition in 1970. Women were admitted for the first time to Lafayette. Despite the welcome addition, the Lafayette men preserved a Lafayette-Lehigh tradition by fighting for the goalposts instead of the ladies on the day of The Game.

Lafayette game.

Though Lehigh eventually punted and the Maroon marched for the winning field goal, Dunlap's daring play captured the essence of the 1970 contest.

Lafayette (6-5) jumped to an early 21-0 lead in the first half with the help of three Engineer miscues. Touchdown runs by Rich McKay and Doug Elgin and a 12-yard touchdown reception by Darrell Johnson followed the turnovers.

McKay, who smashed almost every Leopard passing record during the 1970 season, sprinkled passes on the drives to a fine supporting cast of receivers, including Rick Nowell and Bobby Donofrio.

Trailing by a 21-0 count, Lehigh's vaunted running attack was not able to shift into high gear. Entering The Game, the Engineer backfield needed 56 yards to break the team record for rushing yards in a single season (2,162) which was established by the 1957 Lambert Cup team.

Lehigh prevented a blow-out by scoring before the half ended on an 80-yard touchdown drive. Jack Paget rushed the final 12 yards over right tackle for the touchdown.

The Engineers kept momentum rolling down the tracks after intermission. The Brown and White needed only five plays to drive 78 yards, cutting the deficit to 21-14 early in the third quarter.

After Lafayette countered with a 14-play, 83-yard scoring drive with Tom Conway scoring from the two, the Engineers fought back with a sudden scoring flurry that stunned the crowd of 17,000 at Fisher Field.

In a span of 12 seconds, the Engineers scored two fourth-quarter touchdowns to even the score. First, Paget hit Bill Howard on a 54-yard halfback pass for a touchdown. Then, on the first play from scrimmage after the kickoff, Gary Scheib intercepted a McKay pass and galloped 22 yards to the endzone for Lehigh's only defensive touchdown of the season. "Old

Faithful" Schattenberg kicked his fourth extra point to knot the game at 28.

Nowell's game-winning field goal, combined with his four extra points, punting efforts, and four pass receptions for 31 yards earned him the Most Valuable Player trophy.

Lafayette, known as a passing team, relied primarily on the run in its defeat of Lehigh. The 'Pards rushed the ball 65 times for 248 yards and three touchdowns while connecting on only 11-of-27 passes for 88 yards.

Harry Gamble resigned as coach on College Hill after the 1970 season, finishing with an overall record of 21-19-0, including a 2-2 mark versus Lehigh. Gamble accepted the head position at the University of Pennsylvania in 1971 and later became President of the NFL's Philadelphia Eagles.

I Wish They All Could Be Lehigh Girls!

For the third year in a row, the Lehigh campus was without the traditional bonfire the night before the Lehigh-Lafayette game. In its place were plenty of coeds, as 1971 was the first year Lehigh admitted undergraduate women to the University.

For the first time since 1957, both teams entered The Game with more wins than losses. The winning records of Lafayette (5-4) and Lehigh (7-3) revived interest in the football game, while the addition of women on campus aroused the interest of the male students.

"The warmth of the bonfire was replaced by the coeds on campus in '71."
— anonymous Lehigh student who didn't seem to mind the cancellation of the bonfire.

A victory over Lehigh would complete the

If You Can't Beat 'Em, Join 'Em

With the Leopards up 21-0 and controlling the play in the 1970 game, the Lafayette students in Fisher Field jumped into action. Sensing an early kill, the Maroon undergrads began a chorus of "Lehigh Sucks!"

A handful of Lehigh students, disgruntled with their team's effort in The Game and tired of numerous lackluster seasons, looked at one another, shrugged their shoulders, said "What the hell," and joined in the chorus of "Lehigh Sucks!"

Lehigh's Giant Saint

Lehigh's offensive line was anchored by John Hill in 1971. The All-American center and Lehigh Hall of Famer played in the NFL from 1972 to 1984 for the New York Giants and New Orleans Saints.

The Lafayette

College Hill's school newspaper, *The Lafayette*, celebrated its 100th year anniversary in 1970. Founded in 1870, The Lafayette is the oldest college newspaper in Pennsylvania.

Leopards' second consecutive winning season — something they had not done since stringing two together in 1959 and 1960.

Lafayette coach Neil Putnam, who replaced Harry Gamble after the 1970 season, enjoyed instant success in his rookie season.

Lehigh coach Fred Dunlap, after experiencing six losing seasons in a row, finally reaped the benefits of several hard years of recruiting and rebuilding. Dunlap earned the respect of his veteran players by relaxing some of his stringent policies, like not allowing long hair or mustaches. In return, the seniors provided new-found leadership, instilling faith in the coaching staff and building the players into a close-knit unit.

The Engineer offense, stacked with talented seniors, included running backs Jack Rizzo and Don Diorio, center John Hill, and split end John Aylsworth. And the squad welcomed sophomore QB Kim McQuilken, a 6' 2", 180 pound Allentown native, who would later graduate to an NFL career with the Atlanta Falcons.

Lehigh built an early 14-0 lead before 17,000 frenzied fans at Taylor Stadium. Sophomore Chuck Merolla kicked field goals of 25 and 22 yards and Rizzo ripped off a 22-yard run for a touchdown. Norm Liedtke added a two-point conversion on a botched placement snap.

Lafayette fought back with vengeance, exploding for two scores in a 66-second span late in the second quarter. Sophomore quarterback Tim Grip squeezed off an 84-yard

Powder Puff Football

With the addition of coeds to both campuses in 1971, a new and fresh Lafayette-Lehigh tradition was started — Powder Puff football. The inaugural women's version of The Game was played at Taylor Stadium the Sunday after the men's varsity competition. Proceeds for the charity event were donated to the Multiple Sclerosis Society.

The Leopardettes rolled to an easy 30-0 victory over the Lady Engineers, avenging the defeat of the men's team in 1971.

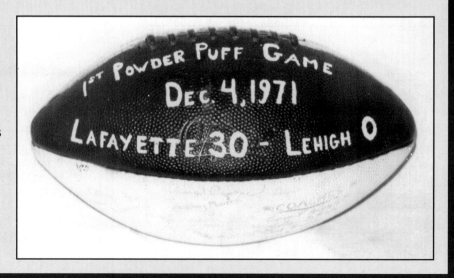

Rizzo's Revenge

The 1971 Lehigh-Lafayette game, tabbed "Rizzo's Revenge," was dominated by the Engineer tandem of Jack Rizzo and Don Diorio, who completed their careers in spectacular fashion. Rizzo and Diorio ripped through the Leopard defense like a pair of crazed animals, rekindling memories of Dick Doyne and Dick Gabriel who terrorized Lafayette in 1949 and 1950. Diorio (32 carries) and Rizzo (31 carries) were the only Lehigh backs to carry the ball in the game. They combined for six touchdowns and 506 yards, surpassing the old team mark (414) set against VMI in 1956.

Rizzo established a new Lehigh single-game record, lugging the leather for 313 yards against Lafayette. The previous milestone (220 yards) was set by Bob Naylor against VMI in 1956. Jack the Ripper finished the 1971 season with 1,143 yards, breaking Dick Gabriel's 1949 single-season rushing record of 1,023 yards.

Rizzo was the unanimous choice for the Most Valuable Player Award. His standout performance was highlighted by four touchdown runs including an 83-yarder. The MVP performance overshadowed a fine effort by teammate Diorio, who finished his career on South Mountain with 193 yards rushing and two touchdowns against Lafayette.

touchdown strike to split end Bob Baumann for the first score. After a Lehigh fumble, Doug Elgin plunged one yard for the neutralizing score. But, a failed extra point attempt left the Leopards trailing by one, 14-13.

In the second half, Lehigh erupted for 34 unanswered points before the Leopards scored on the last play of the game. The Engineers' 48-19 triumph was an impressive ending to Lehigh's best season (8-3) since the 1961 Lambert Cup squad posted a 7-2 record.

The Engineers tallied 664 total yards which shattered the old single-game mark (538 yards) set against Ithaca in 1969.

Lehigh's 48 points against Lafayette boosted its season total to 362 in 11 games making the 1971 squad the highest scoring team in the school's history to date.

Three Lehigh-Lafayette MVP winners in the same backfield during the 1971 game: Kim McQuilken (11), Jack Rizzo (45) and Don Diorio (42).

Lehigh Bonfire Rekindled

After a three-year hiatus on the South Mountain campus, the bonfire was rekindled on the eve of the 1972 Lehigh-Lafayette game. The bonfire and pep rally were relocated from Upper Taylor Field and Grace Hall to Saucon Valley Fields.

McQuilken Shines

Quarterback Kim McQuilken led the 5-5 Engineers into the 1972 Lafayette game. McQuilken rewrote the Lehigh record book, breaking every single-game, season, and career passing record except one — career attempts. The junior field general needed seven attempts against Lafayette to break Rich Laubach's 574.

Lafayette All-American halfback Tony Giglio was questionable for The Game because of a sprained ankle suffered against Drexel. During the season, Giglio became the first Lafayette rusher to gain 1,000 yards in a season. The star halfback entered the Lehigh contest with 1,127 yards, including six games in which he gained more than 100. Without a healthy Giglio, the Leopard offensive attack was severely handicapped.

For Lehigh, the officials were as troublesome as the Leopards. In the first half, the Engineers were penalized more yards than the Leopards gained on offense, 88 to 55. Between yellow flags, the Engineers squeezed a three-yard touchdown run by Bob Stewart for a 7-0 halftime lead.

Lehigh increased its lead to 14-0 in the third period when McQuilken found Norm Liedtke open in the endzone.

The Maroon rallied with a fourth-quarter touchdown run by Frank Campbell. Lafayette continued its comeback effort late in the game, but the Engineer defense rose to the occasion with a goal-line stand to preserve the 14-6 victory. The Leopards were stopped cold after a first-and-goal situation at the Lehigh two-yard line. Lehigh's Chuck Smith sacked quarterback Tim Grip at the Lehigh seven on fourth down to end the threat.

Giglio, playing with a painful ankle injury, was the game's top rusher with 77 yards on 12 carries.

McQuilken won Most Valuable Player to cap his junior season. The Lehigh quarterback found the Lafayette secondary to be as soft as church music, completing 21-of-31 passes for 248 yards and a touchdown. The former Allen High Canary set a new school mark for career pass attempts with 599, completing a sweep of Lehigh passing records.

The MVP had the Fisher Field fans on the edge of their seats during one play in the third quarter. Under a strong rush, McQuilken, a la Fran Tarkenton, retreated 40 yards to elude enemy pursuers, then scrambled forward directing blockers like a dance choreographer before finally completing a pass to Bill Schlegel. The play netted nine yards, but McQuilken's theatrics covered 92 yards of uninhibited excitement.

Richard Harding Davis Honored

The Pennsylvania Newspaper Hall of Fame selected Richard Harding Davis, the Father of Lehigh Football, as one of its first ten distinguished journalists. Other inductees in the inaugural 1972 class included Benjamin Franklin, Elizabeth Cochran Seaman, William Bradford, E.J. Lynett, M. Raymond Sprigle, and Alexander McClure.

Lehigh's Third Lambert Cup

"It's a lovely afternoon, it's a shame there's a game."

— an avid Taylor Stadium tailgater before the 1973 Lehigh-Lafayette game.

In 1973, the Engineers, with a 6-3-1 record, topped the Lambert Cup balloting for the two weeks prior to the Lafayette game. An impressive win over the Leopards would strengthen Lehigh's chances of winning a third Lambert Cup. Lafayette, 6-2-1, was ranked sixth in the Lambert Cup poll and hoped to dethrone number one Lehigh.

The pregame tailgating parties proved to be more exciting than the football game. Lehigh's high-powered offense was too much for Lafayette and the Engineers rolled to a 45-13 yawner.

McQuilken lit up the sky in the 109th Lehigh-Lafayette game with an aerial display that included 17 completions in 26 attempts for 304 yards and two touchdowns to his favorite target, tight end Bill Schlegel.

Take a Walk on The Boardwalk

After the 1973 regular season, Lehigh did not pass "GO" or collect $200 because the Boardwalk Bowl selection committee chose Delaware over Lehigh for the first-round Division II playoff game in Atlantic City. Lehigh later received a bid to play Western Kentucky in Bowling Green, Kentucky in one of the three remaining first-round games of the NCAA Division II football tournament. The postseason bowl was Lehigh's first in 90 years of intercollegiate football competition. The Engineers received four different bowl bids after their undefeated 1950 season, but declined all offers.

After jumping out to an early 10-0 lead, Lehigh bowed to the Western Kentucky Hilltoppers by a score of 25-16.

Green Thumb

The Lafayette students planted a surprise for the crowd of 18,000 at Taylor Stadium in 1973. A group of Leopard prowlers left the succinct message "LEHIGH SUCKS" embedded in the Taylor Stadium turf that became visible only when the grass was cut the day before the kickoff. At halftime, the Lehigh students returned the favor by unveiling a 25-foot sign that reciprocated the distasteful message. The students proceeded to exchange unpleasantries until the Bethlehem police, whose reaction time was considerably faster than the Lehigh secondary, restored order in the stands.

The Lehigh baseball team lived through the fallout of the pranksters' joke. In an era when both football and baseball were played at Taylor Stadium, the Engineers' leftfielder became all too familiar with the "LEHIGH SUCKS" emblem during the spring season. An artistic groundskeeper eventually remedied the situation by camouflaging the message with green spray paint.

"What I remember most about my career at Lehigh is probably beating Lafayette three times. I think the Lafayette games were more exciting to me than any other games I played in, including the NFL games."

— Kim McQuilken '74

The Heisman to South Bethlehem?

Kim McQuilken ended his career at Lehigh by rewriting every Lehigh single-game, season, and career passing record. In addition, he finished the 1973 regular season as the nation's leading passer.

After a fantastic 1973 season, McQuilken was one of 12 nominees for the Heisman Trophy. The Lehigh quarterback was the only Division II player to be nominated in 1973.

The All-American quarterback played his final collegiate game in the annual North-South Shrine Bowl in Miami's Orange Bowl on Christmas night. McQuilken was drafted in the third round in 1974 by the Atlanta Falcons. The former Lehigh standout played seven years in the National Football League with the Atlanta Falcons and Washington Redskins. In 1983, McQuilken came out of retirement for a short time to play with the Washington Federals of the United States Football League (USFL).

Kim McQuilken with the MVP and Winning Team Trophies in 1973.

Lafayette's First 1,000-Yard Rusher

Lafayette's two-time All-American halfback Tony Giglio, who played sparingly in the second half of the 1973 Lafayette-Lehigh game because of a leg injury, picked up 44 yards on 15 carries in his final game. Giglio finished his career at Lafayette with over 4,000 all-purpose yards. He broke the 1,000 yard rushing barrier both as a junior and senior enroute to a then school record 2,519 career rushing yards. Giglio also set records for carries in a season (228) and career (505) while finishing with a 5.0 yard per carry average. The Lafayette Hall of Famer scored 23 touchdowns, exceeded 100-yards rushing 12 times, and broke the 200-yard mark twice during his career.

Lafayette's All-American halfback Tony Giglio.

The sure-handed Schlegel finished the afternoon with 112 yards on six receptions, setting single-season school records for receptions (68), receiving yardage (1,094) and touchdowns (10).

Freshman fullback Rod Gardner was the game's leading rusher with 141 yards on 27 carries and two touchdowns for the Brown and White.

McQuilken's air show earned him an unprecedented second Most Valuable Player award. The Heisman Trophy nominee not only became the first player to win MVP honors twice, but also became the first to win the award two years in a row.

After overwhelming Lafayette, Lehigh (7-3-1) tied Delaware (8-3) for first place in the Lambert Cup poll after the Blue Hens pounded Bucknell 50-0 in its regular season finale. The Lambert Cup crowning was Lehigh's third since the award was established in 1957.

The Year of the Russian Election

"It was as suspenseful as a Russian election."
— Bethlehem <u>Globe-Times</u> Sports Writer Jack Collins's description of the
1974 Lehigh-Lafayette game.

Lehigh's strong offensive line and stubborn defense overpowered the Leopards in 1974. The Engineers racked up 575 yards rushing on way to a 57-7 demolition of Lafayette at Fisher Field. The 50-point spread was Lehigh's largest margin of victory since 1917 when the Brown and White defeated Lafayette 78-0. In the process, Lehigh's Class of 1975 became only the second class in the school's history to defeat Lafayette four years in a row.

The lopsided score enticed the students to find an alternate form of entertainment — goalpost destruction. The goalpost at the west end of the field was ripped down by the Lafayette students with 9:23 remaining in the third quarter, setting a new record for early destruction. The Lehigh students, equally uninterested in the football game, responded by tearing down the east post seconds later. The missing goalposts didn't seem to bother the Lehigh offense which continued its scoring barrage with three fourth-quarter touchdowns and a pair of two-point conversions.

For the third straight year, a Lehigh quarterback from Allentown won the Most Valuable Player trophy. Joe Alleva followed in the footsteps of fellow Allentownian Kim McQuilken by capturing the 1974 Most Valuable Player award. Alleva connected on 14-of-21 passes for 285 yards and three touchdowns against the Leopards.

Powder Puff Update

In 1974, the fourth annual Powder Puff football game was played before a crowd of 600 at Taylor Stadium. The Lady Engineers defeated the Leopardettes 46-0 to even the series at two games apiece. Quarterback Pam Watson's precision passing guided the Lady Engineers to victory for the second year in a row. The Powder Puff trophy, donated by Vernon Macke, was presented to the winners. The game raised approximately $500 for the Multiple Sclerosis Society.

Playoff-Bound Once Again

In 1975, the 8-2 Engineers took a playoff berth and a season-long, home win streak into the 111th Lehigh-Lafayette game.

Coach Fred Dunlap, in his eleventh season at Lehigh, was riding a four-game win streak against the Leopards. Dunlap's success came at the expense of Lafayette's fifth-year coach Neil Putnam, who had not defeated Lehigh since taking over in 1971.

The Brown and White jumped to an early 26-0 lead in the first half and cruised to a 40-14 triumph at Taylor Stadium.

Despite the lopsided score, Lafayette outgained the Engineers in almost every category except the final score.

Competing with a painful shoulder injury, Lehigh fullback Rod Gardner paved the way by rushing for three touchdowns and 116 yards.

Greg DeSanty led the Leopards with 96 yards on 23 rushes and two touchdowns.

In the passing category, Joe Sterrett completed 13-of-19 passes for 165 yards, scoring one touchdown through the air and another on the ground.

Lafayette quarterback Rob Stewart connected on 17-of-28 attempts for 190 yards but tossed two costly interceptions, including one that was returned for a Lehigh touchdown.

Sophomore Mark Weaver won the "EXCEDRIN Pain Killer of the Game" award. Weaver, who was knocked unconscious on the opening kickoff, returned to kick two extra points for Lehigh. Both times, teammates had to point the still-groggy Weaver toward the uprights.

Sterrett edged Gardner in the press box ballot, 23-20, for Most Valuable Player honors. Sterrett was on his way through the tunnel to the locker room when he heard his name announced over the Taylor Stadium public address system. The future Lehigh Athletic Director promptly returned to the field to accept the award and offer praise to his teammates, particularly the inspirational play of Gardner.

With the victory, Lehigh recaptured the Brass Cannon from Rutgers and won its fourth Lambert Cup, outpointing New

1975 Game at a Glance

	Lafayette	Lehigh
First Downs	23	20
Yards Rushing	199	197
Yards Passing	190	165
Total Yards	389	362
Passes Attempted	28	19
Passes Completed	17	13
Intercepted by	0	2
Punts	5	3
Avg. Distance (yds)	37	34
Fumbles Lost	1	1
Yards Penalized	59	49
SCORE	**14**	**40**

Halftime Melee

During the 1975 game, a combination of excessive drinking, a one-sided score, and a three-man slingshot resulted in one of the biggest halftime battles in Lehigh-Lafayette history.

The disruption started early in the game when a three-man slingshot was used to fire objects from the Lafayette side into Lehigh's student section. The Lehigh students did not take kindly to the aerial maneuvers and retaliated by making a personal visit to the Leopard command post. This prompted a series of fist fights that spread through the stands quicker than a round of free drinks at the Tally Ho Tavern. By halftime, nearly 300 students were rioting on the field. The west goalpost took the brunt of the attack, setting a new record for early destruction. The east post lasted until early in the third period. Eventually, enough order was restored to complete the game.

Without goalposts, the Lehigh and Lafayette field goal kickers, whose job suddenly became very uneventful, took a number and waited in the unemployment line.

A Record-Setting Season

The defeat of archrival Lafayette in 1975 completed a fine regular season for the Engineers, who finished with a 9-2 record and were undefeated at Taylor Stadium for the second year in a row.

Senior quarterback Joe Sterrett set a new season passing record with 22 touchdown passes and finished his career at Lehigh with a quarterback rating of 155.43, the highest in Lehigh football history. During the 1975 season, Sterrett and Mark Weaver combined for the school's longest completion (86 yards).

Rod Gardner, as a junior, established new records for career rushing yardage (2,595) and career points scored (272).

The Engineer squad set a new team rushing mark (2,692 yards) and total yardage milestone (5,037 yards). Lehigh scored 409 points during the regular season — the highest regular season point total in the school's history.

Hampshire 67 to 58 in the final standings.

Lehigh was not as fortunate in its postseason playoff game against the UNH Wildcats at Taylor Stadium. The Yankee Conference champions won a thriller, 35-21, scoring three touchdowns in the fourth quarter to break open a tight game and end the Engineers' two-season home winning streak.

Party Time On College Hill

Veteran Neil Putnam initiated John Whitehead into the circle of Lafayette-Lehigh coaches by handing the rookie a 21-17 defeat in the 1976 game. Putnam and his Leopards put an end to the talk about how the Lafayette and Lehigh football programs had grown too far apart.

The 1976 game re-established the true meaning of The Rivalry — great football. For the first time in many years, the pregame tradition and hype were overshadowed by a well-played and excitingly-close football game with a storybook ending.

Lafayette turned the tide from the 1975 game when the Leopards outgained the Engineers in every category except the score. Although bullied by the Brown and White statistically in the 1976 contest, the Leopards posted a victory much to the delight of 15,000 partisan onlookers at Easton's Fisher Field.

Coach Putnam, a deeply religious man, must have thought he had died and gone to football heaven after reviewing the game summary. At the final gun, Lehigh had 16 more first downs, 141 more rushing yards, 69 more passing yards, and ran 43 more plays from scrimmage than Lafayette. But, Lehigh turned the ball over six times to Lafayette's four and Lafayette outscored the Engineers 21-17.

The veteran Lafayette-Lehigh spectator knew the 1976 contest was not going to be the typical, run-of-the-mill game. Although the contest was played at Lafayette's Fisher Field, the Leopards wore visiting white uniforms. The '76 Lafayette team wanted to keep the momentum from its three previous road victories in the whites. "Besides," co-captain George O' Shaughnessy explained, "we thought we looked better in them."

Once the dress code was established, the teams engaged in a see-saw affair. Lehigh started the scoring in the first quarter with Mark Weaver connecting on a 42-yard field goal. The Leopards fought back in the second quarter to take a 7-3 lead on John Orrico's three-yard run.

Rod Gardner put Lehigh back on top at the start of the second half with a two-yard scoring plunge. The Leopards retaliated with a 32-yard scoring connection between quarterback Mark Jones and wide receiver Orlando Wright and the score swayed back in Lafayette's favor, 14-10.

Defensive back Tom Crouse set up Lafayette's final score with his first of two critical interceptions.

Moments later, Jones, who could be mistaken for a California surfer with his long blonde hair, caught a cool breeze and a tasty wave and rode the Leopard offense to the end zone for a 21-10 lead.

Lehigh made a late-game charge with a 65-yard scoring drive that narrowed the lead to 21-17. Monday morning quarterbacks questioned why Whitehead did not try a two-point conversion that, if successful, would allow Lehigh to tie the game with a field goal. After the game, Whitehead made it clear that he would not have gone for the field goal and a tie. The Lehigh-Lafayette contest was a game to win or lose; a tie would be like kissing your sister.

Lafayette's defense preserved the victory late in the game. With 1:52 remaining, the Engineers had the ball at the Lafayette 16 and were poised to strike for the go-ahead score and its sixth consecutive victory in The Rivalry. On first down, Mike Rieker rifled a pass to tight end Larry Henshaw in the end zone. Henshaw was well-covered and the pass deflected off several hands before Crouse pulled in his second interception of the game.

For the first time in six years, the final score flashed in Lafayette's favor, prompting the ringing of the church bells on College Hill and the mother of all "spinning" parties at the fraternity houses that night.

And for the first time in The Series' long history, co-

Dunlap Returns to His Alma Mater

With Lehigh's victory in 1975, Fred Dunlap became the first Engineer coach to defeat the Leopards five times in row and to record eight career victories over Lafayette. Dunlap accepted the head coaching job at Colgate after the 1975 season and later became his alma mater's Athletic Director. Nine-year Lehigh assistant John Whitehead replaced Dunlap as head Engineer. Dunlap coached in South Bethlehem from 1965 to 1975 and compiled an overall record of 49-62-2, including an 8-3 record against archrival Lafayette. Dunlap led Lehigh to its first playoff appearances in 1973 and 1975.

"Man, are we going to party tonight!"

— excerpt from Lafayette QB Mark Jones' acceptance speech after winning the 1976 Lafayette-Lehigh Most Valuable Player trophy.

Brass Cannon	
<u>Year</u>	<u>Winner</u>
1937	Lafayette
1938	Rutgers
1939	Rutgers
1940	Lafayette
1941	Lafayette
1942	Lafayette
1943	Lafayette
1944	Lafayette
1945	Rutgers
1946	Rutgers
1947	Rutgers
1948	Rutgers
1949	Rutgers
1950	Lehigh
1951	Lehigh
1952	Lehigh
1953	Lehigh
1954	Lehigh
1955	Lafayette
1956	Lehigh
1957	Lehigh
1958	Rutgers
1959	Rutgers
1960	Rutgers
1961	Rutgers
1962	Rutgers
1963	Rutgers
1964	Rutgers
1965	Rutgers
1966	Rutgers
1967	Rutgers
1968	Rutgers
1969	Lehigh
1970	Lehigh
1971	Lehigh
1972	Rutgers
1973	Rutgers
1974	Rutgers
1975	Lehigh

Little Brass Cannon Defunct

At the end of the 1975 season, the Little Brass Cannon and Middle Three Championship came to an end after 39 years of competition between Lafayette, Lehigh, and Rutgers. Rutgers discontinued Lafayette from its schedule in 1976 and Lehigh in 1978.

During the span, Rutgers possessed the Cannon 21 times, Lehigh 11, and Lafayette seven. Lafayette won the inaugural Cannon and Middle Three Championship in 1937. The Scarlet Knights held the titles for 11 consecutive years from 1958 to 1968, the longest streak in the series. Lehigh was the last winner of the Cannon and Middle Three Championship in 1975.

Most Valuable Players were named. Lafayette's Jones and Lehigh's fullback Gardner shared top honors. Lafayette's senior quarterback played the game of a lifetime in his farewell performance. Gardner was only the second player on the losing team to win the Most Valuable Player trophy since the award was established in 1960. Gardner once again displayed great courage in a losing effort. Suffering from a knee injury and shoulder separation, Lehigh's all-time leading rusher gained 92 yards on the ground and 102 yards receiving in his final game.

The Lafayette locker room was an emotional scene after the game. The tears in coach Neil Putnam's eyes were washed away by the champagne poured over his head during the victory celebration. As the team kneeled in postgame prayer led by Putnam, a poster in the background read:

1971	Lehigh 48	Lafayette 19
1972	Lehigh 14	Lafayette 6
1973	Lehigh 45	Lafayette 13
1974	Lehigh 57	Lafayette 7
1975	Lehigh 40	Lafayette 13
1976	It's Up To You!	

The last line had been covered boldly with a hastily written "Lafayette 21 Lehigh 17."

We Are The Champions!

— Lehigh University:
1977 Division II National Champions

The Engineers brought a powerful offensive machine and 8-2 record into the 1977 game. Lehigh, ranked 8th in the nation, was led by quarterback Mike Rieker. Going into the Lafayette game, Lehigh was ranked fourth in passing (247 yards per game), fifth in total offense (416 yards per game), and fifth in scoring (32.9 points per game). Rieker led the nation in total offense (227 yards per game) and his favorite target, Steve Kreider, topped the Lehigh receiving corps with 11 touchdowns, 49 catches, and 1,102 yards.

Lafayette had a few offensive weapons of its own, including quarterback Rob Stewart who was rated among the nation's Division II passing leaders. The 6'5" Stewart ranked third in completions per game with 14.4 and passed for 1,560 yards going into the final game with Lehigh. Lanky soccer-style placekicker Dave Heverling added a new dimension to the Leopard offense. The 6' 0", 157-pound Heverling successfully converted on 13-of-17 field goals, including 5-of-6 from 40 yards or more, and was 18-of-20 in PAT's for a team leading 57 points. The Leopard running duet composed of tailback Brian Musician and fullback John Orrico combined for 1,200 yards in the first ten games.

On defense, coach Neil Putnam relied on middle guard Tom Padilla, who led the team with eight sacks, to pressure Rieker and contain Lehigh's running game.

The capacity crowd watched the Engineers rally from a 17-14 deficit to score 21 points in the final 25

Lehigh's Division II National Championship Trophy won in 1977.

Steve Kametz

The 1977 Lehigh-Lafayette game marked the 69th in a row for 85-year old Steve "Boozie" Kametz. The faithful fan attended every game since 1910, including doubleheaders in 1943 and 1944. The Bethlehem native saw his first game in 1900 when he was eight-years old by climbing under the fence at old Lehigh Field to watch Lafayette defeat Lehigh 34-0. His first official entry through the gates was six years later at age 14. A custodian at Lehigh, he was recognized as an honorary member of the football team in 1968 and awarded an Engineer football T-shirt and hat.

Boozie did not get his nickname because of his fondness of alcoholic beverages. Instead, the nickname stemmed from a childhood experience during which Kametz was swimming with some friends. After an extended swim under water, Kametz surfaced with a red face. His friends said he looked like a boozer and the name stuck.

50-Game Club

The list of Lehigh 50-Game Club members grew to 22 in 1977. Members of the elite crew who attended 50 or more Lehigh-Lafayette games included:

Al Chenoweth-Bethlehem, Pa.
George Desh-Bethlehem, Pa.
Jack Conneen-Bethlehem, Pa.
Morgan Cramer-New York City, N.Y.
John Maxwell-Allentown, Pa.
Bob Harrier-Pen Argyl, Pa.
George Stutz-Palmerton, Pa.
Mickey Seward-West Caldwell, N.J.
Robert Watson-Gibson Island, Md.
Roy Coffin-Merion, Pa.
Lathrop Bevan-Virginia Beach, Va.
Bill Davis-Monmouth Beach, N.J.
Ed Snyder-West Orange, N.J.
Tom Conley-Philadelphia, Pa.
John Shigo-Bloomsburg, Pa.
Mack White-Camp Hill, Pa.
Edward Garra-Ambler, Pa.
Ed Curtis-Doylestown, Pa.
Larry Kingham-Verona, N.J.
James Law-Bloomsburg, Pa.
Ted Jones-Ambler, Pa.
Herb Cresswell-Wherabouts Unknown

minutes and defeat Lafayette 35-17. Second-year coach John Whitehead patiently waited until the second half to unleash Lehigh's passing attack so Lafayette could not make defensive adjustments during the intermission.

The turning point of the game came midway through the third quarter with Lafayette leading 17-14. Lehigh free safety Pete Fenton blocked a 50-yard field goal attempt and the Engineers took possession at their own 41-yard line.

Rieker immediately hit a double-covered Kreider on two consecutive passes of 44 and 15 yards for an Engineer touchdown. Freshman placekicker Ted Iobst converted the point-after to put Lehigh ahead 21-17. A fumbled punt and an interception led to two more Lehigh touchdowns and put the game out of reach, 35-17.

Rieker fired the last two scoring strikes to Don Van Orden and Matt Ricketson, setting a new school record for most touchdown passes in a season (23). Lehigh had two other touchdowns that were called back on penalties, including a 62-yard touchdown catch by Kreider.

Rieker-Kreider Rewrite the Playbook

To no one's surprise, senior quarterback Mike Rieker and junior split end Steve Kreider rewrote the Lehigh record books during the 1977 season. What most people didn't realize, including coach John Whitehead, was that the tandem also rewrote a page in the playbook. Rieker and Kreider devised their own play which they called "Steve go long." According to Rieker, "Steve would line up standing up because he had a bad back, and the guys covering him would think he wasn't all he was made up to be. Next thing they knew Steve was gone. He just loves to run."

Lehigh was penalized a whopping 123 yards in the Lafayette game, which concerned the coach of the playoff-bound Engineers. Whitehead knew the Brown and White would have to play better against the top-rated Division II schools in order to win in the postseason.

Lehigh's defense was led by linebackers Bruce Rarig (12 tackles) and Jim McCormick (11 tackles). Lafayette's Kevin McCarthy turned in a rib-cracking performance leading all defensive players with 14 tackles.

Rieker, whose strong second-half performance won him Most Valuable Player honors, finished 10-of-17 for 153 yards and three touchdowns. The former Catasauqua Rough Rider, whose personal best in the 40-yard dash was 5.2 seconds, galloped for eleven yards including two runs which converted critical first downs.

Lehigh finished the 1977 regular season with a 9-2 record and was voted the surprise winner of the Lambert Cup. The Engineers, who had not been ranked number one in the polls all year long, won five of seven first-place votes. Massachusetts (8-2) and Clarion State (9-0-1) were named on top of the other two ballots. UMass led the Lambert Cup polls the last two weeks of the season before getting dusted by Boston College, 24-7, in its final game. Meanwhile, Lehigh's 35-7 victory over Lafayette propelled the Brown and White to its fifth Lambert Cup.

> ## Toohey's Travels
>
> Bill Toohey, Class of 1941, ran his streak of attending Lehigh football games to 84 games in a row after traveling to all three of the Engineers' playoff games. Maintaining the unbroken streak, which included both home and away games, was quite a test of endurance considering Lehigh played games in nine different states during the 1977 season.

Lehigh's Second Season

Flying high from the victory over Lafayette and Lambert Cup crowning, Lehigh took the battlefield against the Massachusetts Minutemen in the first round of the 1977 Division II playoffs. The game was played under muddy conditions as the crowd of 5,700 spectators endured a cold and rainy day at Alumni Stadium in Amherst.

The Engineers picked-up where they left off against Lafayette, then held-on for a 30-23 victory. On the first play from scrimmage, Rieker hit Kreider on a 71-yard bomb good for a Lehigh touchdown and 7-0 lead 14 seconds into the game. The touchdown was Kreider's first of four in the game. The game's initial play call was an off-tackle run, but Rieker changed the play to "Steve go deep on two" in the huddle.

Lehigh jumped ahead of the Yankee Conference champions 23-0 before the startled Minutemen scored a touchdown and two-point conversion late in the second quarter.

Massachusetts regrouped at halftime and staged impressive scoring drives of 74 and 73 yards to even the score at 23-23 with 5:14 remaining in the third period.

The Engineers regained the lead in the fourth quarter on Rieker's fourth touchdown pass of the day to Kreider.

Punter Jim McCormick and the Lehigh defense preserved Lehigh's first playoff

A Heart of Gold

Some of Whitehead's ex-players describe him as a mean old man, while his colleagues brand him as a tough, honest, and proud individual. After the Cal-Davis victory, Whitehead showed why he was respected not only as a great football coach, but also as a great person. Upon returning to Bethlehem after a grueling overnight plane ride from California, Whitehead instructed his players go to their rooms for some badly needed rest, while he and his staff unloaded the equipment at the field house.

The mean old man's kindness paid off wonderfully as a well-rested and well-prepared Engineer squad shut out Jacksonville State University of Alabama, 33-0, in the Pioneer Bowl to capture the 1977 Division II National Championship.

A former player summed up Whitehead's character best when he said, "John Whitehead is a better person than he was coach. And he was a great coach."

victory in three tries. Lehigh previously lost first-round games to Western Kentucky in 1973 and New Hampshire in 1975.

Rieker finished the game 25-of-40 for 351 yards passing and four touchdowns. Former UMass head coach Vic Fusia, who mentored NFL quarterback Greg Landry when he was a Minuteman undergrad, had high praise for the Engineer quarterback.

"I had Greg Landry, of the Detroit Lions, when he was undergraduate here, and he was a great one. But he never had a day like Mike Rieker had this afternoon."
— Vic Fusia, Former UMass Head Coach

Lehigh Visits Knute Rockne

The victory sent the Engineers to the west coast to face undefeated Cal-Davis (11-0) in the Knute Rockne Bowl. The Cal-Davis Aggies had not lost at home in 20 games spanning four years.

ABC-TV regionally televised the contest between Lehigh and Cal-Davis with Bill Fleming handling the play-by-play and Ara Parsegian doing the color commentary.

The crowd of 10,500 hostile spectators at Toomey Field witnessed an offensive fireworks display that would have made Keith Jackson say "Whoa Nellie!" The teams combined for 69 points and 884 yards on the afternoon. Lehigh used excellent offensive balance (235 yards rushing and 271 yards passing) and an opportunistic defense (one fumble recovery and five interceptions) to advance to the finals of the Division II National Championship playoffs by a 39-30 count.

Coach Whitehead's Engineers outlasted Cal-Davis despite a feisty comeback effort led by Aggies' quarterback Mike Moroski. Moroski finished the game with 353 yards passing, all four Cal-Davis touchdowns, and a confused look on his face after five of his passes were caught by the men in Brown and White uniforms.

The small contingent of Lehigh fans in the stands, numbering approximately 300, was not surprised that one of Lehigh's five touchdowns was scored on an 81-yard pass from Rieker to Kreider. They were surprised by Lehigh's running attack and the emergence of engine number 35, Mike Ford.

The big sophomore fullback from Kansas City, Missouri — a second-stringer who saw action after starter Matt Ricketson was shaken-up — was the game's leading ground-gainer with 66 yards. Ford scored Lehigh's last two touchdowns, one rushing and one receiving, to ice the victory and send the Engineers to the Big Show.

ABC-TV's Fleming and Parsegian selected Lehigh quarterback Mike Rieker and linebacker Mike McCormick as the Chevrolet Offensive and Defensive Players of the Game.

The victory left the Lehigh students, fans, and administration scampering to their travel agencies to find the closest airport to Wichita Falls, Texas — the site of the 1977 Division II National Championship showdown in the Pioneer Bowl. Bethlehem area sportswriters flipped through NCAA handbooks to learn more about Lehigh's next opponent, Jacksonville State (Alabama).

The Road to Wichita Falls

NCAA Division II National Champions
Lehigh University (12-2)

1977 Season

Connecticut	49-0	W
Baldwin-Wallace	16-28	L
Pennsylvania	19-7	W
Davidson	43-7	W
Rhode Island	42-16	W
Rutgers	0-20	L
VMI	30-20	W
Bucknell	47-13	W
Gettysburg	47-0	W
C.W. Post	36-10	W
Lafayette	35-17	W

NCAA Division II Tournament

Massachusetts	30-23	W

Knute Rockne Bowl @ Davis, California

Cal-Davis	39-30	W

Pioneer Bowl @ Wichita Falls, Texas

Jacksonville St. (Ala.)	33-0	W

The Big Show

An ABC-TV national television audience and a live crowd of 14,114 in Wichita Falls saw the "Mighty Engineers Who Could" claim the national championship in the Pioneer Bowl, whitewashing Jacksonville State 33-0.

The defense dominated, as Lehigh blanked Jax State for the first time in 93 games, a string started in 1968. A hard-hitting tone was established early by the Brown and White.

First, defensive back Pete Fenton and linebacker Keith Frederick sandwiched Jax State quarterback Bobby Ray Green, knocking him out of the game with a concussion.

Which Way Did He Go?

Lehigh's wing-T offense thoroughly confused Jacksonville State. In fact, at one point in the game, senior offensive guard Tom Stine was tempted to tell the Jax State linemen which way the play was going so that he would have someone to block. Against Lehigh's wing-T offense, the Jax State linemen were constantly running the wrong way, and Stine was left with no one to hit.

After regaining consciousness, Green staggered to the sideline thinking he had four first names instead of just two.

Next, a savage hit by Lehigh defensive end Greg Clark forced an early fumble at the Lehigh five-yard line. Dale Visokey recovered the ball in the end zone for a touchback and Lehigh escaped Jax State's only serious scoring threat of the day. Clark, who was named ABC-TV's Chevrolet Defensive Player of the Game, led Lehigh's defense which forced four Jax State fumbles.

Meanwhile, the Lehigh offense kicked into high gear for a 423-yard performance, including 305 yards rushing. Lehigh turned to its running game when gusty winds and double-coverage in the secondary made passing difficult.

Ironically, Ford was selected as the *Chevrolet* Offensive Player of the Game by ABC-TV. The backup tailback was Lehigh's leading ground gainer for the second week in the row, picking up 92 yards on 13 carries and one touchdown.

Lennie Daniels complemented Ford with 89 yards rushing. Rieker and halfback Dave April rushed for touchdowns and Rieker added two touchdown passes to favorite target Steve Kreider.

Mike Rieker (15), on the shoulders of his teammates, reminds the crowd who's number one after Lehigh's 1977 Pioneer Bowl victory.

After building a 33-0 advantage in the fourth quarter, coach Whitehead cleared the bench and gave every player in a Lehigh uniform a chance to see action in the National Championship game. Since one-fourth of Lehigh's team were graduates of area high schools, Lehigh Valley viewers especially enjoyed the late action.

After an exhausting 14-game season which included a trouncing of rival Lafayette, a fifth Lambert Cup, and three playoff victories over state schools with student bodies twice its size, Lehigh University was crowned NCAA Division II National Football Champions.

Over 1,000 Lehigh football supporters met the team at A-B-E airport to congratulate the Engineers on their accomplishment.

Lehigh University received approximately $60,000 from the NCAA as part of an eight-team financial arrangement for the Division II playoffs. The six-figure television contracts paid to the big time Division I-A football powers did not apply to Division II schools, even though Lehigh and Jacksonville State played more games than any other school in the nation. Lehigh won 12 games in 1977, more than any other college football team at any level. Notre Dame was crowned Division I National Champions the same year with an 11-1 record.

The Friendly Skies

Greg Clark was one of the meanest pass rushers ever to wear the Brown and White. The senior defensive end destroyed opposing quarterbacks during Lehigh's 1977 National Championship season. But, the gentle giant showed his heart on the flight to the Pioneer Bowl when he stood up in the aisle and presented the game ball from the Cal-Davis victory to fellow defensive end Glenn Skola, who was injured and missed the final two playoff games. Clark showed his humorous side on the return flight from Wichita Falls when he donned a stewardess apron and wig while serving peanuts and drinks to his teammates. Witnesses claim the moonlighter collected $18 in tips which went unreported to the NCAA violations committee.

Lehigh's Greg Clark earned his wings along with the Chevrolet Defensive Player of the Game honors in the Pioneer Bowl.

And The Band Plays On ...

The Marching 97 staged a fund raiser to help pay for the trip to Wichita Falls. The band arrived barely in time for the Pioneer Bowl parade on the eve of the big game. As the Marching 97 made its way through the streets of Wichita Falls, the Lehigh football players blocked its path to show their appreciation for a job well done all season long. The players would not let the band continue along the parade route until every Lehigh fight song was played. When the band finally started marching again, senior halfback Lennie Daniels emerged as the new Marching 97 drum major.

Choosy Mothers Chose Lehigh

For Mike Ford, winning the National Championship and Chevrolet Offensive Player-of-the-Game award in the Pioneer Bowl were his second and third biggest thrills that day. The sophomore fullback's biggest thrill was discovering that a group of alumni had flown his mother in from Kansas City to see him play football for the first time.

Ford's mother was one of many Lehigh moms to attend the game. In fact, Pioneer Bowl officials announced that the group of Lehigh moms was the largest ever to attend from a participating team. Even honorary Lehigh mother, Helen Chro, who ran the South Side Luncheonette, attended the game after team members chipped in to pay for her expenses.

Lehigh Firsts in 1977

- First Lehigh athletic team to win a NCAA Championship.
- First private institution to win the NCAA Division II National Championship.
- First Eastern football team to win the Division II title.
- First football team in Lehigh history to win 12 games in a season.
- Only football team in the nation to win 12 games during the 1977 season.
- Lehigh and Jacksonville State (Ala.) were the only football teams in the nation to play 14 games in 1977.
- First team to record a shutout in the Pioneer Bowl.

Postseason Honors

Along with the Division II National Championship, numerous other postseason honors were bestowed upon the Brown and White in 1977.

- John Whitehead was named Division II Coach of the Year in only his second season as Lehigh head coach. Whitehead summed up his first two years as head coach by saying, "What a difference a year makes."
- The New York Sportswriters Association named Whitehead as the Eastern College Coach of the Year.
- Senior quarterback Mike Rieker was selected to the Kodak All-American First Team.
- Junior split end Steve Kreider was named to the Associated Press All-American First Team.
- Rieker, Kreider, and defensive end Greg Clark were selected to the *New York Times* All-East squad. Rieker and Kreider were the only Division II players at their positions to be selected on the team.
- Six Lehigh players were named to the ECAC Division II All-Star team including Rieker, Kreider, Clark, offensive guard Jim Schulze, defensive end Glenn Skola, and defensive back Pete Fenton.
- Lehigh was designated as the Team-of-the-Year by the National Football Foundation Hall of Fame, the Washington D.C. Touchdown Club, the Eastern Collegiate Athletic Conference, and the New Jersey Sportswriters Association.

Division II Coach of the Year John Whitehead leaves Witchita Falls, Texas with a cowboy hat and a National Championship.

The Champn

In 1978, Larry Holmes, nicknamed the Easton Assassin, won the World Heavyweight Boxing Championship by knocking out Ken Norton. Later the same year, Lafayette couldn't deliver the knockout punch against Lehigh as the Eastonians lost a 23-15 decision.

"I was very fortunate to have played in a Super Bowl, but for me there was nothing more thrilling than playing in some of the big rivalry games at Lehigh."
— Steve Kreider '78

Steve Kreider with the 1978 Lehigh-Lafayette MVP trophy.

The Family Feud

The Lafayette-Lehigh football game fueled its share of feuds over the years, but none quite like the feud of 1978.

The 1978 Lafayette-Lehigh game pitted brother against brother — Lehigh's Vince Rogusky against younger brother Ed Rogusky, who played for Lafayette. Vince, a 6'2", 215 pound sophomore halfback, missed the Engineers' National Championship season with a knee injury and played mostly as a reserve in 1978, gaining 106 yards on 29 carries. Vince finally got his day in the spotlight when Whitehead designated him as the starting tailback for the Lafayette game. Ed, a 5'11", 198 pound freshman tailback, was the Leopard workhorse and leading ground gainer with 450 yards on 111 carries. Although Ed was smaller than his older brother, he was known for his power running, while Vince was a more fluid and elusive runner who relied on speed and guile.

After playing on undefeated football teams at Catasauqua High School, the Rogusky brothers chose Lehigh and Lafayette for purely academic reasons. Vince wanted to study Mechanical Engineering at Lehigh while brother Ed chose Pre-Med at Lafayette. The brothers had a chance to settle their differences on the football field during the 114th Lafayette-Lehigh game. Each hoped the other would perform well, but not at the expense of the other team winning the game.

When Mr. and Mrs. Rogusky were asked which team they would be rooting for, they responded, "That's easy. We just root for the team with the ball."

Older brother Vince won the 1978 episode of the Family Feud as Lehigh completed its sixth consecutive winning season with a 23-15 victory over Lafayette at Fisher Field. The Engineers finished 8-3 while the Leopards closed at 4-7.

Senior All-American Steve Kreider became the first wide receiver to win the Most Valuable Player award. Kreider continued his football career after graduating from Lehigh for the NFL's Cincinnati

Bengals from 1979 to 1986. Kreider played in Super Bowl XVI with the Bengals against Joe Montana's San Francisco 49ers.

The Engineers Keep Rolling ...

The tremendous interest in the 1979 Lafayette-Lehigh game was undoubtedly due to the success enjoyed by both teams during the season.

Lafayette traveled to sold-out Taylor Stadium with a 5-2-2 record to meet the 8-2 Engineers, who were ranked sixth in Division I-AA.

Although Lafayette held a commanding 63-46-5 margin in the historic series with Lehigh, the Engineers were optimistic about the 1979 game after winning nine of the last 11 against the Leopards. The Engineers were riding a seven-year streak of winning seasons, the longest in the school's history. The last time Lafayette defeated Lehigh at Taylor Stadium was in 1967 when the Maroon shut out the Brown and White 6-0.

Coach Neil Putnam was understandably tired of Lehigh's dominance in recent years and was looking for his strong defense to derail the Engineers. Only two opponents scored more than seven points against a Leopard defense which allowed a mere 9.6 points per game. Lafayette's two ties were low scoring affairs against Bucknell, 0-0, and Colgate, 7-7. The Lafayette defense was led by linebacker Brent Beyer (89 tackles), speedy cornerback Dave Shea (4.5 seconds in the 40-yard dash), and Lafayette's best defensive tackle in John Best of Beaver Falls, Pennsylvania.

Coach Whitehead's defense was just as impressive, allowing only 7.6 points per game. The Engineer defense held opponents to an average of 92.8 yards rushing and 81.4 yards passing while forcing 34 turnovers. The Lehigh defense was anchored by linebacker Jim McCormick, a four-year starter with a National Championship ring. Going into the Lafayette game, McCormick led the team in tackles for losses (11) and fumble recoveries (5).

Both offenses had trouble scoring during the season, but strong defenses kept the teams com-

Lafayette and Lehigh Join the Big Leagues

In 1978, Lehigh and Lafayette switched from Division II to Division I-AA as the NCAA did its own version of corporate restructuring.

Parnell Lewis

In 1978, veteran newswriter Parnell Lewis retired from *The Express* newspaper of Easton after 42 years.

Lewis, an Easton native, lived on College Hill since 1942 and covered numerous Lafayette-Lehigh football games. Lewis remembered the 1922 and 1981 games as the greatest games of all time. Of course, the Leopards won both contests. In 1922, a late Bots Brunner field goal gave the Leopards a 3-0 victory. In 1981, Bill Russo's Lafayette team upset the Engineers by a score of 10-3.

The University of Pennsylvania grad is endeared to Lafayette as an associate member of the Class of 1925. Lewis's brother, Bob, was a graduate of Lafayette's Class of 1939.

Referee Proving Grounds

Lehigh-Lafayette games have had their share of referees, but few were more prominent than Don Guman and James Egizio. The Bethlehem duo officiated several Lehigh-Lafayette games in the late 1970's and remember The Game having a bowl-type personality all its own.

"Being selected to referee the Lafayette-Lehigh game at the end of the season was an honor — it was like being selected to referee a bowl game," said Guman, who officiated in numerous bowl contests. "Emotions ran high during the game and the hardest part was controlling the taunting and trash talking between the players."

According to Egizio, there was as much action in the stands with the fights between students as there was on the field. Egizio left the refereeing in the stands to the police, while he focused on the football game.

The Lehigh-Lafayette game acted as a proving ground for the two local referees, who went on to referee 18 college bowl games between them, including two National Championship Orange Bowls in 1988 (Oklahoma-Miami, Fla.) and 1994 (Florida State-Nebraska).

petitive.

Lafayette's most dangerous offensive weapon was soccer-style placekicker Dave Heverling, who never kicked a football before his senior year in high school. The veteran kicking specialist started four years breaking virtually every school kicking record including career field goals (27), field goals in a season (14), and career scoring (153 points).

The Engineer defense lived up to its pregame billing and held the Leopards to a field goal in Lehigh's 24-3 victory. The three points marked Lafayette's lowest point total against Lehigh since 1960 when the Engineers won 26-3. Lafayette finished the game with 94 total yards — all through the air. The Leopards laid a goose egg on the ground, netting zero yards on 33 carries. Lafayette's 94 yards were the fewest total yards allowed by the Lehigh defense during the 1979 season.

Meanwhile, Lafayette's highly touted defense buckled under the pressure of Lehigh's offense, which turned in one of its best performances of the year. The Engineers racked up 351 total yards and scored 24 points including cornerback Lou D'Annibale's 30-yard interception return for a touchdown.

Sophomore Joe Rabuck was the Engineers' leading rusher with 113 yards on 27 carries which included carrying away the Most Valuable Player Trophy for the 115th Game.

The Engineers parlayed their 24-3 victory over Lafayette into a Division I-AA playoff berth and a second-place finish in the Lambert Cup balloting. Lehigh finished second to Delaware, replacing Boston University which held the number two spot the final two weeks of the season.

The BU Terriers barked in protest after Lehigh (9-2) was awarded the final playoff spot. Although the 8-1-1 Terriers owned the best overall record of any Division I-AA school, Lehigh was 5-0 and BU was 5-1-1 against Division I-AA opponents.

The regular season polls ranked Lehigh fourth while BU slipped to fifth after its season-ending tie with Bucknell. The Terriers went home whimpering and the Engineers packed their bags for a trip to Murray, Kentucky.

Lehigh faced second-ranked Murray State University (9-1-1) in one of the two semifinal playoff games. Upon hearing the good news, several Lehigh football players climbed the University Bell Tower and sounded a playoff cheer across the entire campus.

Coach Whitehead and the Engineers executed their patented ball control offense to grind out an impressive 28-9 victory against the Murray State Pacers. Lehigh ran a total of 77 plays during the game while Murray State was limited to 58 snaps.

Senior Rich Andres quarterbacked the Lehigh offense, completing eight-of-13 passes for 113 yards. Andres's two touchdowns, one passing and one rushing, helped earn him ABC-TV's Offensive Player-of-the-Game award.

The Lehigh ground attack was led by halfback Jeff Bernstein, who rushed for 80 yards on 11 carries.

A Second Trip to the National Championship Game

The 1979 National Championship game in Orlando, Florida, matched Lehigh against the Eastern Kentucky Colonels, who outlasted Nevada-Reno 33-30 in overtime to advance.

ABC-TV's Bill Fleming and Frank Broyles handled the commentary for the nationally-televised championship game. The 5,200 spectators at Tangerine Bowl Stadium watched Eastern Kentucky take a page from Coach Whitehead's 1977 National Championship playbook as the Colonels defeated Lehigh 30-7.

Eastern proved to be too tough for Lehigh in the trenches. The Engineers had an early indication that they were in for a long day when, on its first possession, Eastern Kentucky drove 72 yards on 20 consecutive rushing plays to take a lead it never relinquished.

EKU attempted only five passes the entire game, completing one to an Eastern receiver and two to Lehigh defensemen. The Colonels' strong rushing attack which netted 288 yards and four touchdowns more than compensated for the inept passing game. EKU's offensive statistics were impressive considering Lehigh had given up an average of 85 yards rushing and one touchdown per game for the season.

On offense, Lehigh was held to 91 yards rushing and 102 in the air. The Engineers were never able to establish an offensive rhythm, as Andres was a dismal 6-of-23 in the passing department.

ABC-TV selected Paul Anastasio as the Player-of-the-Game for Lehigh. Anastasio had two spectacular pass receptions and hustled downfield on special team coverage to bat a Lehigh punt out of bounds at the EKU one-yard line.

For the second time in his career, John Whitehead, who led the Engineers to a 10-3 record and number two finish in 1979, was named Division II Coach of the Year.

Lehigh's Second Undefeated Season

Lehigh brought its undefeated record (8-0-2) and number one Division I-AA ranking to Fisher Field for the 116th renewal of the Lehigh-Lafayette game in 1980. The Engineers were heavily favored over the 3-6 Leopards, but Lafayette hoped to spoil Lehigh's bid for its second undefeated season in the school's history.

Lehigh surprised many football critics by rebounding with a great season after falling one victory short of its second National Championship in 1979. Unheralded junior quarterback Larry Michalski took over where Rich Andres left off and guided the Engineers to an impressive record that included a 24-24 tie with Division I-A Army at West Point. Michalski's favorite target was split end Mark Yeager, who hauled in 45 passes for 797 yards and 11 touchdowns in the first 10 games.

Lehigh possessed big offensive and defensive front lines, averaging 240 pounds per man. The Lehigh defense was anchored by defensive end and co-captain Mike Crowe.

Lafayette was counting on quarterback Hal Hocking and running backs Roger Curylo and Ed Rogusky to jump-start its struggling offense. In the first nine contests, the Leopards scored touchdowns in just two of them and averaged a scant eight points per game.

Lehigh completed its second undefeated regular season as a crowd of 17,000 at Easton's Fisher Field watched the Engineers whitewash the home team, 32-0. Lafayette never had a chance in the 116th chapter of the Lehigh-Lafayette storybook.

Coach Whitehead gave the *Reader's Digest* condensed version of the game during his postgame interview: "Our defense was just too tough for them." After two quarters of play, Lafayette had zero points, zero first downs, one yard rushing, and 11 yards passing. After the same two quarters of play, Lehigh collected 26 points, 20 first downs, 160 yards rushing, and 179 yards passing.

Whitehead held a brief staff meeting at halftime and decided to play the reserves in the second half. The scoring was limited to two Ted Iobst field goals, but the second string defense preserved the shutout. The last time Lehigh shutout the Leopards was in 1951.

The Final Episode of The Family Feud

The Rogusky family feud between brothers Vince and Ed ended after the 1980 game, with older brother Vince, a Lehigh running back turned tight end, retaining the family bragging rights. Younger brother Ed, a two-time Academic All-American halfback for the Leopards, painfully endured four Lehigh victories during his stay on College Hill.

Yeager hauled in his 12th touchdown pass of the season in the first half to tie Kreider's school record set in 1977.

Lehigh defensive end Mike Crowe became only the second defensive player to be named MVP since the award was established in 1960. The crowning marked the 10th year in a row that a Lehigh player won or shared the MVP trophy. The "Human Mummy" demonstrated guts and determination by overcoming several injuries acquired during the season.

"Mike Crowe was so beat up for the 1980 Lafayette game," recalled center Bill Brennan, "that he was literally taped from

Neil Putnam

The 116th Lafayette-Lehigh game was the last for Neil Putnam, who resigned after the 1980 season. Putnam completed the second longest tenure of any Lafayette coach, behind only Herb McCracken who coached 12 seasons at Lafayette from 1924 to 1935. In 10 seasons on College Hill, Putnam won 44, lost 55, and tied three games.

Putnam, highly regarded as a man of integrity and character in the football circle, graduated from Miami of Ohio where he was an outstanding lineman. Putnam played on the Miami Redskins undefeated 1955 team coached by the legendary Ara Parsegian, who later coached the Notre Dame Fighting Irish. Putnam served as an assistant coach at Yale under Carmen Cozza for six years before taking over for Harry Gamble at Lafayette.

Putnam became Lafayette's 26th head football coach in 1971 and led the Leopards to upset victories over Penn, Rutgers, and Co-lumbia during a 5-5 season. Putnam completed his best season in 1973 with a 6-3-1 record. During the decade that Lehigh became a National powerhouse, Putnam defeated Lehigh only once in 10 tries, a 21-17 upset in 1976.

head to toe. To win the MVP award in his condition shows what a tremendous competitor he is." Another ex-teammate described Crowe as having a high threshold for pain, both for himself and his opponents.

If At First You Don't Succeed, Try Again!

The Brown and White's victory over Lafayette in 1980 clinched its sixth Lambert Cup and sent the Engineers into the playoffs ranked number one in the nation. Lehigh (9-0-2) was the only Division I-AA school to finish the regular season with an undefeated record.

Lehigh hosted its semifinal playoff game against Eastern Kentucky in a rematch of the 1979 National Championship game which EKU won 30-7.

A stubborn Lehigh team gave the defending National Champions all they could handle before bowing 23-20 in front of 11,500 spectators at Taylor Stadium.

The Engineers tallied the first and last touchdowns, but in between EKU outscored the Brown 23-6. A last ditch Lehigh scoring drive fizzled at midfield, as the ball was turned over on downs with 2:03 left in the contest.

Engineer Playoff Summary

The NCAA implemented the playoff format in 1973 for Division II schools. The Engineers made the playoffs five times in eight years from 1973 to 1980, establishing a dynasty-like presence in Division II and I-AA football world. After first round losses in 1973 and 1975, Lehigh won the Division II National Championship in 1977. The Brown and White moved into the newly created I-AA Division in 1978 and posted an 8-3 record and barely missed a playoff bid. In 1979, Lehigh rallied with a 9-2 regular season record only to lose the Division I-AA Championship game to Eastern Kentucky. In 1980, the Engineers entered the playoffs as the only undefeated Division I-AA school with a 9-0-2 record. Lehigh bowed 23-20 in the first round to defending champs Eastern Kentucky.

Year	Record	Division	Opponent	Winner	Score
1973	7-4-1	II	at Western Kentucky	Western Kentucky	16-25
1975	9-3	II	New Hampshire	New Hampshire	21-35
1977	12-2	II	at Massachusetts	Lehigh	30-23
			at Cal-Davis	Lehigh	39-30
			Jacksonville State (Ala)*	Lehigh	33-0
1979	10-3	I-AA	at Murray State	Lehigh	28-9
			Eastern Kentucky **	Eastern Kentucky	7-30
1980	9-1-2	I-AA	Eastern Kentucky	Eastern Kentucky	20-23

OVERALL PLAYOFF RECORD = 4-4

* at Wichita Falls, TX
** at Orlando, Fla.

Quarterback Larry Michalski started the scoring with a five-yard pass to tight end Paul Anastasio. The Lehigh score was set up by Keith Conley's interception on Eastern's third play from scrimmage.

Eastern Kentucky fought back at the end of the first quarter with a touchdown but missed the extra point, cutting Lehigh's lead to 7-6.

Lehigh continued to apply the pressure in the second quarter with two Iobst field goals from 47 and 38 yards, extending its lead to 13-6. The Colonels mounted a touchdown charge at the end of the half to knot the score 13-13.

Eastern regrouped at the half and took advantage of its superior offensive speed to take a 23-13 lead into the fourth quarter.

Lehigh rallied with the Michalski-Rogusky Polish connection for a touchdown in the final period. Iobst added the conversion and Lehigh was within striking distance, 23-20, with 8:50 remaining. But, the nation's top-ranked team could not generate one last score.

ABC-TV selected Lehigh quarterback Larry Michalski and Eastern Kentucky tailback Anthony Braxton as Players-of-the-Game. Michalski completed 12-of-27 passes for 156 yards and two touchdowns. Braxton, the game's leading rusher, carried 20 times for 84 yards, including a 21-yard touchdown run.

An Even Matchup

Lehigh once again had playoff hopes and the Lambert Cup riding on The Game in 1981, while Lafayette entered with its best record since the undefeated 1940 squad. In fact, both teams entered the contest with identically impressive 8-2 records. The teams were so closely matched that their losses were to the same opponents, Colgate and New Hampshire.

During an era when Lehigh had won 11 of the last 13 games against Lafayette, the even pairing aroused interest from supporters of both schools. The renewed attention was apparent from the early ticket sales for the game which was declared a sellout a week before kickoff. This was despite the opening whistle being moved to high noon in an attempt to control excessive tailgating.

Sparked by the heavy interest, WLVT-TV of the Lehigh Valley telecast The Game live for the first time.

First-year coach Bill Russo hoped for some rookie magic in his inaugural Lafayette-Lehigh game, while veteran coach John Whitehead looked forward to welcoming Russo, a former Brown University player and coach, to the "other" Ivy League.

The Leopards knocked Lehigh from atop of the Lambert Cup polls and bounced the Engineers from a post-season bid by handing the

Ten Years After

A decade after Lafayette and Lehigh first admitted women, men were still trying, and failing, at the socialization game.

After a Lehigh-Lafayette contest in the early 1980's, a Lehigh coed was at a fraternity party when she was approached by a slightly inebriated Lafayette alumnus of that house.

"The fellow grabbed me by the arm and kissed my hand," recounted Carol McAdam, the chosen recipient of the pass. "Drooling all over himself, he said, 'We didn't have people like you when I was in school.' Of course, they didn't. Neither school had women students when he attended. The gentleman was in his seventies."

Lafayette's 100th Season

Lafayette celebrated its 100th season of football in 1981 and appropriately ended the centennial celebration with a 10-3 upset victory over longtime rival Lehigh.

Kodak All-American Middle Guard Tony Green.

Engineers a 10-3 defeat before 19,414 fans — the most ever to attend a football game at Taylor Stadium.

The game featured a pair of stalwart linebackers. Lafayette's two-time All-American Joe Skladany speared a defense which held the Engineer ground attack to 58 yards on 40 carries. With the help of middle guard Tony Green, a future All-American, the Leopards caged the Engineer offense inside its own 39-yard line for the entire second half.

John Shigo anchored the Lehigh defense. The 6'2", 229-pound sophomore from Bethlehem's Freedom High School registered 18 tackles, a fumble recovery and a broken-up pass.

Tied 3-3 at half, thanks to field goals by Lehigh's Mike Whalen and Lafayette's Mark Petty, the Leopards squandered three different scoring opportunities in the red zone during the third quarter.

The first ended abruptly at the Lehigh 19-yard line when Shigo recovered a Frank Corbo fumble. The second fell short when Petty missed a 33-yard field goal. Lafayette struck out a third time after a first-and-goal situation at the Lehigh three-yard line. The Engineers bowed their necks with a tough goal line stand and stopped the Leopards on four consecutive rushing attempts.

Allergic Reaction

After receiving a bone-crushing hit from the Leopard defense in the 1981 game, a Lehigh running back was helped to the sideline to shake the cobwebs from his head. Upon looking at the running back's watering and blood-shot eyes, a concerned teammate asked the player if his allergies were bothering him. The player responded, "The only thing I'm allergic to is Green and Skladany."

Lafayette would not be denied for a fourth time. Frank Luzi's fourth-quarter interception at the Lehigh 31-yard line set-up the Leopards' game-winning score.

After a personal foul penalty against Lehigh moved the ball to the 16, Frank Novak hit Corbo for an eight-yard gain, setting the stage for Roger Shepko's heroics. The 6'1", 200 pound junior running back boasted a Walter Payton-like 7.0 yards per carry average and had already established a new Lafayette rushing record with 1,231 yards prior to the Lehigh game.

Against an Engineer defense that was anticipating a run around right end, Shepko breezed through the middle for the final eight yards, scoring easier than a hooker on Bourbon Street. The Game's only touchdown gave Lafayette a hard-fought 10-3 victory.

Lafayette's vaunted ground attack was shut down early by a fired-up Engineer defense. Shigo stalked Shepko with Dick Butkus-like intensity, limiting the Division I-AA's second-leading rusher to 19 yards on 15 carries at the half.

Once Shigo figured out what flavor gum Shepko was chewing, Lafayette turned to its passing game with Novak lining up in the shotgun formation. The Leopards threw the ball routinely on first down, and at one point in the second quarter, passed six plays in a row. The Lafayette passing game proved effective in moving the ball but ineffective in putting points on the scoreboard.

Lehigh's offense had the odor of a two-month old "Greeker" hot dog with extra onions. Lehigh's running chores, shared by Bethlehem Catholic's Ed Godbolt and Chris Sexton whose combined season rushing total fell 342 yards short of Shepko's, generated little spark.

Maxwell Club award-winning quarterback Larry Michalkski was limited to 11 completions in 29 attempts for 95 yards and was pressured into throwing three interceptions, including one to junior defensive back Bob Mahr. Mahr ended the season with 10 interceptions to tie for the Division I-AA lead.

The sophomore Novak, playing in his first Lafayette-Lehigh game, completed 19-of-37 passes for 164 yards. Novak was a near-unanimous choice for the Most Valuable

Joe Skladany '82
- **First Lafayette football player to be selected to the Associated Press All-American First Team.**
- **Two-time Associated Press All-American Linebacker (1980-81)**
- **Lafayette Athletic Hall of Fame Inductee (November 1990)**

Player award after he successfully redirected the Lafayette offense to the air when the running game faltered.

"He (quarterback Frank Novak) is a combination of poise and confidence."
— Lafayette coach Bill Russo

The record crowd was well-behaved, partly due to the early starting time and a close game that kept the interest of the students.

While the Lehigh administration figured out the winning combination for crowd control, coach Russo was left scratching his head trying to figure out how to win the Lambert Cup and a playoff bid. After defeating the number one contender for the Lambert Cup on enemy turf, the 9-2 Leopards were snubbed by the Division I-AA playoff selection committee. Lafayette finished third in the Lambert Cup poll, while Lehigh tumbled from first to fourth. The Leopards ended eighth in the final Division I-AA poll.

Spoken in the true spirit of The Rivalry, future Lafayette Hall of Famer Tony Green put the 1981 season into perspective: "If we're not going to the playoffs, they're not going either."

Russo's Offensive Machine

The successes of 1981 carried into 1982 for the 6-3 Leopards. Back-to-back winning seasons, for the first time since 1959-60, were assured on College Hill. Meanwhile, Lehigh brought a dismal 4-5 record into The Game, which was broadcast live on WLVT-TV for the second consecutive year.

In his second season as coach, Bill Russo developed an explosive offense. Lafayette averaged 33 points per game and was led by quarterback Frank Novak, who broke almost every Lafayette passing record in just two years of play. The 6'2", 190-pound junior with sophomore eligibility was Division I-AA's top-rated passer (152.49 rating) and was ranked fourth in total offense.

A huge offensive line that averaged 253 pounds protected Novak and opened holes for tailback Nick "Special K" Kowgios. Kowgios filled in for 1,000-yard rusher Roger Shepko, who was sidelined for the season with an ankle injury. Special K proved to be a worthy replacement, rushing for 970 yards and 15 touchdowns while maintaining a lofty 5.7 yard per carry average. Kowgios was tops in Division I-AA scoring with a 10.6 point per game average.

Work Stoppage

In 1982, the NFL experienced its first strike in the league's 63-year history. While the NFL players and owners sat at the bargaining table, Lehigh and Lafayette prepared for their 118th meeting in 99 years. The only work stoppage in The Rivalry occurred in 1896 when a player eligibility dispute resulted in the cancellation of the two Lehigh-Lafayette games scheduled for that year.

Fullback Craig Williams cleared the way for Kowgios. The 6'2", 230-pound Williams, a converted defensive end, was nicknamed "The Human Thigh" because of his muscular physique and Bronko Nagurski-like blocking style. "You didn't want Williams to hit you with a full head of steam or your picture could end up on the side of a milk carton," recalled an ex-Lehigh defenseman.

On special teams, freshman Ryan Priest, a former Parade All-American and Big 33 All-Star, entered The Game as the nation's leading punt returner.

The Lafayette offense faced a stiff challenge against a stingy Lehigh defense that allowed 15 points per game. Middle linebacker John Shigo headed the Lehigh defense with 121 tackles, including 17 for losses.

Ed Godbolt provided veteran leadership for Lehigh's young offense. The senior tailback was the leading rusher for the Engineers with 766 yards and five touchdowns. The Lehigh offense, averaging just over 17 points per game, struggled to put points on the scoreboard.

The heavily-favored Leopards rolled to a 34-6 demolition of the Engineers.

Lehigh's offense controlled the ball for 11 of 15 minutes in the second quarter and ran 37 offensive plays to Lafayette's eight, but trailed by 24 at half.

By the time Lehigh completed its first pass of the game 11 minutes into the second quarter, Lafayette had registered three touchdowns and a field goal. Lafayette scored touchdowns on a tipped pass completion, a 92-yard punt return, and a 54-yard interception return.

The Lafayette defense held Lehigh in check most of the afternoon. Bob Sharr snared two of Lafayette's four interceptions in the game.

The Leopards completed the season with a 7-3 record and a number 20 ranking in the final regular season Division I-AA poll. The margin of victory was the largest for Lafayette since the Leopards defeated Lehigh 35-6 in 1955. The 335 points scored by the 1982 team marked the most in Lafayette football history at the time.

After a decade of dominance, Lehigh slipped to 4-6, its first losing season since 1972. The Lafayette victory marked the first time since 1966-67 that the Leopards defeated Lehigh two years in a row.

Lafayette's Jack Gatehouse won the MVP award even though his pass receiving chores were completed before the half. Gatehouse made

Two-Point Frenzy

In Princeton's game against Lafayette in 1982, Tiger quarterback Brent Woods set a new Division I-AA record for most successful two-point conversion passes (3) in a game. The coach of Princeton at the time was Hank Small, who would later haunt Lafayette as Lehigh's head coach in 1986.

Ryan's Return

In 1982, Ryan Priest was the nation's leading punt returner with an average of 22.6 yards per return. Priest was the only freshman in Division I-AA to lead a category. Priest's performance moved him to number two on the NCAA's all-time leaders for highest punt return average in a single season.

Lafayette's Jack Gatehouse turned in a fabulous first half performance to win the 1982 Lafayette-Lehigh MVP award.

Stolen Helmet Award

Bethlehem's Ed Godbolt finished his last game in a Brown and White uniform with 37 carries, a plethora of bumps and bruises, and a career-high 187 yards rushing. Godbolt scored Lehigh's lone touchdown on a 13-yard run in the third period of the 1982 game. The Engineer workhorse deserved recognition for his fine rushing performance, but instead he got his helmet stolen by an overzealous fan at the end of the game.

the most of his abbreviated performance, catching five passes for 115 yards in a little over one quarter of play. The MVP made the 11 o' clock news highlight reel with his diving, one-handed, 11-yard touchdown grab from Novak, which was his last catch in a Maroon and White uniform. Gatehouse finished his career owning five school records, including most career touchdowns catches (10), most touchdown catches in a season (8) and in a game (3), along with most yards receiving in a season (850).

Lehigh's 100th Season

Lafayette, a preseason favorite for a Division 1-AA playoff bid after finishing 7-3 in 1982, brought a 6-4 record into the '83 version of The Game. Lehigh sporting a surprising 7-3 mark, hoped to cap its 100th season of football with a win over its archrivals.

Bill Russo was looking for his third victory over Lehigh in as many years. The last Lafayette coach to complete the hat trick against Lehigh was Steve Hokuf in '53, '54, and '55.

Lafayette brought a potent running attack, ranked 10th in Division I-AA, to Taylor Stadium to take on the Engineers. The Lafayette offensive backfield was deep in talent with Priest, Shepko (1,280 yards rushing in 1981), and Kowgios (1,018 yards rushing in 1982).

Novak continued to be the franchise of Russo's offense. The three-year letterman started every game for Lafayette since Russo came to College Hill in 1981.

The Engineers' offense was powered by the Jersey Connection — sophomores Marty Horn and Rennie Benn, who played high school football together in Short Hills, New Jersey.

Lafayette's Kodak All-American middle guard Tony Green anchored the nation's 10th best rushing defense.

The Lehigh defense was just as intimidating with middle linebacker John Shigo of Hanover Township doing his "Terminator" impersonation on Saturday afternoons. Shigo led Lehigh with 128 tackles going into the showdown with the 'Pards. Jim Gum, who was ranked sixth in the nation with seven interceptions, directed the secondary.

The sellout crowd of 19,162 watched the Lehigh defense dominate, setting-up all of the Engineer scores in the 22-14 triumph over the Leopards.

The Lehigh "D" limited Lafayette to minus two yards in the first quarter and two first downs and 40 yards by the half. By the time the 'Pards retreated to the locker room at the intermission, Lehigh jumped to a 15-0 lead.

The Lehigh defense was a big part of the Lehigh offense. In the second quarter, Shigo intercepted a Novak pass and returned it 22 yards to the Lafayette six-yard line, setting up a field goal by Jim Scott. Four plays later, left cornerback Blair Talmadge picked off a tipped Novak pass and blazed 66 yards for a touchdown.

A fumble recovery at the Lafayette 27-yard line by defensive tackle Kevin Zlock set up Lehigh's final score of the afternoon. Four plays later, freshman tailback Joe Svede powered into the end zone for the score.

The game ball belonged to the Lehigh defensive line — Kevin Zlock, Wes Walton, and Wayne Kasbar. The front three applied the big hurt to Novak the entire afternoon and forced the standout quarterback to throw three interceptions.

Novak's hard-earned 162 passing yards moved him into fourth place on the Division I-AA career yardage list.

Despite a knee injury, Kodak All-American linebacker John Shigo finished his career at Lehigh with 12 tackles against Lafayette, giving him a total of 140 for the season. Shigo left the Taylor Stadium locker room for the last time wearing a Lafayette baseball cap which he had donned all week in preparation for The Game. Shigo's relentless pursuit from his middle linebacker position left a lasting impression on his cross-town rivals. A former opponent perhaps best described Shigo's intimidating style of play: "Shigo would hit you so hard, he'd knock the taste right out of your mouth."

By 1983, the list of MVP winners read like a classic novel. Marty Horn completed the latest chapter by passing for 160 yards and a touchdown. The 6'3", 195-pounder, plagued by interceptions in his first two seasons, avoided turning the ball over to the Leopards. Instead of forcing long passes to a double-covered Benn, Horn patiently worked the offense with short passes to his backs, none covering more than 24 yards. When all the passing routes were covered, Horn tucked the ball under his arm and danced like John Travolta through the Lafayette defense. Several of Horn's runs in the last quarter were helpful in killing the clock. After the game, Lehigh's offensive coordinator Barry Fetterman joked about Horn's scrambling ability: "With his speed, he could kill the clock."

Third Quarter Wrap-Up (1950-1983)

The first 100 years of College Football's Most-Played Rivalry came to a conclusion in the Third Quarter. Both The Rivalry and the game of football evolved during the Modern Era (1950-1983). Equipment and rule changes dramatically impacted college football while coaches developed sophisticated strategies to outsmart their opponents. The evolution of football changed The Rivalry to the point where participants from a century earlier would barely recognize what they saw on the gridiron. Of course, off the field, the pranks, ploys, and traditions that created the foundation of The Rivalry continued in the true spirit of past eras.

✔✍ Penalty flags changed from red to yellow, but students were not yellow in the mischief department.

✔✍ Rent-a-leopard, and a leopard finds itself in a beer mug.

✔✍ Girls, girls, girls. Both schools admit women, adding a "Powder Puff" version of The Game to the tradition.

✔✍ An undefeated team and an end to an unlucky 13-year streak.

✔✍ Bowl bids were bypassed, but university students were not denied their bid for an extra vacation day from class to celebrate a perfect season.

✔✍ A duo of Dazzling Dicks did their darnedest to out-do the other.

✔✍ A tailback-sized tackle makes All-American.

✔✍ The Game moved from a high school stadium to a "new and improved" stadium.

✔✍ A new spirit director is welcomed but bad haircuts are still unwelcome.

✔✍ In a game featuring a sleeper, one player accounts for 212 yards and three touchdowns on just four plays.

✔✍ A fake so real that the officials were fooled, nullifying an apparent touchdown.

✔✍ Lassie visited the offensive backfield on a game's first play. The defense spent the rest of the afternoon there.

✔✍ Facemasks were attached to helmets to make the game safer. Unfortunately, the safety features were not implemented as part of the postgame battle for the posts.

✔✍ A rubber match between two stalwart quarterbacks required snow tires, as a snowstorm greeted The Game.

✔✍ Lambert Cups, top-ten teams, playoff games, and a National Championship visit The Rivalry.

✔✍ One head coach later becomes an assistant at the other school.

✔✍ The goalposts came down a day early in the freshman contest, as did the scoreboard and a pair of flagpoles.

✔🖎 A pitcher punts.

✔🖎 Postgame awards are instituted.

✔🖎 Six turnovers, two penalties, a UFO sighting, and a "Hail Mary" in a contest's final quarter — and a last second field goal by a player who had never kicked one, ends a most memorable Game.

✔🖎 The Game includes a fast start, a lonesome end, a Go, a Go-Go, a Stop, and a shoelace play.

✔🖎 A Game is postponed, but not because of the teams' combined 1-15 record.

✔🖎 The 100th Game is contested, but not before a major player has a nightmare that it's only number 99.

✔🖎 Horns, bells, buzzers, and whistles greet a national media contingent for Game 100. The excitement in the stands exceeds that on the field, as the game finishes deadlocked at six.

✔🖎 A winless team wins The Game, prompting the coach to celebrate with an eight-week old bottle of champagne.

✔🖎 Both schools instituted "back every year" clubs for The Game. A senior member attends his 94th.

✔🖎 Pajama parades and bonfires are cancelled. In their place, the ECO 1 pep rally tradition starts.

✔🖎 A Heisman hopeful and numerous NFL players flourish in The Rivalry, as do national coaches of the year.

✔🖎 National TV, national radio, and national newspapers become acquainted with the schools and The Game.

✔🖎 A mean old man with a heart of gold and a family feud feed the folklore.

✔🖎 A Ford wins a prize from Chevy.

✔🖎 Years after nixed bowl games, a school makes some trips. It's California dreamin', a Texas two-step, and a Florida fantasy.

Coaches Notepad

Third Quarter (1950-1983)

Lafayette Coaches: Record vs Lehigh

Coach	Season	Wins	Losses	Ties
Maurice "Clipper" Smith	1950-51	0	2	0
Steve Hokuf	1952-57	3	3	0
James McConlogue	1958-62	1	3	1
Kenneth Bunn	1963-66	1	2	1
Harry Gamble	1967-70	2	2	0
Neil Putnam	1971-80	1	9	0
Bill Russo	1981-83	2	1	0
Total		**10**	**22**	**2**

Lehigh Coaches: Record vs Lafayette

Coach	Season	Wins	Losses	Ties
Bill Leckonby	1950-61	7	4	1
Mike Cooley	1962-64	2	0	1
Fred Dunlap	1965-75	8	3	0
John Whitehead	1976-83	5	3	0
Total		**22**	**10**	**2**

Third Quarter (1950-1983) Summary

Year	Where Played	Winner	SCORE Lafayette	Lehigh
1950	Easton	Lehigh	0 –	38
1951	Bethlehem	Lehigh	0 –	32
1952	Easton	Lehigh	7 –	14
1953	Bethlehem	Lafayette	33 –	13
1954	Easton	Lafayette	46 –	0
1955	Bethlehem	Lafayette	35 –	6
1956	Easton	Lehigh	10 –	27
1957	Bethlehem	Lehigh	13 –	26
1958	Easton	Tie	14 –	14
1959	Bethlehem	Lafayette	28 –	6
1960	Easton	Lehigh	3 –	26
1961	Bethlehem	Lehigh	14 –	17
1962	Easton	Lehigh	6 –	13
1963	Bethlehem	Lehigh	8 –	15
1964	Easton	Tie	6 –	6
1965	Bethlehem	Lehigh	14 –	20
1966	Easton	Lafayette	16 –	0
1967	Bethlehem	Lafayette	6 –	0
1968	Easton	Lehigh	6 –	21
1969	Bethlehem	Lehigh	19 –	36
1970	Easton	Lafayette	31 –	28
1971	Bethlehem	Lehigh	19 –	48
1972	Easton	Lehigh	6 –	14
1973	Bethlehem	Lehigh	13 –	45
1974	Easton	Lehigh	7 –	57
1975	Bethlehem	Lehigh	14 –	40
1976	Easton	Lafayette	21 –	17
1977	Bethlehem	Lehigh	17 –	35
1978	Easton	Lehigh	15 –	23
1979	Bethlehem	Lehigh	3 –	24
1980	Easton	Lehigh	0 –	32
1981	Bethlehem	Lafayette	10 –	3
1982	Easton	Lafayette	34 –	6
1983	Bethlehem	Lehigh	14 –	22
			488	724

	Wins	Losses	Ties
Lafayette	10	22	2
Lehigh	22	10	2

FOURTH QUARTER
The Patriot League Years
(1984-1995)

Lafayette and Lehigh marked a new allegiance in 1984, as both schools became charter members of the Colonial League. Dismayed with the evolution of college sports, a group of university presidents founded a league where the student-athlete vision would be true to itself. Based on the principles of admitting athletes who were representative of their academic class, awarding need-based scholarships, and maintaining presidential control of athletics, the league kicked-off play in 1986 as a football-playing conference. The league's charter members included Lafayette, Lehigh, Bucknell, Holy Cross, Colgate, and Davidson. Holy Cross defeated Lehigh 17-14 in the inaugural Colonial League football matchup.

By 1989, Davidson had dropped out of what was now called the Patriot League. Fordham joined, the league expanded to competition in 22 sports, and Army and Navy became members in all sports but football.

Since league play started in the 22 sports for the 1990-91 academic year, 31 teams have been selected for postseason play in the NCAA, ECAC, or National Invitational Tournaments. Twenty-six student-athletes have qualified for NCAA Championships. Member institutions have hosted 12 NCAA or eastern championships, with league representatives participating in nine.

The Patriot League ranks fourth among the 33 Division 1 conferences in the total number of sports offered and second in the number offered for women.

In its short existence, the Patriot League has featured 41 Academic All-Americans, including 13 GTE/CoSIDA Football Academic honorees, and more than 2,300 student-athletes have qualified for the league's Academic Honor Roll by earning a 3.2 grade point average and a varsity letter. Twelve student-athletes have received NCAA Postgraduate Scholarships, and the league has produced both a Fulbright and Luce Foundation Scholarship winner.

Each of the schools in the Patriot League finished in the NCAA Division 1 top-20 for graduation rates, all above 80 percent.

Patriot League institutions are among the

Snakebitten Huskies

Both Lafayette and Lehigh defeated UConn on the final play of the game in 1984. On September 15th in a snow and sleet storm in Storrs, Connecticut, Lehigh's Dave Melick kicked a 45-yard field goal as the gun was fired to give the Engineers a 10-7 victory.

A month later, Lafayette's Ryan Priest scored on a two-yard blast as the whistle sounded to give the Leopards a 20-13 win at Fisher Field.

Simone The Leopard

The 1984 Lafayette press guide was intended to have a unique pairing on the cover — captain Frank Corbo with a live leopard cub named Simone. Borrowed for the photo shoot from Hoxie Brothers Circus, the 150-pound cat did not take kindly to sharing the spotlight.

Corbo, in his Leopard football uniform, was repeatedly mauled by the rambunctious "co-star" during the photo shoot. The football prop suffered an even worse fate, as the playful leopard punctured and destroyed the ball.

After much ado, Simone received the star billing on the front cover of the fall sports guide. Submitting defeat to one of his tougher opponents of the season, Corbo watched the photo shoot from the sidelines.

oldest in the nation and most prestigious on the historic, academic, and athletic fronts. The College of Holy Cross is the oldest Jesuit college in New England; Fordham televised the first men's basketball game from its Rose Hill Gymnasium in 1940; Colgate has one of the top five collegiate golf courses in the country; college football's most-played rivalry is contested under the league's flag; and only one school in the nation can boast of more Academic All-Americans than Bucknell.

For ancient rivals Lafayette and Lehigh, it would be 10 years before The Game decided the Patriot League Championship.

With the formation of the Colonial League imminent, both squads entered the 1984 edition of The Game with five losses. The Leopards also entered with a quarterback controversy, as record-breaking signal-caller Frank Novak bypassed his final year of eligibility. Splitting time at the vacant spot was junior Dean Rivera and freshman Jim Johnson.

At game time, Johnson got the nod from coach Bill Russo. Making only his third start, Johnson threw two touchdown passes and ran for another in directing the Leopards to a 28-7 mauling of Lehigh.

After twice thwarting Lehigh's offense inside the Leopard five yard-line in the first quarter, Lafayette tallied 21 unanswered points in the second stanza.

Frank Corbo caught scoring strikes for the first two Maroon touchdowns. The split end, who shares the school record of 11 receptions in a game, also threw a 19-yard completion off a reverse pitch from Johnson to set-up the first touchdown.

Johnson was 9-for-17 passing for 166 yards, with two touchdowns and no interceptions. He rushed for 63 yards on 13 carries and another touchdown. For his efforts, Johnson was honored as the first freshman MVP.

In The Game, halfback Ryan Priest became the first Leopard player to pass the 2,000-yard mark in career rushing totals. On the day, he finished with 174 yards and one touchdown on 36 carries.

Lehigh's Marty Horn threw for 205 yards in the contest. The effort increased his season total to 2,605 yards which shattered the previous single-season mark held by Kim McQuilken. Surpassing another of McQuilken's marks, Horn also became the Engineers' all-time leader in passing attempts.

End Of Record-Setting Era

The 1985 version of The Game marked the final chapter in John Whitehead's coaching career, as he would soon become Athletic Director. The Game also brought the end to the "Horn to Benn" era.

Marty Horn and Rennie Benn, the most prolific pitch and catch combination in Lehigh football history, gave Coach Whitehead a memorable retirement present, as the duo led the Engineers to a 24-19 triumph over Lafayette. This was Lehigh's 50th victory in The Classic Series.

In winning a second Most Valuable Player award, Horn connected on 22 of 36 passes for 263 yards and two

Tres Hombres

After finishing the year with a 5-6 record in 1984, the Engineers placed three players on the Associated Press All-American squad. Nose guard Wes Walton and split end Rennie Benn were named to the Second Team. Center Dave Whitehead, the son of coach John Whitehead, was named as Honorable Mention. It was the second straight season Walton and Benn received honors.

Leopard Leader

Ryan Priest earned Associated Press All-American Honorable Mention for his performances in the 1984 season. Priest finished his career on College Hill as the Leopards' career rushing leader. In later years, Tom Costello and Erik Marsh would surpass Priest in career rushing yardage bumping him to third on the all-time list.

The Women of Lafayette

The 1984 Game marked the debut of the Women of Lafayette Calendar. It was circulated in the Friday, November 16th edition of *The Lafayette* as part of the Lafayette-Lehigh Week festivities.

touchdowns. Benn led all receivers, nabbing six for 101 yards. Closely-defended all afternoon, Lehigh's all-time reception leader also did an effective decoy job, as fellow wide-out Todd Melton snared an additional six balls — two for touchdowns.

The Brown and White scored on four of five first-half possessions, then held on as the Leopards rallied to narrow the score to 24-19 in the third quarter. Lehigh freshman safety Glenn Comisac intercepted a Frank Baur pass at the Lehigh 15 yard-line with 30 seconds remaining in the contest to end the Maroon's late comeback charge.

Lehigh took the game's opening kickoff and marched 51 yards behind the passing of Horn and the running of diminutive halfback Lee Blum. The compact 5'6", 185-pound freshman sneaked four yards through left guard for the contest's initial score.

Lafayette, playing without All-American running back candidate Ryan Priest who went down with a knee injury in the season's second game, rallied to tie the game after Dave MacPhee recovered a fumbled Lehigh punt at the Engineer 24. One play later, Baur hit Gordie Bullock for a 24-yard scoring strike to knot the score.

Lehigh countered with a 16-play, 65-yard scoring drive. Mike Beattie's 25-yard field goal put Lehigh ahead.

After a Cliff Hubbard interception, Lehigh took four plays to score. Melton collected his first touchdown pass of the day, a 10-yard strike from Horn.

Whitehead then ordered his troops to try an onside kick from the huddle formation in hopes of catching Lafayette napping, but the Leopards' Andy Nygren recovered at midfield.

It made little difference, as moments later, Matt Cichocki intercepted another Baur pass at the Lehigh 35. This set-up Lehigh's final

"Iron Leopard" Craig Parsons (below) set a Lafayette College football record by starting in his 42nd game in the season-ender against Lehigh in 1985. The versatile 6'3", 230-pounder played fullback and tight end for the Leopards during his four years on College Hill.

MVP Trophy Fumbled

Before the 1985 contest, the Most Valuable Player trophy was fumbled, booted, and kicked around the Taylor Stadium press box like a slippery pigskin in a muddy quagmire.

As the trophy was being delivered to the press box high above the south stands before opening kick-off, the courier stumbled and bobbled the trophy as he climbed the last step into the box. The prized-award went crashing to the floor of the box. Unfortunately, it didn't bounce like a football. Parts went everywhere.

During the first-half, there was as much action in the press box as on the field. A bevy of scribes, sports information interns, and medical types performed surgery on the award so that it could be presented in one piece to The Game's MVP.

Afterwards, one of the repairmen quipped, "There's probably more athletic tape on the trophy than the MVP."

---

score on a controversial play.

First, a Horn to Benn 41-yarder moved the ball deep into Lafayette territory. Then, on a first-and-goal from the Leopard five, Horn dropped to pass and was forced to roll right from the pocket. As the pursuit intensified, Horn retreated to the Lafayette 35, scrambled toward the left sideline, then heaved a pass against the grain into the right side of the end zone. Melton and Lafayette defensive back Joe Yanek leaped for the ball and both players hit the ground with their arms wrapped around the pigskin.

The near referee at first signalled a touchdown, but then held a conference with the other officials. After a brief discussion, a touchdown was officially awarded to Lehigh.

Coach Bill Russo, whose high-powered offense had established 52 school records in five seasons, argued vehemently at the referee's decision. The heated discussion

Sympathy Card

Pregame pranks began early in the week leading to the 1985 contest. Lafayette supporters left an ominous message for Lehigh at its Saucon Valley practice fields. The "greeting" was a coffin-sized box complete with funeral floral arrangements and an epitaph that read:

Here Lies Lehigh
Rest in Peace
Born: ?
Died: Nov. 23, 1985
Condolences, the 'Pards

A Laughing Matter

A stand-up comedy show was part of the pregame pep rally before the 1985 contest. National headliners Patti Leary, Tom Clark, and Dennis Leary performed in Stabler Arena as a warmup to the bonfire at the Saucon Valley Fields. Fireworks were added at the end of the evening for the grand finale.

did not change the call and the touchdown stood, much to the dismay of coach Russo.

Emerging from the intermission trailing 24-7, Lafayette's Dave Rankin set the tone. The Leopard safety's interception of a Horn pass on the first play of the second half swung the momentum toward Lafayette.

Behind the running of Bruce McIntyre, Lafayette's fifth all-time leading rusher who on the day gained 100 yards on 23 carries, the Leopards took control. This led to three

Two-Timing

Lehigh's Marty Horn joined fellow quarterback Kim McQuilken '73 as the only two Engineers to earn the Lehigh-Lafayette Most Valuable Player award more than once. McQuilken was the recipient in 1972 and 1973. Horn took the accolades in 1983 and 1985.

After the ceremony presenting the 1985 trophy, Horn relayed McQuilken's comments on Marty's career. Said Horn, "Kim said to me after the game 'since I had all of his other (passing) records, I might as well get this (trophy) too.'"

Quarterback Marty Horn — only the second Engineer to win the Lehigh-Lafayette MVP award twice.

successive scores — a Mike Renzi field goal, a Baur to Carl St. Bernard touchdown pass, and another Renzi field goal before Comisac closed the door on the Leopards with his big interception.

All-American Combo

Quarterback Marty Horn and wide receiver Rennie Benn earned All-American status in 1985. Benn was a Kodak All-American; both were Associated Press Honorable Mentions.

This was the third consecutive year Benn reaped Associated Press All-American honors. In 1984, Lehigh's career leader in receptions, receiving yardage, and touchdown receptions, was selected as a second team All-American. As a sophomore in 1983, he earned Honorable Mention status.

Against Indiana University (Pa.) in the 1985 season-opener, Benn tied Jerry Rice's Division 1-AA record for most touchdown pass receptions in a game with five.

As the other half of the combination, Horn re-wrote many of the school passing records. Horn is the all-time completion (744), yardage (9,120), and touchdown (62) leader.

Rennie Benn — Lehigh's All-Time leading receiver and three-time All-American.

End Of The Whitehead Era

The 1985 contest was the final time head coach John Whitehead led his troops into battle. In 10 highly-successful seasons, Whitehead took the Engineers to levels never experienced on South Mountain. His accomplishments included a national championship, a national runner-up, three playoff bids, two Lambert/Meadowlands Cup awards for Eastern supremacy, and the two winningest seasons in Lehigh football history.

During his reign, the Lehigh record book was written numerous times at both an individual and team level.

After suffering a 6-5 inaugural campaign in 1976, which dismayed boosters accustomed to the playoff appearances under previous coach Fred Dunlap, Whitehead molded the 1977 team into Division II National Champions. The 12 wins remains a school record, as does the 466 points scored.

For his efforts, Whitehead was named Coach of the Year, an award also received in 1979 for leading the Engineers to the Division 1-AA runner-up spot.

After stepping down, Whitehead took over the role of Athletic Director, a position he held until 1989.

Whitehead finished with a 75-38-2 record, for a .661 winning percentage, second best among all Lehigh mentors who coached more than one season. Included in that mark is a 6-4 record against Lafayette.

Lehigh's Father-Son team of John Whitehead and Dave Whitehead played their last football game together as coach-player in the 1985 Lehigh-Lafayette game.

Colonial League Kickoff

Like the 1985 contest, the 1986 edition wasn't settled until time expired, as an interception closed the book on a potential game-winning drive.

This time, Lafayette got revenge 28-23, as Leopard safety Mike Joseph intercepted a Mark McGowan pass at midfield as the gun sounded.

Behind a massive offensive line that averaged 276 pounds, Bruce McIntyre once again led a ground game which netted 303 yards on the day. Against a Lehigh defensive front whose biggest man barely tipped 230, the MVP accounted for 251 yards, just five yards shy of Jack O'Reilly's 1927 school record for most yards rushing in The Game.

On the other side of the field, sophomore quarterback Mark McGowan established a Lehigh record for passing yards against Lafayette. Playing with a cast on his broken left wrist, the mid-season replacement for injured starter Jim Harris completed 32-of-55 for 397 yards and three touchdowns. This passing yardage record against Lafayette would be obliterated twice in the next six years.

The Game featured 11 turnovers, but was also marked by 800-plus yards of total offense. And this was without the quarterbacks who were expected to direct their teams at the start of summer practice. After the fifth game, Harris was sidelined for the season with mononucleosis. Lafayette's Frank Baur, who later would hold all the major Leopard passing records, was forced to miss the season with a non-football related suspension.

Lafayette scored a touchdown in each quarter and three of the biggest names in the Lafayette offensive record books each scored a six-pointer. Priest and McIntyre each reached the end zone from the backfield and all-time reception-leader Philip Ng caught a

Lafayette's Bruce McIntyre rushed for 251 yards against Lehigh in 1986 earning him MVP honors.

Defensive back Mike Joseph holds the career interception record at Lafayette.

scoring strike from Paul Struncius. Taking the helm at mid-season from Baur's replacement Clayton Evans, Struncius also sneaked from one-yard for the fourth Leopard score. A week earlier, Struncius threw for a school-record five touchdown passes against Army.

All three Lehigh touchdowns were tallied by fullback Rich Curtis on screen passes from McGowan.

Defensive back Steve Banco intercepted three Leopard passes. Lafayette's four interceptions of Lehigh aerials set a school-record 27 for the year and included career-leading number 19 by Mike Joseph on the contest's last play.

With the win, Bill Russo's squad finished at 6-5 for the second straight season. The Lehigh troops, under new head coach Hank Small, closed at 5-6 for the third consecutive year.

First All-Colonial Team

The first All-Colonial Football Team was announced at the end of the 1986 season. Lehigh and Lafayette each placed three members on the squad.

For the Leopards, The Game MVP Bruce McIntyre was named to a running back spot. One of his blockers, offensive tackle Chris Thatcher, and punter Joe Genduso were also honored.

All three Engineers named were linemen. Offensive tackle Joe Uliana, tight end Randy Miller, and defensive tackle Mike Kosko received recognition. Quarterback Mark McGowan was honored as Rookie of the Year, as he stepped into the starting line-up with the Engineers at 1-4 and directed the team to four wins in the last six games.

National accolades were also earned by Uliana and Kosko. Both were chosen as Honorable Mention Associated Press All-Americans.

Uliana received a different type of accolade upon graduation, as he was elected to the Pennsylvania House of Representatives for the district which included Lehigh and South Bethlehem. After two terms, the populace voted him into the State Senate.

The Turkey Bowl

Lehigh All-Americans John Shigo and Joe Uliana grew up in the same Bethlehem neighborhood and were three years apart in age. Though teammates and neighbors, some of the most competitive action between the two occurred in the annual Turkey Bowl held at the local Asa Packer grade school playground each Friday after Thanksgiving.

What started as a friendly game of pick-up football in the mid-1970's has turned into an annual spectacle. With crowds almost rivaling those at early Lafayette-Lehigh football games, this sandlot contest has featured former players from Lafayette, Lehigh, Temple, West Virginia, Moravian, Muhlenberg, East Stroudsburg, and Kutztown — all of whom were raised in the same Bethlehem neighborhood.

In true spirit of The Game, kegs of beer and a deli spread are provided for pregame tailgating and postgame celebration. An MVP trophy is presented annually by Turkey Bowl Commissioner Tom Baldo — a modern day Bots Brunner who attended five different colleges in his journeyman academic career and who reportedly has a year of college football eligibility remaining. After numerous postgame beers, the MVP trophy usually rested in the hands of Uliana or Shigo.

A "bull session" caps the evening at South Bethlehem's famous Tally Ho.

It was during one such instance when Uliana compared the Turkey Bowl to Lehigh-Lafayette and uttered the immortal words, "It's a backyard brawl! There's no room on the field for pansies. There are no winners, only survivors!"

Joe Uliana — Colonial League All-Star, All-American, State Representative ... and Turkey Bowl MVP Award winner.

Taylor's Last Stand

"This game just presents a great opportunity. This is our bowl game, this is our playoff game, this is the game of the season."
                    — Lehigh coach Hank Small on the final game at Taylor Stadium.

Taylor Stadium, home to Lehigh football for 74 years, was gone with the wind after the 1987 Lehigh-Lafayette game.

Forty mile per hour winds coupled with temperatures in the mid-20's sent wind chills into the minus-20's by the opening whistle. Fans of both schools braved the conditions to witness the last game held at the country's fifth-oldest college football arena. Most stayed to the end, hoping to take home a memory from the venerable concrete coliseum.

Some took home a chunk of the stadium, a hunk of turf, or a piece of the goalpost. Others just left with the chilled memory of Lehigh's 17-10 triumph in the final Taylor Stadium game of College Football's Most-Played Rivalry.

The game was a nail-biter in more ways than one. In ever-worsening conditions, Mark McGowan engineered the game-winning drive, marching Lehigh 60 yards on 11 plays for a touchdown as the sun set over a scoreboard showing 5:08 to play.

With the gale-force west-winds at his back, McGowan connected with Tom Marron and Vance Cassell for a pair of first downs. Rich Curtis earned another first down with 13 yards on two carries.

McGowan took the game into his own hands. With the ball resting at the Lafayette 22, the call from the bench was a halfback sweep toss left. However, Lehigh's field general defied orders and faked the pitch left then bootlegged right.

By the time any Leopard defender could react, McGowan made it to the one-yard line. Two plays later, he sneaked into the end zone behind guard Aaron Frantz for the winning score.

Lafayette got the ball back with five minutes remaining, but cannon-armed quarterback Frank Baur could not overcome the numbing cold and stiff wind in his face.

During the game, the gusts wreaked such havoc that coaches used time-outs at the end of the quarters to keep the wind at their team's backs for an extra set of plays. Any type of kick was an adventure and passes went sideways as often as down field.

The teams scored only with the wind at their backs. The lone exception was a 25-yard Lafayette field goal that was almost blown back through the uprights to start the fourth stanza. This came after Baur, using

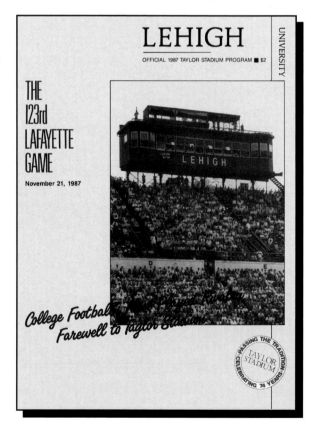

LEHIGH
UNIVERSITY
OFFICIAL 1987 TAYLOR STADIUM PROGRAM ■ $2

THE 123rd LAFAYETTE GAME
November 21, 1987

College Football
Farewell to Taylor Stadium

PASSING THE TRADITION
CELEBRATING 74 YEARS
TAYLOR STADIUM

Taylor Treasures

Fans exhibited ingenuity in their efforts to salvage a piece of history following the conclusion of the final game at the ancient concrete memorial called Taylor Stadium.

A pair of Daniel Boone "wannabees" took a hatchet and Bowie knife to the 50-yard line number painted on the turf.

Another man in a custom-tailored blazer and houndstooth overcoat used an ax and shovel to remove the "LU" insignia from midfield. How he managed to get the garden tools past security is still an unsolved mystery.

A group of sorority sisters, not willing to enter the goalpost fracas, stripped wood boards from the temporary bleachers along the north sideline and were later seen parading their trophies around South Bethlehem.

In the south stands, one person pulled a carpenter's hammer from under his trench coat and pounded out chunks of the grey concrete seating bowl.

Just rows away, another fellow wielded a sledge hammer. Unfortunately, the hammer was no match for Taylor's sturdy construction, as the handle cracked before a piece of history could be carved.

In the upper deck, a student tried to lasso one of the "L-E-H-I-G-H" letters off the exterior face of the press box. Alongside stood a fan who ripped a section of the aluminum seating bench from its base and used the plank to poke the fabricated letters from their press box mountings into the waiting arms of compatriots below.

Two fans dissect the 50-yard line turf from the Taylor Stadium field after the 1987 Lehigh-Lafayette game.

The Dreaded "L"

An unidentified Lehigh Theta Xi fraternity brother escaped with the "L" from the Lehigh press box after the 1987 game — the last game played at Taylor Stadium. As he was returning up South Mountain with his souvenir, the student was mugged by a group of fellow students who abducted the "L" and fled. The Theta Xi brother made a valiant stand for his prize but was left with only a black eye as a final memory of Taylor Stadium.

**Lehigh's Mark McGowan
shaking the cold and a
Lafayette tackler in the final
game at Taylor Stadium.**

his time outs, directed the Maroon into scoring position with the wind during the third period.

Although four of Lehigh's defeats were by a total of nine points, McGowan came under fire all season for directing Lehigh to a lackluster 5-5-1 record in '87.

Expectations were high for the campaign on the strength of McGowan's monster 397-yard performance in the 28-23 loss to the 'Pards to close out '86.

In the last game at Taylor Stadium, McGowan threw for a less-than-monstrous 120 yards. Given the bitterly-cold weather conditions, McGowan turned in a hot performance that slayed the Leopards. McGowan didn't seem to mind the cold and willfully braved the elements after the game when he accepted the MVP trophy.

"Heck, at the end of the day, it felt like it was sunny, and 75 degrees out there."
— Lehigh Quarterback Mark McGowan,
1987 MVP Award Winner

A win in The Game could leave a player delirious, while a loss could leave one numb.

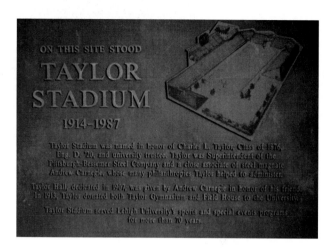

This memorial is found on Lehigh campus near the site where Taylor Stadium stood. It reads:

Taylor Stadium was named in honor of Charles L. Taylor, Class of 1876, Eng. D. '20, and university trustee. Taylor was Superintendent of the Pittsburgh-Bessemer Steel Company and a close associate of steel magnate Andrew Carnegie, whose many philanthropics Taylor helped to administer.

Taylor Hall, dedicated in 1907, was given by Andrew Carnegie in honor of his friend. In 1913, Taylor donated both Taylor Gymnasium and Field House to the University.

Taylor Stadium served Lehigh University's sports and special events programs for more than 70 years.

Final Game Improv

The bone-chilling weather for the last contest at Taylor Stadium left some pregame partiers searching for a warmer climate. A group of tailgaters just west of the stadium found a more temperate environment when one reveler discovered an unlocked door to the nearby Physics Building.

Instead of sitting on the cold concrete of Taylor, the group moved the party into the Physics Auditorium. One person located the light switch. Another uncovered the microphone controls. Before long, the venue turned into a comedy club — complete with cocktails, as aspiring comedians took turns doing their best Jerry Seinfeld, Robin Williams, and Billy Crystal.

As the mercury plummeted outside at The Game, the audience grew inside at the Physics Improv.

One member of the troupe, architecture student Paula Sagerman, couldn't recall The Game, but remembered the stand-up gigs.

"The last game was very cold and I wasn't too happy to see Taylor go," she recounted. "So I boycotted the game and continued the party inside the Physics Building. It was more fun than sitting in the bitter weather."

Now a historic preservationist, Sagerman has not been to the modern Goodman Stadium. "I've got such great memories of historic Taylor Stadium, I just can't bring myself to go to the new stadium."

Number 1 versus Number 2

The 1988 Game was one for statisticians, mathematicians, and record books. The number one and two Division 1-AA offenses met at Fisher Field in a game that will be remembered through the ages. Even Lafayette-Lehigh superfan Roger Conners, who attended every game in The Rivalry since 1912, witnessed something new in the 124th rendition of College Football's Most-Played Series. In fact, a point was nearly scored for each of the 104 years of The Rivalry's existence.

In a game contested in a cold, damp mist, *both* teams tallied over 625 yards in total offense. One quarterback threw for 372 yards *in the first half*, and the *losing* squad scored 45 points. Who knows what records would have been shattered had the weather conditions been better.

In spite of the gloomy weather, the action on the field captivated and thrilled the capacity crowd. Ninety-seven points were scored. Just as many cases of fan whiplash were reported as fans in the stands strained to keep pace with the tennis-match-type action up and down the field.

In the offensive slugfest, Lafayette was the last one standing, holding on for a 52-45 triumph and its first Colonial League title with a perfect 5-0 mark.

What a wild finish it was to a championship season!

Consider that Lafayette's Tom Costello, The Game's Most Valuable Player, rushed for 216 yards, but had only the third-best offensive stats.

Consider that the spectacular performance of Leopard quarterback Frank Baur, who missed on only five passes in going 21-26 for 309 yards with four touchdowns via the air and one more on the ground, was overshadowed by his Engineer counterpart.

Lehigh quarterback Jim Harris completed 23 of 29 for 372 and two touchdowns — *in the first half* — directing the nation's number one offense to a 35-30 lead at intermission. His performance was one-yard shy of the NCAA halftime record.

Harris led Lehigh to touchdowns in its first five

Lehigh's Jim Harris (above) and Lafayette's Frank Baur (below) lit up the sky in the 1988 game which matched the nation's top-ranked offenses.

1988's Biggest Celebration

After Frank Baur scored on a one-yard quarterback sneak to give Lafayette a 36-35 lead to start the second half, the 'Pard defense stiffened. Surrendering five consecutive scoring drives on Lehigh's first five possessions, the Leopard defense finally forced Lehigh to punt. This set off a wild celebration on the Maroon bench and among the Lafayette faithful akin to winning the Super Bowl.

Ng, Costello Earn Accolades

Frank Baur was not the only Leopard to receive post-season laurels for the outstanding 1988 season.

Phil Ng, the school's career reception leader, was named Honorable Mention Associated Press All-American. Freshman tailback Tom Costello also received similar honors.

offensive possessions and completed 14 of his first 15 for 201 yards. All he had to show for it was a 21-21 deadlock early in the second quarter.

Before leaving with a rib injury in the fourth quarter, Harris threw for a then school record 430 yards on a 28 for 46 performance. The senior broke Mark McGowan's two-year-old school record also set against Lafayette.

The Game featured 1,257 yards in total offense, an amazing 172 plays from scrimmage, 58 first downs, and only one turnover and three punts.

Lehigh's 495 yards passing established a new school record, as did the Leopards' 628 yards in total offense. Lafayette's 420 points scored during the season was the most in Leopard history.

The 97 points scored easily surpassed The Rivalry's previous combined total of 78 set by Lehigh's 78-0 whitewashing of Lafayette in 1917.

The wide receivers logged more miles in this aerial spectacular than if on a Boston Marathon training run. Three players went over the century mark in receiving yards for The Game.

Rob Varano took the long distance award and established a then school record in a Lafayette game, covering 189 yards on 12 catches. Flanker John Gorman added 125 yards on seven receptions. Lafayette's Phil Ng totalled 127 receiving yards on eight catches, including a game-long 59-yarder for a touchdown.

Costello's MVP rushing performance paced a ground attack which balanced the passing game. The Leopards passed for 309 and rushed for 320. In the process, the tailback became only the second freshman to win the MVP trophy.

Connecting on four of four extra points in the contest helped Lafayette placekicker Jim Hodson establish a Division-IAA record for most consecutive extra points converted in a season. He was a perfect 51 of 51 in 1988.

Lafayette finished 8-2-1 on the season, its best mark since Bill Russo's first team in 1981 which went 9-2.

Lehigh posted its first winning season in five years despite the loss to its long-time rival. The Engineers ended at 6-5 in the first season at Murray H. Goodman Stadium in Saucon Valley.

1988 Game Summary

Scoring Summary:
- LU - Torain 1 run (Bird kick)
- LC - Caldwell 11 pass from Baur (Hodson kick)
- LU - Curtis 19 run (Bird kick)
- LC - Ng 59 pass from Baur (Hodson kick)
- LU - Torain 22 pass from Harris (Bird kick)
- LC - Costello 5 run (Hodson kick)
- LU - Gorman 43 pass from Harris (Bird kick)
- LC - Hodson FG 23
- LU - Torain 20 run (Bird kick)
- LC - Ng 18 pass from Baur (run failed)
- LC - Baur 1 run (pass failed)
- LU - Bird 20 FG
- LC - Miller 1 run (run failed)
- LC - Grau 34 pass from Baur (Hodson kick)
- LC - Hodson FG 19
- LU - Gorman 6 pass from Brunner (Bird kick)

	Lehigh	Lafayette
First Downs	29	29
Rushes-Yards	26-133	58-320
Yards Passing	495	309
Total Yards	628	629
Passes Attempted	59	26
Passes Completed	35	21
Intercepted by	0	1
Punts-Average	2-36	1-38
Fumbles-Lost	1-0	3-0
Penalties-Yards	11-102	8-75
3rd Down Conversions	9-18	7-15
Possession Time	26:05	33:55

	1st	2nd	3rd	4th	Total
Lehigh	21	14	3	7	**45**
Lafayette	14	16	6	16	**52**

INDIVIDUAL STATISTICS:

RUSHING - Lehigh: Curtis 8-59, Torain 14-58, Brunner 1-8, Harris 2-6, Varano 1-2; Lafayette: Costello 37-216, Baur 6-51, Miller 11-45, Adams 3-7, Mallozzi 1-1.

PASSING - Lehigh: Harris 28-46-1 for 430 yards, Brunner 7-13-0 for 65 yards; Lafayette: Baur 21-26-0 for 309 yards.

RECEIVING - Lehigh: Varano 12-189, Gorman 7-125, Torain 8-89, Curtis 5-51, Cassell 3-42; Lafayette: Ng 8-127, Caldwell 6-85, Grau 2-55, Baird 2-18, Winters 1-19, Costello 1-7, Miller 1-(-2).

Record-Setting Pianist

The offensive machines created by coach Bill Russo finally received national recognition in 1988. Record-breaking quarterback Frank Baur was named first team All-American by both the Associated Press and *Football Gazette*, and was named second team by *The Sports Network*. He was also named ECAC Player of the Year for leading the nation in passing efficiency with a 171.1 rating — good for #2 on the NCAA's Division I-AA all-time list. In his remarkable season, Baur completed better than 64% of his passes for 2,621 yards and 23 touchdowns. His numbers ranked ahead of Division I-A quarterbacks Steve Walsh of Miami and Troy Aikman of UCLA, who later guided the Dallas Cowboys to a Super Bowl Championship.

Baur was such a highly-touted pro prospect after his junior season that he was on the cover of the 1989 *Sports Illustrated* college football preview edition and the subject of an extensive feature article.

An accomplished pianist, Baur holds every major Lafayette passing and total offense record and was the first Leopard player to play in the postseason Hula Bowl All-Star game in Hawaii.

Unfortunately, elbow problems during his last season on College Hill scared away scouts. He was signed as a free agent by the New York Giants, but never made it past the exhibition season.

Russo Named Coach of the Year

The mastermind behind the juggernaut Lafayette offensive machine that set 15 school records en route to an 8-2-1 record received national recognition in 1988. Bill Russo received the Eddie Robinson "Coach of the Year" award as the top coach in Division I-AA.

During his tenure, Russo-coached teams appeared in 53 of the 65 entries in the Lafayette offensive record book, including a school and nation-leading 38.2 points per game scoring average in 1988.

His Colonial League championship team of 1988 was ranked as high as fifth in Division I-AA polls. For this, Russo was named Colonial League "Coach of the Year" and was the winner of the Scotty Whitelaw Award from the New York Sportswriters as the Northeast's best I-AA coach.

In 1990, Russo became the winningest coach in Lafayette football history. A 59-14 victory over Fordham gave the Brown University graduate win number 60 on College Hill. The mark surpassed the total of 59 set by Herb McCracken from 1924-35.

Russo took Lafayette by storm in his first season in Easton. In 1981, the former Wagner College head coach directed the Leopards to a 9-2 record and a national ranking as high as eighth in his break-through season. A year earlier, the Leopards limped through a 3-7 mark. His first game as the Lafayette leader was a 51-0 blanking of Central Connecticut, a stark reversal for a team which went six games without scoring a touchdown the year before he took over the reigns on College Hill.

His inaugural season efforts earned Russo the District 2 "Coach of the Year" honors from a vote of peers in the American Football Coaches Association.

Through 1994, Russo compiled an 84-64-3 record at Lafayette and three Colonial/Patriot League championships. Russo-coached quarterbacks have eclipsed the 2,000-yard mark in eight seasons - the only times it has happened in school history. Running backs from his squads have accounted for eight of the ten 1,000-yard rushing seasons in Lafayette history.

Before coming to Lafayette, Russo led Wagner to its first postseason competition in its 50-year history. His overall record is 99-79-3 entering the 1995 season.

The Eddie Robinson Coach of the Year award (above) was won by Lafayette's Bill Russo in 1988.

Lafayette won the NCAA Division I-AA scoring title in 1988.

From Taylor to Goodman

In 1988, the home of Lehigh football moved from the main campus in South Bethlehem to Saucon Valley and the Goodman Campus. On October 1, 1988, Lehigh defeated Cornell 27-14 in the first game played at the 16,000 seat Murray H. Goodman Stadium.

Nestled in a natural bowl at the wooded base of South Mountain amidst the Lehigh athletic grounds, the oval-shaped facility has also hosted NFL scrimmages featuring the New York Giants, Washington Redskins, and New York Jets; U.S. Soccer games contesting Olympic Qualifying and World Cup exhibition action; the Pennsylvania Keystone State Games; and the NCAA Women's Lacrosse Championship.

The stadium features a two-story structure at midfield atop the west grandstand, housing a fully-enclosed press box and a level of private club suites. A field house featuring offices, locker and equipment rooms, and an athletic training facility is located at the stadium's north end behind the bleachers and directly below the scoreboard.

Standing-room only crowds of 18,623 and 19,110 witnessed the Lafayette contests of 1989 and 1991, establishing attendance records for the new stadium that replaced venerable Taylor Stadium.

Ancient Rivals Christen New Stadium

Since 1914, Taylor Stadium played host to and became part of the folklore of College Football's Most-Played Series.

In 1989, a new venue welcomed the 125th renewal in the long and storied Rivalry. On November 18th, Murray H. Goodman Stadium was christened with all the fanfare and pageantry deserving of the spirited fall classic . . . including the ceremonial goalpost destruction.

And like the first Lehigh-Lafayette game held at Taylor Stadium 74 years earlier, Lafayette was victorious.

With offensive weapons Frank Baur and Tom Costello returning from the explosive Lafayette team that won the shoot-out at Fisher Field a year earlier, the Leopards rolled to a 36-21 win before 18,623, then the largest crowd in Goodman Stadium history.

Lafayette was among the nation's leaders in scoring. Lehigh led the nation in total offense and passing yardage with a 485.6 and 330.1 yards per game average respectively. There would be no shortage of offensive firepower in The Game.

Generating over 600 total yards for the second straight time against the Engineers, the Leopard offense took advantage of both the weakened Lehigh defense and the wintry elements.

Trailing 20-14 at half, coach Hank Small expected the wind and snow to be in Lafayette's face to start the second half. With the teams in the locker room at half, the blustery conditions shifted. So did Lehigh's hope of a comeback. The Leopards not only received the ball to start the third quarter, they also had the wind at their backs.

"To my amazement, when we came out (for the second half of the 1989 Lehigh-Lafayette game), all of a sudden the wind had changed, and snow was blowing in the opposite direction. So we gave them (Lafayette) the wind and the football."

— Lehigh Coach Hank Small

The weather made little difference to Lafayette, as they controlled the ball for 25 of 30 minutes after intermission. When faced with the wind, it was Ground Costello. With the 25-to-30 mile per hour gales at their tails, the Leopards went to Air Baur.

Winning The Game's MVP trophy for the second consecutive season, Costello went through the Lehigh defense for 245 yards and three touchdowns. In the lopsided second half, Costello toted the ball 30 times for 150 yards of real estate. It was the second straight time the Lafayette tailback shredded Lehigh's defense for 200-plus yards.

It was also the second straight 300-plus yard passing performance by the Leopards against the Engineers. Once again, Baur paved the way, completing 17 of 28 for 290 yards. Of Lafayette's 336 yards passing, 227 came on just five big plays, including a surprise 45-yard flanker-around scoring strike from Dave Baird to Mike Grau.

When the Leopard offense stalled short of the end zone, Jim Hodson booted three field goals to cap scoring drives. Hodson became Lafayette's all-time scoring leader with 254 points, and still holds the school record for field goals in a game (four — accomplished

A Fair Trade?

The dream of an offensive lineman is to score a touchdown. Lehigh's Brian Hensel fulfilled this fantasy in the 1989 Lafayette game.

On a third and six from the Leopard 10 yard-line, Engineer coach Hank Small called Hensel's number on the old "fumblerooskie." The Lehigh right guard scooped up the ball set on the ground by the center, and went untouched around left end for a touchdown that brought the Engineers to within six just before half.

Later, Small ran out of tricks and the Engineers bowed 36-21 to their ancient rival.

Reflecting on the meaning of The Rivalry after the game, Hensel said, "It (the touchdown) was the pinnacle of my career, but I'd trade in 100 touchdowns for a win today."

Scholar-Athlete

Lehigh's 1989 high-powered, nationally-ranked offense was led by scholar-athlete split end Rob Varano. In addition to earning Second Team All-American status from both the Associated Press and *The Sports Network*, he was named the Patriot League Co-Scholar Athlete of the Year.

Fourth on Lehigh's career receiving list with 152, Varano still holds the single-game reception mark of 14 with Rennie Benn.

two times).

Lehigh's nationally-ranked offense was relegated to running trick plays. Quarter-back Todd Brunner set seasonal marks for pass completions (273), passing yards (3,516), and touchdown passes (26), but was ineffective against a Leopard defense spearheaded by Keith Grant. The Engineers' offensive highlight was right guard Brian Hensel scoring a touchdown on a "fumblerooskie."

Freshman Flash

Tom Costello was a young 18-year old when he won his first Lafayette-Lehigh Most Valuable Player award, rushing for 216 yards and one touchdown on a workhorse-like 37 carries. He was also named Associated Press Honorable Mention All-American as a freshman.

That first year was merely a warm-up. A year later in 1989, he carried the ball 45 times for 245 yards and three scores and won a second straight MVP

trophy. Lehigh re-engineered its defense from a 3-4 to a 4-3 that season to specifically stop Costello. It failed.

In his junior season, Costello managed 76 yards and one touchdown against a defense that found a way to control the record-setting Leopard.

Injuries finally stopped Costello. Elected captain as a senior, he was forced to sit-out his last year because of chronic shoulder problems.

Though playing only three seasons, he became Lafayette's all-time leading rusher with 2,936 yards and 28 touchdowns.

It was a short-lived mark. Just as a young Lou Gehrig filled in for the Yankees at first base for a headache-plagued Wally Pipp, a young Erik Marsh took over the tailback spot for the injured Costello. As Gehrig rewrote the baseball record book, so would Marsh rewrite the Lafayette records.

Joe's Attendance Count

Before Goodman Stadium, fan headcounts were an inexact science at Lehigh. A review of Taylor Stadium game chronicles revealed attendance numbers that were suspiciously even.

All spectator counts were rounded to the nearest 500 people, or to the nearest thousand on a hectic day.

Fans wondered how these mysteriously-even numbers were tabulated, as Taylor had no turnstiles to count the bodies entering the stadium.

It was a well-guarded secret to which only those in the press box were privy.

Early in the third quarter of each home game, one of the media members, self-anointed in advance, would yell, "Hey, Joe! What's the number?"

Long-time Sports Information Director Joe Whritenour would adjust his bi-focals, chomp down a bit harder on his ever-present pipe, and stick his head out the press box window.

Like a small child waiting to cross a busy street, Joe would check left, scan right, and check left again, surveying the fans in the stands. Then he would duck back into the press box like a wise turtle retreating its head into its shell. Rotating his noggin' just enough to be able to keep one eye on the field, he'd blurt out the attendance figure while blowing a big puff of pipe smoke.

"Twelve thousand, five hundred," he'd say in a gruff baritone voice befitting a grandfatherly war veteran, and all the scribes used that number in the newspaper accounts and on the airwaves.

If the game was against a weaker school or in dreary weather, his number would be "Ten thousand."

For an important regular season game or a playoff game, his visual attendance count totalled "Fifteen thousand."

For the season-ending game against Lafayette, Joe would not even bother sticking his neck out the window. His reasoning? "Too cold. Besides, it's a sell-out. You know it's seventeen thousand."

Except 1979, when Joe deviated from the norm and announced the attendance as 18,778. Of course, that was just days before Joe had scheduled a visit to the eye doctor.

Tailgate Twists

Before Goodman Stadium, Lehigh and Lafayette fans tailgated curbside along row homes, among smoke stacks, or on a parking structure.

The first Lafayette-Lehigh game at Goodman in 1989 provided a pastoral setting in which to enjoy food, drinks, and camaraderie.

The barbecues were such a big part of the tradition that the game almost became secondary, especially since the fans could see the scoreboard while tailgating.

Gradually, rules were implemented which reduced the amount of revelry outside the gates before The Game. In an effort to place the focus back on the game on the field, admission was denied after 2:00 and no re-entry was permitted.

Murray H. Goodman prepares to pass the tradition to Saucon Valley Fields. In the background, the site for Goodman Stadium is seen in its pre-construction days.

Lehigh football fans, players, alumni, and administration pass the tradition from Taylor Stadium to Murray H. Goodman Stadium.

Taylor Stadium played host to The Rivalry since 1914. Taylor passed the tradition to Goodman after the 1987 season.

Goodman Stadium hosted its first Lehigh-Lafayette football game in 1989.

From Colonial To Patriot

Effective with the 1990-91 academic year, the Colonial League officially became the Patriot League with competition in 22 men's and women's sports.

The name change took place to avoid confusion with a southern athletic conference that was also using the "Colonial League" name.

Lehigh Ends a Decade of Frustration at Fisher

With the ghost of Frank Baur gone from College Hill in 1990 and Lafayette suffering only its second losing season in ten years under Bill Russo, Lehigh posted its first win in Easton since 1980. This capped a 7-4 record for the Engineers, their most wins in eight seasons.

Lehigh's potent offense led the Engineers to the brink of its first Patriot League title in the circuit's initial year under the new banner.

The Engineers had their hopes to win the very first Patriot sports title dashed the week before The Game, as Bucknell rallied for 21 third-quarter points to defeat Lehigh 30-27. The stunning loss knocked the Engineers from atop the Patriot League standings.

The Game went from "The Championship Game" back to just The Game.

As had been the case in The Rivalry's recent

Lehigh's Erick Torain ripped through the Lafayette defense for a career-high 224 yards against Lafayette in 1990.

years, offense ruled the show. The two schools fell 15 yards short of combining for 1,000 total yards in offense. A record-breaking back went over 200 yards rushing for the day. A quarterback passed for over 300 yards. His counterpart fell seven yards shy of the mark. And Lehigh's nationally-ranked offense topped the 5,000 total yard mark for the third straight season.

Relying on the MVP work of Erick Torain, Lehigh bested Lafayette 35-14 for its most-lopsided victory in The Series since the 32-0 shut out in 1980 at Fisher Field.

Torain rushed for 224 yards and one score on 36 carries behind the blocking of Kodak All-American guard Keith Petzold. "ET" recorded 148 of those in the second half and broke the 1,000-yard barrier in the process.

Assisting Torain in igniting the 539-yard offensive arsenal was quarterback Glenn Kempa. With 293 yards passing on a 21 for 40 performance, Kempa surpassed Marty Horn and set the second-best season yardage mark with 3,000. Rich Clark, number two on Lehigh's career reception list and Academic All-American, snared 12 Kempa passes for 143 yards. On the day, Kempa threw for one TD and ran for another.

Tom Kirchhoff hit the 300-yard passing mark and connected for two scoring strikes for the 'Pards, but was twice intercepted in the end zone by free safety Adam Ciperski.

Ciperski was joined on the turnover parade by middle linebacker Lee Picariello, who recovered two Lafayette fumbles, made 14 solo tackles, and led the charges in silencing Lehigh-killer Tom Costello. Lafayette's junior tailback was stifled in his attempt to "three-peat" with the MVP trophy. He finished with 76 yards.

For his efforts, Picariello was recognized as the Patriot League defensive player of the week.

E.T. Joins Select Company

With 20 seconds left in The Game's 1990 edition, Erick Torain took a toss and swept around left end for five yards to become only the fourth player in Lehigh history to surpass the 1,000 yard rushing mark.

The tailback's two-yard touchdown run earlier in the fourth stanza set a school scoring record. Torain's 306 points bumped him to the top of the career scoring list, four better than Rod Gardner's 302 established from 1973-75.

In finishing with 1,017 yards rushing, Torain trailed only Jack Rizzo's season-best 1,143 set in 1971, Gardner's 1,112 established in 1975, and Dick Gabriel's 1,023 recorded in 1949.

"ET" became the first Lehigh back to rush for over 200 yards in more than one game, peppering Towson State for 201 yards earlier in the season in addition to the 224 against Lafayette. Torain also tied Rennie Benn's Lehigh single-game record by scoring 30 points against Colgate.

TWO MINUTE WARNING:
Fantastic Finishes

1915

Lafayette's Joe Dumoe grabbed a short sideline pass from teammate John "Bodie" Weldon, out-fighting two Lehigh players. Spinning away from one opponent, straight-arming a second, and side-stepping a third, Dumoe crossed the goal line in the game's waning moments giving The Maroon a 10-6 victory.

1922

In the lowest scoring game in Series' history, former Lehigh player Bots Brunner drop-kicked the winning field goal with 45 seconds left to give Lafayette a 3-0 win.

1930

A year earlier, Lehigh bested the Leopards for the first time in a decade. Lafayette avenged that defeat in 1930, rallying for 16 points in the game's last eight minutes against a veteran Engineer squad that returned nine of eleven starters.

1952

With the score tied at seven, reserve quarterback Jack Conti, who played only 20 minutes all season, drove the Engineers 55 yards in ninety seconds through a torrential downpour for the winning score. Tommy Gunn made a diving catch in the mud between two Leopard defenders with 1:30 left to give Lehigh the 14-7 win.

1958

With the score tied at 14 in the fourth quarter, Lehigh's Frank Koziol missed a decisive extra point by inches. The Engineers got the ball back and marched to the Lafayette five before the Leopards' Don Westmaas intercepted. The kicking game also deserted the Leopards, as two 29-yard field goal attempts failed in the final stanza, leaving the final score deadlocked.

1961

Tied at 14, the fourth quarter of this Game featured six turnovers, two penalties, a "Hail Mary" pass, and a UFO sighting. With six seconds on the game clock, Lehigh's Andy Larko, who had not converted a field

TWO MINUTE WARNING:
Fantastic Finishes (cont.)

goal all season, set-up on the right hash for a 19-yard attempt. The ball spun sideways, just clearing the on-rushing defensemen before knuckling through the lower-left corner of the uprights, giving the Engineers a 17-14 victory.

1964
The 100th Game ended in a 6-6 deadlock, with both teams squandering scoring chances late in the contest. First, Lafayette was stopped on downs after having a first and goal at the Lehigh five. After a quick exchange of possessions, Lehigh drove to the Leopard 17 before Hal Yeich lost his third fumble of the day. Lafayette recovered with 1:55 to play but could not mount an offensive.

1985
In the last game of Lehigh's Horn-Benn era, the Engineers scored on four of five first-half possessions, only to see future *Sports Illustrated* cover boy Frank Baur rally the Leopards in the second half. With 30 seconds left in the contest and Lafayette marching, freshman safety Glenn Comisac intercepted a Baur pass at the Lehigh 15 to preserve a 24-19 victory.

1986
Two rookie quarterbacks generated more than 800 combined total yards, but their offenses committed 11 turnovers. Mike Joseph's interception of a Mark McGowan pass as time expired guaranteed Lafayette's 28-23 victory.

1988
Lafayette's Frank Baur outlasted Lehigh's Jim Harris in this wild shoot-out that ended with the Leopards on top 52-45. Establishing a new Series' record for total points scored, it was a "fantastic finish" when this seemingly endless battle finally ended, giving Lafayette its first Patriot League championship.

1992
Lafayette's Erik Marsh rushed for 251 yards and Lehigh's Scott Semptimphelter passed for a school record 480, but it was Tramont Evans' interception of a Semptimphelter aerial on the game's last play that gave the Leopards a 32-29 win and their second Patriot League title.

Two Points From Perfect

The Game of 1991 matched an up-and-coming Leopard squad against a veteran Lehigh team that was only two points from a perfect record. One-point losses to Holy Cross and Colgate prevented Lehigh from entering The Classic with a perfect 10-0 record.

Led by a trio of All-Americans — quarterback Glenn Kempa, wide receiver Horace Hamm, and offensive lineman Mike Moriarty — the Engineers' passing offense was ranked first in the Patriot League and fifth in the nation entering The Game.

Kempa broke Todd Brunner's seasonal passing records in the Lafayette contest, as Lehigh rolled to a 36-18 victory before a record Goodman Stadium crowd of 19,110.

Finishing 26 of 38 for 276 yards and one touchdown, "The Rifle" was voted Most Valuable Player. For the season, Kempa established new school records in touchdown passes with 31, passing yardage with 3,565, and completions with 286.

Kempa was supported by senior tailback Larry Arico, who rushed for 116 yards and a six-pointer on 28 carries. It was Arico's sixth time over the century mark in 1991 and the eighth contest a Lehigh back broke the 100-yard plateau in 11 games.

Second team back Mark Lookenbill chipped in three rushing touchdowns.

As the case in previous Games, a losing squad's performer overshadowed the victors. Freshman Erik Marsh, a Bethlehem native who selected Lafayette over Lehigh, ran for a game-high 164 yards on 26 carries. Substituting for standout tailback Tom Costello, who was forced to sit out his senior year due to shoulder problems, Marsh was the Leopards' leading rusher for the year and was named the Patriot League

The 1991 Engineers were two points from a perfect season.

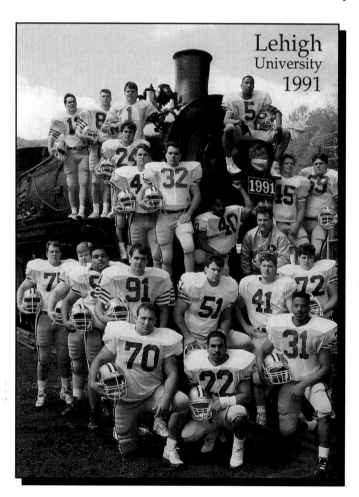

Rookie of the Year.

Cornerback Pete Sczerbinski led Lehigh's defensive assault on Marsh and quarterback Tom Kirchhoff. The 5'-7", 172-pound senior, who four years earlier was burned badly by Frank Baur in the legendary 52-45 shoot-out, repeatedly came up with big plays to thwart the Leopards.

First, it was an interception in the end zone to kill Lafayette's opening drive. Lehigh's offense took advantage of the momentum swing and marched 80 yards for a TD.

Next, "Too Small," as *Express-Times* sportswriter Bob Flounders penned, set up Lehigh's second touchdown when he forced a fumble by Marsh. The loose ball was recovered by fellow cornerback Tommy Clark.

In the third quarter, "Too Small" took the snap on a fake punt from the up-back position and handed to teammate Mike Wetzel on a derivation of the ol' fumblerooskie. The play netted a first down, and one play later, Lookenbill scored.

After the ensuing kick-off, "Too Small" intercepted another Kirchhoff misfire at the 'Pards' 41 and returned it to the 30. Three plays later, Kempa hit wide-out Rich Clark on an 18-yard scoring strike to make it 33-6.

"Two Small" was runner-up in the MVP voting.

Lafayette Wins Second Patriot League Championship

Lafayette needed a victory in its 1992 game against Lehigh to secure a second league championship in five years. The final obstacle in its path was a Lehigh team whose offense over the last four years had gained more yards than any other 1-AA football team. During those four years, the Engineers played 43 games. Lehigh quarterbacks passed for over 300 yards 24 times, and on seven additional occasions they threw for more than 400 yards.

The Leopards entered with an equally offensive offense, ranked eighth in the nation in scoring and eleventh in total offense. Once again, The Game figured to test the scoreboard operator and statisticians.

"Too Small" Sczerbinski

Pete Sczerbinski was a heavily recruited running back/defensive back at Bishop Hendricken High School in Cranston, Rhode Island. Lafayette was perhaps his hottest pursuer.

Set to sign with the Leopards and spend the next four years in Easton, the interest from College Hill suddenly disappeared. Apparently, the coaching staff got word of how big Sczerbinski really was. He stood a towering 5'7", and tipped the scale at 155 pounds "on a good day." So Lafayette said "Good Day."

He decided to enroll at Lehigh by chance. Sczerbinski wasn't even aware Lehigh had a rivalry against Lafayette.

After four years on South Mountain wearing a Brown and White uniform and culminating his career as the second-place finisher in The Game's MVP voting, the guy who was too small for one school played a big role in a big rivalry.

Riot Of '91

The postgame goalpost wars are as much a part of the tradition of The Rivalry as The Game itself. With well-lubricated students and fraternities battling one another for bragging rights to the biggest chunk of the post, the event became a major safety concern.

The police, who had the unenviable task of protecting the goalpost and assuring fan well-being, were confronted with a rude twist of fate in the 1991 game at Goodman Stadium.

Upset by the administrations' heavy handed tactics and implementation of indestructible steel goalposts, the students turned their frustrations toward the law enforcers.

With 40 officers guarding each post and a private security firm patrolling the field, the first wave of students did not set foot on the field until well after the final whistle. Once the first group hit the gridiron, a swarm followed.

But instead of the usual violence pitting student against student, it was now student against police. Unable to demolish the well-protected steel goalposts, the students began to hurl chunks of muddy sod at the police. As the swell of students closed in on the officers surrounding the post, the patrolmen responded by using mace to counter the advances.

The goalpost crashers retreated as nightsticks were brandished. A combat zone formed, as screaming, hysterical students grappled with the authorities. Only after a protracted battle was order restored.

One photojournalist on the field said it was one of the scariest riot scenes he had ever experienced.

Led by the nation's ninth-ranked rusher Erik Marsh and three-year starter Tom Kirchhoff at quarterback, the Leopards edged the Engineers 32-29 in another vintage offensive spectacular that had become characteristic of College Football's Most-Played Rivalry.

Playing with an injured shoulder that caused him to miss the better part of two games, Marsh ran for 251 yards on 46 carries and the game-winning touchdown with 5:58 left in the contest.

Yet, like other games in The Series over the past decade, this one was not decided until the final play when Lafayette's Tramont Evans intercepted a Scott Semptimphelter pass.

Moments earlier, Semptimphelter orchestrated a scoring drive to bring the Engineers to within three. The junior, who threw for a school-record 480 yards in The Game, drove the Engineers to paydirt immediately after Marsh's TD, using only 1:54 off the clock before connecting with Jason Cristiano for his third touchdown reception of day. The score and Jason Mastropierro's two-point conversion narrowed the Leopard lead to

The Morning Show

Lafayette College Administrators set a 10:45 a.m. kick-off time at Fisher Field for 1992 edition of The Game. This was the earliest opening whistle in the long-playing series and an effort to curb excess fan revelry both on and off the field.

Express-Times columnist Jack Schlottman described it this way, "a ploy by college administrators who hoped the early start would deter those who wished to engage in the quaint, alcohol-fueled ritual of tearing down the goal posts and trying to use the crossbars to behead their equally inebriated buddies."

32-29 with 4:04 left.

Lehigh got the ball back into the hands of its strong-armed quarterback at its own 47 with 24 seconds left and the opportunity for one more scoring strike, but Evans sealed the Lafayette win with the interception.

Semptimphelter's 480 yards passing on a 25 for 39 effort eclipsed the previous Lehigh single-game record of 467 set by Todd Brunner against Colgate in 1989.

It also overshadowed Kirchhoff's performance. The senior connected on 70% of his passes, going 14 of 20 for 228 yards and three touchdowns. He hit speedy flanker Jamal Jordan on two long scoring bombs in a five and one-half minute span for Lafayette's first two scores. Seven of Jordan's eleven touchdown receptions on the season exceeded 69 yards.

Deep threat Cristiano set a Lehigh and Patriot League single-game record for receiving yards. The Associated Press and *The Sports Network* second team All-American caught 11 balls for 319 yards against the Leopards' blitzing man-to-man coverage. His yardage was 10th best in Division 1-AA game history. Cristiano's seasonal mark of 1,282 also established a new Lehigh mark.

Ironically, it was the much-maligned Lafayette defense that saved the day for

Quarterback Tom Kirchhoff led the Leopards to a victory over Lehigh and the Patriot League title in 1992.

Long-ball threat Jamal Jordan.

the home team. During a mid-season three-game losing streak, the "swiss cheese" defense allowed points as fast as the offense scored them.

In the Lehigh contest, the Leopards surrendered 262-yards passing in the first half, and 561 total yards for the day. But, they also stopped the Engineers from scoring inside the ten on three different occasions in the first half.

After intermission, Marsh gave his defensive counterparts a break. The Game MVP carried 30 times for 184 yards in the final two quarters, keeping the ball out of Semptimphelter's hands and resting the Leopard defense in the process.

Marsh won the Patriot League rushing crown for the 8-3 Leopards, gaining 1,365 yards. This was 32 yards shy of Tom Costello's 1989 school record — a mark Marsh would earn before he left College Hill.

Action from the 1992 Lafayette-Lehigh game.

Title Match

For the first time in the 129-game history of The Game, a league title would belong outright to the victor of the 1993 contest.

Lafayette entered the season finale with a 5-3-2 record behind the legs of Erik Marsh. With veteran signal-caller Tom Kirchhoff graduated, the junior tailback became Lafayette's all-time leading rusher by mid-season.

Lehigh came into the title-tilt with a 6-4 record, including three losses to teams ranked in the top 20. Somehow, the Engineers succeeded with a running game ranked 111 out of 114 schools in Division 1-AA, a pass defense ranked 105, and a run defense at 106. Among the losses was a season-opening 62-21 thrashing by Delaware, and a 77-14 blasting at Idaho.

Of course, Lehigh did have its high-octane passing offense. The passing attack ranked third in the nation and was once again directed by the record-setting Scott Semptimphelter. In his last year on South Mountain, he was sixth in the country in total offense and 11th in passing. Semptimphelter also had last season's record-setting wide-out Dave Cecchini to play catch. The senior end led the nation in receptions and receiving yards and was named to three 1993 first team All-American squads.

In The Game, Semptimphelter connected for a Lehigh-record six scoring strikes, passing for 373 yards on a 27 of 43 effort. He also scrambled for 90 yards on 11 carries and was named MVP in Lehigh's 39-14 defeat of Lafayette, giving the Engineers their first Patriot League title.

Cecchini, the primary target of Semptimphelter during the league championship season, caught nine

Paving The Way

Most offensive linemen toil in relative anonymity, but not Lafayette's Ed Hudak. Opening the holes for the Leopards' stable of thoroughbred tailbacks for four years (1989-92), the offensive guard became the most-highly decorated blocker in College Hill history.

In his career, he was selected to five All-American teams, including two first and one second team selections in his senior season.

Lafayette coach Bill Russo flyin' high with the 1992 Patriot League trophy.

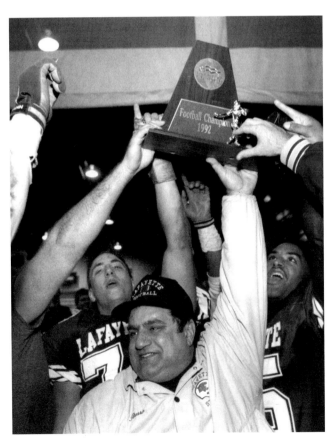

Slingin' Semptimphelter

Had Scott Semptimphelter played all his games against Lafayette, the Lehigh record book would be renamed Scott's record book.

In two games against the rivals from Easton, Semptimphelter took possession of two single-game passing records.

In 1992, the Lehigh quarterback passed for a school-record 480 yards in the season finale.

In 1993, Semptimphelter peppered the Leopards for a school-record six touchdowns and 463 yards in total offense in winning The Game's MVP.

The MVP numbers were recorded in just over three quarters, as SLINGIN' Scott ruptured an achilles tendon while celebrating teammate Greg Amon's interception of a Mike Talerico pass with 13:58 left on the clock.

The joyous leap on the sideline was about the only misstep the Lehigh signal-caller made against the Maroon.

aerials for 88 yards and two touchdowns. In the process, the future Canadian Football League player set single-season school records for pass receptions (88), receiving yards (1,318), and TD receptions (15).

The Engineers' leading receiver in The Game was actually Mark LaFeir, a burly 6' 6", 248-pound tight end. He lassoed a career-best 10 balls, then bulled his way through the Leopards defense for 141 yards and two scores.

Injury-plagued tailback Mark Lookenbill closed his college-playing days by catching two touchdowns and rushing for 120 yards on 25 carries.

For Lafayette, Marsh was a one-man gang. He ran 25 times for 249 yards, including a 62-yard dash down the right sideline for a touchdown which brought Lafayette to within 19-14 with 5:16 left in the half. His three-game rushing performance against Lehigh totalled 664 yards — a career for most ordinary players. In The Game, the former Bethlehem Catholic All-Stater broke the Patriot League career rushing mark of 3,461 held by Holy Cross' Joe Segreti. Marsh's season total of 1,441 rushing yards surpassed Tom Costello's school mark of 1,397.

Three in a Row

Lehigh-Lafayette soon became synonymous with the Patriot League Championship game. For the third consecutive year, the

Cradle Of Quarterbacks

During Hank Small's eight years on South Mountain, Lehigh became a haven for strong-armed quarterbacks who filled the air with pigskins and filled the scoreboard with points. A passing offense ranked in the nation's top ten became common-place.

From 1988 through 1993, Lehigh QB's passed for over 3,000 yards each season.

Jim Harris and Mark McGowan combined for 3,484 in 1988, and Todd Brunner passed for 3,516 yards in 1989. Glenn Kempa followed with back-to-back 3,000-yard seasons in 1990 and 1991. Kempa's 3,565 yards in 1990 still stands as a school record. Scott Semptimphelter repeated the feat with 3,000-yard seasons in '92 and '93.

The yardage marks from 1989 through 1993 are the top-five in Lehigh seasonal history.

The top three single-season leaders in TD passes and completions (Kempa — 31 TD's and 286 completions in '91; Semptimphelter — 30 and 249 in '93; and Brunner —26 and 273 in '89) were all established under Small's reign.

Kempa is third on the all-time passing yardage list with 6,732 and third in touchdowns with 49. Semptimphelter stands fourth in career passing yardage with 6,668 and second in TD's with 50, while McGowan ranks fifth in career yardage with 4,838.

Brunner, McGowan, Semptimphelter, and Kempa are one, two, three, and five in career completion percentage.

The top eight single-game passing yardage marks (all over 420 yards per game) were established during Small's tenure.

Patriot League title was decided in the season-ending contest.

With the hope of defending its Patriot crown, Lehigh entered The Game with a 3-1 league mark and a 5-4-1 overall under new coach Kevin Higgins.

Meanwhile, Lafayette lost its first six games of 1994 against non-conference opponents. The Leopards then won their next five against Patriot League foes, including a 54-20 rout of Lehigh for a third league title in seven years.

Lafayette's 54-point outburst against Lehigh was the most by the 'Pards in The Game since a 64-0 blanking of the Engineers in 1944 and third highest in series' history by the Eastonians.

From the opening snap, it was the Erik Marsh and the Leopards show. On the first play from scrimmage, Lafayette's all-time leading ground-gainer took a sweep pitch around left end. Thirty-eight yards later, with Lehigh defenders left clutching at nothing but air, Lafayette was on its way to capping an astonishing turn-around season.

The senior tailback went out in style. Before the afternoon was over, Marsh made three appearances in the end zone. It was his third straight 200-yard day against the

A Gentleman's Bet

The mayors of Easton and Bethlehem shook hands and agreed to a friendly wager on the outcome of the Lafayette-Lehigh game.

Tom Goldsmith, mayor of Easton and Lafayette Class of '63, wagered a case of Crayola crayons donated by its Easton-based manufacturer Binney and Smith on his Leopards.

Bethlehem mayor Ken Smith, a Lehigh grad Class of '61, offered an assorted case of Mike and Ikes candy provided by its Christmas City producer Just Born Inc.

Each company donated 500 boxes of its goodies for the wager with the winning mayor's local Boys and Girls Club receiving the prize.

Ground Marsh

Erik Marsh made the Lehigh game his own personal showcase. The Hellertown native used four huge games against the Engineers as the springboard to propel him to the top of the all-time Patriot League and Lafayette College record books.

His 4,824 yards rushing is a Patriot League and Lafayette career standard. He also holds the school-record for most yards in a season with 1,441, and rushing attempts in a game, season, and career.

Marsh's 878 yards rushing in his four Lehigh games would place him 11th on the all-time Lafayette career list.

Lafayette's Erik Marsh rushed for 878 yards in four games against Lehigh.

Engineers and his 214 yards upped his four-year total against Lehigh to 878 yards. He was a unanimous selection for The Game's MVP award which was his second.

Former defensive back Tremont Evans, the man who made the game and title-clinching interception of a Lehigh pass as time expired in the 1992 contest, caught two scoring rockets from his new position. The wide-out split double coverage for one TD, triple coverage for another. Freshman-eligible quarterback Shawn McHale threaded the seams on both strikes.

McHale was the third quarterback of the season for Lafayette. The uncertainty at the position, along with an inexperienced offensive line, created the early-season problems. Defenses were able to overload against Marsh and ignore a non-existent air attack. In fact, Marsh was held under 100 yards in each of Lafayette's first four games but erupted as usual against the Brown and White.

While the Leopard offense was running like uncaged animals over the Fisher Field turf, the defense was caging the Engineers. The 'Pards

Tailback U.

Against Lehigh, Lafayette is a regular Tailback U. During the Colonial/ Patriot League years, every Leopard victory over the Engineers was marked by "career games" by the person manning the tailback post.

In 1984, Ryan Priest rushed for 174 yards and one touchdown on 36 carries in Lafayette's 28-7 triumph.

In 1986, Bruce McIntyre gained 251 yards on 35 carries and the Most Valuable Player Trophy in the Leopard's 28-23 win.

Tom Costello ran for 216 yards and one TD on 37 handles - winning the 1988 MVP award in leading Lafayette to a 52-45 victory.

Repeating as the Most Valuable Player in 1989 on the strength of a 45-carry, four-touchdown, 245-yard performance, Costello paced the Leopards' 36-21 conquest of Lehigh.

Erik Marsh set a school record with his 46 carries in the 1992 Lehigh game. He ran for 251 yards and a six-pointer and rushed off with the MVP award in the Leopards 32-29 triumph.

It was more Marsh in 1994, unanimously selected The Game's MVP for a record-tying second time. On the strength of the captain's 34 carries for 221 yards and three touchdowns, the Leopards won 54-20.

Five of the top fifteen Lafayette single-game rushing marks were set against Lehigh during these 10 years.

Coach Bill Russo reflected on the successes experienced in the Lehigh game. "Every time we've won this game, we've had a monster performance from our tailback. Tommy Costello, Bruce McIntyre, Erik Marsh . . . the bread and butter guys in our offense. Our plan was to get the most from our tailback in the last game of the season.

"You'd think they'd figure out our game plan by now," Russo added jokingly.

recovered two LU fumbles, picked-off five passes, and tallied three sacks.

Defensive end Harrison Bailey's sack of Bob Aylsworth in the first quarter was his school-record 25th, surpassing Mike King's standard of 24 set in the early 80's.

Maroon placekicker Jason McLaughlin booted a school and league-record 41st career field goal in the final stanza to join Marsh and Bailey as record-setters in the 130th renewal of college football's most-played rivalry.

Jason McLaughlin's field goal against Lehigh in 1994 established a new school and Patriot League record for career field goals (41).

Harrison Bailey's 25 sacks are the most in Lafayette history.

Fourth Quarter Wrap-Up (1984-1994)

The final gun sounds, the teams shake hands in the spirit of competition, the bands play on, and fans swarm the field. The Fourth Quarter becomes part of the history of College Football's Most-Played Rivalry. As The Game moves into its second century, the stories and glories continued to roll during the Patriot League years.

- ✔✎ A student-athlete sports league is established, producing NCAA championship qualifiers, Academic All-Americans, and a Fulbright scholar.

- ✔✎ Fantastic finishes and freshmen phenoms hit the spotlight.

- ✔✎ Foes and friends are mauled by a leopard, and female Leopards are unleashed in a calendar.

- ✔✎ The Game turns offensive both on and off the field. Air wars and ground attacks fill game-time strategy, while postgame battles feature hand-to-hand combatants.

- ✔✎ A Priest saves the day, while a Horn strikes at the right time for big Benn.

- ✔✎ Records are buried as is an ancient stadium, but spirits remain high in spite of a sympathy message at practice.

- ✔✎ Comedians take center-stage for the pregame pep rally, which goes out with a bang.

- ✔✎ Fumblerooskis score big on the gridiron, but a big medal gets booted in the press box.

- ✔✎ Two hundred-yard individual rushing performances fall like goalposts in The Game, as do 300, then 400-yard passing efforts.

- ✔✎ A national championship coach retires at one school, and another coach restores national prominence to the other.

> ## Overtime and Postseason Play
>
> The Patriot League's Council of Presidents approved two changes for the 1995 season. First, the league's presidents voted to allow its football playing members to participate in postseason play. Previously, the football teams were not eligible for the Division I-AA playoffs. Second, the presidents announced overtime would be played in league games. If a game is tied after regulation, the team winning the coin toss will be given the ball on the opponent's 25-yard line. The first team to score more than its opponent after an equal number of possessions wins.

✔✍ Sub-zero wind chills greet the farewell to Taylor. Nevertheless, fans stay to bid farewell with chain saws, sledge hammers, and hatchets.

✔✍ Ninety-seven points, 1,250-plus total yards, and 372-yards passing in the first half by the losing quarterback greet fans in The Game which secures a first Colonial League championship.

✔✍ A quarterback is named first team All-American. Another records better stats than a future Super Bowl-winning quarterback. A third graces the cover of *Sports Illustrated.*

✔✍ The 125th renewal welcomes a new state-of-the-art stadium.

✔✍ Morning kick-offs are started, and students mourn the demise of the goalpost destruction.

✔✍ Betting action takes a new twist, as politicians get involved.

✔✍ A team finishes two points from perfect but doesn't win the league championship.

✔✍ The schools combine for four titles.

✔✍ The Game becomes a match of "Tailback U" against the "Cradle of Quarterbacks."

Fourth Quarter (1984-1994)

Lehigh Coaches: Record vs Lafayette

Coach	Season	Wins	Losses	Ties
John Whitehead	1984-85	1	1	0
Hank Small	1986-93	4	4	0
Kevin Higgins	1994-	0	1	0
Total		5	6	0

Lafayette Coaches: Record vs Lehigh

Coach	Season	Wins	Losses	Ties
Bill Russo	1984-	6	5	0

Fourth Quarter (1984-1994) Summary

			SCORE	
Year	Where Played	Winner	Lafayette	Lehigh
1984	Easton	Lafayette	28	7
1985	Bethlehem	Lehigh	19	24
1986	Easton	Lafayette	28	23
1987	Bethlehem	Lehigh	10	17
1988	Easton	Lafayette	52	45
1989	Bethlehem	Lafayette	36	21
1990	Easton	Lehigh	14	35
1991	Bethlehem	Lehigh	18	36
1992	Easton	Lafayette	32	29
1993	Bethlehem	Lehigh	14	39
1994	Easton	Lafayette	54	20
			305	296

	Wins	Losses	Ties
Lafayette	6	5	0
Lehigh	5	6	0

OVERALL SUMMARY	Lafayette			Lehigh		
	Wins	Losses	Ties	Wins	Losses	Ties
First Quarter (1884-1905)	21	16	2	16	21	2
Second Quarter (1906-1949)	34	11	1	11	34	1
Third Quarter (1950-1983)	10	22	2	22	10	2
Fourth Quarter (1984-1994)	6	5	0	5	6	0
Grand Total (1884-1994)	71	54	5	54	71	5

Legends: Postgame Wrap-Up

MVP Award Winners

Year	Player	Team	Position	
1960	Al Richmond	Lehigh	RB	
1961	Boyd Taylor	Lehigh	RB	
1962	Walt King	Lehigh	QB	
1963	Les Kish	Lehigh	QB	
1964	George Hossenlopp	Lafayette	QB	(first Lafayette player to win)
1965	Hal Yeich	Lehigh	RB	
1966	Rick Craw	Lafayette	RB	
1967	Art Renfro	Lehigh	LB	(first defensive player to win; first player on losing team to win)
1968	Jim Petrillo	Lehigh	RB	
1969	Don Diorio	Lehigh	RB	
1970	Rick Nowell	Lafayette	WR/PK	
1971	Jack Rizzo	Lehigh	RB	
1972	Kim McQuilken	Lehigh	QB	
1973	Kim McQuilken	Lehigh	QB	(first to win twice and back-to-back)
1974	Joe Alleva	Lehigh	QB	
1975	Joe Sterrett	Lehigh	QB	
1976	Mark Jones	Lafayette	QB	
	Rod Gardner	Lehigh	RB	(first and only co-MVP winners)
1977	Mike Rieker	Lehigh	QB	
1978	Steve Kreider	Lehigh	WR	
1979	Joe Rabuck	Lehigh	RB	
1980	Mike Crowe	Lehigh	DE	(second defensive player to win)
1981	Frank Novak	Lafayette	QB	
1982	Jack Gatehouse	Lafayette	WR	
1983	Marty Horn	Lehigh	QB	
1984	Jim Johnson	Lafayette	QB	
1985	Marty Horn	Lehigh	QB	(second player to win twice)
1986	Bruce McIntyre	Lafayette	RB	
1987	Mark McGowan	Lehigh	QB	
1988	Tom Costello	Lafayette	RB	
1989	Tom Costello	Lafayette	RB	(second player to win twice in a row)
1990	Erick Torain	Lehigh	RB	
1991	Glenn Kempa	Lehigh	QB	
1992	Erik Marsh	Lafayette	RB	
1993	Scott Semptimphelter	Lehigh	QB	
1994	Erik Marsh	Lafayette	RB	

Hall of Fame

Lehigh Hall of Fame

	Inducted
John Hill '72	1992
Bill Leckonby (Coach)	1992
V.J. Pat Pazzetti Jr. '15	1992
Dick Gabriel '51	1994
John Whitehead (Coach)	1995
Kim McQuilken '74	1995
Steve Kreider '79	1995
Allen Ware '32	1995

Maroon Club Athletic Hall of Fame

	Inducted
Charles Berry '25	1976
G. Herbert McCracken (Coach)	1976
Charles Rinehart 1898	1976
Frank J. "Dutch" Schwab '23	1976
Walter Zirinsky '42	1976
Walter "Scrappy" Bachman '02	1977
Mike Gazella '23	1977
Edward "Hook" Mylin (Coach)	1977
Donald J. Nikles '60	1977
George "Mike" Wilson '29	1978
Tony Giglio '74	1981
George "Rose" Barclay 1898	1984
George McCaa '10	1985
George "Sammy" Moyer '41	1985
Harold Bellis '40	1986
John "Jock" Sutherland (Coach)	1987
James T. Farrell '41	1989
John M. Quigg '40	1990
Joseph Skladany '82	1990
David W. Brown '66	1991
Tony Green '83	1992
Joe Bozik '58	1993
William McKnight '43	1993

Lafayette All-Americans

Player	Year	Position	All-American Team
Charles Rinehart	1897	Guard	Walter Camp (2nd Team)
George Walbridge	1897	Back	Walter Camp (3rd Team)
Henry Trout	1899	Guard	Walter Camp (3rd Team)
David Cure	1900-01	Fullback	Walter Camp (2nd Team)
Walter Bachman	1900-01	Center	Walter Camp (2nd Team)
George McCaa	1908-09	Fullback	Walter Camp (3rd Team)
Joseph DuMoe	1919	End	Walter Camp (2nd Team)
Frank Schwab	1921-22	Guard	Walter Camp (1st Team)
Arthur Deibel	1923	Tackle	Walter Camp (2nd Team)
Charles Berry	1924	End	Walter Camp (1st Team)
George Wilson	1926	Halfback	*New York Sun* (2nd Team)
			New York Telegraph (3rd Team)
Frank Kirkleski	1926	Halfback	*New York Telegraph* (2nd Team)
			The New York World (3rd Team)
Bill Cothran	1926	Tackle	*New York Telegraph* (2nd Team)
Tony Cavallo	1937	Halfback	Associated Press (Honorable Mention)
James Farrell	1940	Halfback	Associated Press (Honorable Mention)
George Mayer	1940	Halfback	Associated Press (Honorable Mention)
Tony Giglio	1972	Halfback	Associated Press (Honorable Mention)
Blake Steele	1977	Defensive Tackle	Associated Press (Honorable Mention)
Rob Stewart	1977	Quarterback	Associated Press (Honorable Mention)
Tim Gerhart	1978	Defensive End	Associated Press (Honorable Mention)
	1979	Defensive End	Associated Press (2nd Team)
Bob Rasp	1979	Defensive Back	Associated Press (Honorable Mention)
Dave Shea	1979	Defensive Back	Associated Press (Honorable Mention)
Joe Skaldany	1979	Linebacker	Associated Press (Honorable Mention)
	1981	Linebacker	Associated Press (1st Team)
Rich Smith	1979	Tight End	Associated Press (Honorable Mention)
Steve Biale	1981	Offensive Guard	Associated Press (Honorable Mention)
Rodger Shepko	1981	Halfback	Associated Press (Honorable Mention)
Tony Green	1982	Middle Guard	Kodak
			Associated Press (Honorable Mention)
Frank Novak	1982	Quarterback	Associated Press (Honorable Mention)
Ed Stahl	1982	Offensive Tackle	Associated Press (Honorable Mention)
Ryan Priest	1984	Running Back	Associated Press (Honorable Mention)
Frank Baur	1988	Quarterback	Associated Press (1st Team)
			Football Gazette (1st Team)
			Sports Network (2nd Team)
	1990	Quarterback	Hula Bowl Selection
Tom Costello	1988	Running Back	Associated Press (Honorable Mention)
Phillip Ng	1988	Wide Receiver	Associated Press (Honorable Mention)
Ed Hudak	1991	Offensive Guard	Sports Network (Honorable Mention)
	1992	Offensive Guard	Kodak
			Football Gazette (1st Team)
			Associated Press (2nd Team)
			Sports Network (Honorable Mention)
Dave Pyne	1993	Offensive Guard	Hula Bowl Selction
Ed Sasso	1993	Defensive Tackle	Sports Network (Honorable Mention)
Erik Marsh	1993	Tailback	Sports Network (Honorable Mention)
	1993	Tailback	All-Fraternity (1st Team)

Lehigh All-Americans

Player	Year	Position	All-American Team
D.M. Balliet	1891	Center	Walter Camp (2nd Team)
C.E. Trafton	1893	Guard	Walter Camp (3rd Team)
Pat Pazzetti	1912	Quarterback	Walter Camp (2nd Team)
Billy Cahall	1914	Halfback	Walter Camp (2nd Team)
Dick Gabriel	1949	Running Back	Associated Press (1st Team)
Robert Numbers	1949	Center	Associated Press (1st Team)
Bill Ciarvino	1950	Guard/Linebacker	Associated Press (1st Team)
Dick Doyne	1950	Running Back	Associated Press (1st Team)
Walt Meincke	1959	Tackle	Associated Press (1st Team)
John Hill	1971	Center	Associated Press (1st Team)
Kim McQuilken	1973	Quarterback	Associated Press (1st Team)
			Kodak
Bill Schlegel	1973	Tight End	Associated Press (2nd Team)
Rod Gardner	1975	Running Back	Associated Press (2nd Team)
Joe Sterrett	1975	Quarterback	Kodak
Mark Orcutt	1976	Offensive Tackle	Associated Press (2nd Team)
Steve Kreider	1977	Wide Receiver	Associated Press (1st Team)
Mike Rieker	1977	Quarterback	Associated Press (3rd Team)
			Kodak
Dave Melone	1979	Offensive Tackle	Associated Press (1st Team)
			Kodak
Jim McCormick	1979	Linebacker	Associated Press (2nd Team)
			Kodak
Mark Yeager	1980	Wide Receiver	Associated Press (3rd Team)
Bruce Rarig	1980	Linebacker	Kodak
John Shigo	1983	Linebacker	Kodak
Wes Walton	1983	Defensive Tackle	Associated Press (3rd Team)
	1984	Defensive Tackle	Associated Press (2nd Team)
Rennie Benn	1983	Wide Receiver	Associated Press (Honorable Mention)
	1984	Wide Receiver	Associated Press (2nd Team)
	1985	Wide Receiver	Associated Press (Honorable Mention)
			Kodak
Dave Whitehead	1984	Center	Associated Press (Honorable Mention)
Marty Horn	1985	Quarterback	Associated Press (Honorable Mention)
Joe Uliana	1986	Offensive Guard	Associated Press (Honorable Mention)
	1987	Offensive Guard	Associated Press (Honorable Mention)
Mike Kosko	1986	Defensive Tackle	Associated Press (Honorable Mention)
Kent Weaver	1988	Offensive Tackle	Sports Network (Honorable Mention)
Bob Varano	1989	Tight End	Associated Press (2nd Team)
			Sports Network (2nd Team)
Keith Petzold	1990	Offensive Guard	Kodak
			Sports Network (Honorable Mention)
Horace Hamm	1991	Wide Receiver	Associated Press (2nd Team)
			Sports Network (1st Team)
Mike Moriarty	1991	Offensive Line	Sports Network (2nd Team)
Glenn Kempa	1991	Quarterback	Sports Network (Honorable Mention)
Jason Cristino	1992	Wide Receiver	Associated Press (2nd Team)
			Sports Network (2nd Team)
Dave Cecchini	1993	Wide Receiver	Associated Press (1st Team)
			Kodak
			Sports Network (1st Team)
Craig Melograno	1993	Punter	Associated Press (3rd Team)
			Sports Network (2nd Team)

Game Records

Team

Rushing Yardage
528 yards　　Lafayette　　vs Lehigh 1943
506 yards　　Lehigh　　vs Lafayette 1971

Passing Yardage
495 yards　　Lehigh　　vs Lafayette 1988
309 yards　　Lafayette　　vs Lehigh 1988

Most Pass Attempts
52 attempts　Lafayette　　vs Lehigh 1943

Total Offense
664 yards　　Lehigh　　vs Lafayette 1971
628 yards　　Lafayette　　vs Lehigh 1988

Most Punts
22 punts　　Lafayette　　vs Lehigh 1938

Individual

Most Passing Yardage
480 yards　　**Semptimphelter**　Lehigh　　vs Lafayette 1992
309 yards　　**Frank Baur**　　Lafayette　vs Lehigh 1988

Most TD Passes
6 TD's　　　**Semptimphelter**　Lehigh　　vs Lafayette 1993

Most Pass Receiving Yardage
319 yards　　**Jason Cristino**　Lehigh　　vs Lafayette 1992
167 yards　　**Dave Baird**　　Lafayette　vs Lehigh 1990

Most Rushing Yardage
313 yards　　**Jack Rizzo**　　Lehigh　　vs Lafayette 1971
256 yards　　**Jack O' Reilly**　Lafayette　vs Lehigh 1927

Most Rushing Attempts
46 attempts　**Erik Marsh**　　Lafayette　vs Lehigh 1992
36 attempts　**Erick Torain**　Lehigh　　vs Lafayette 1990

Most Points Scored
30 points　　**Fred Robbins**　Lafayette　vs Lehigh 1944
24 points　　**Jack Rizzo**　　Lehigh　　vs Lafayette 1971

Longest Punt Return
92 yards　　**Ryan Priest**　　Lafayette　vs Lehigh 1982

Most Punts
22 punts　　**Sam Moyer**　　Lafayette　vs Lehigh 1938

Longest Interception Return
99 yards　　**Steve Boyanoski**　Lafayette　vs Lehigh 1978

Most Interceptions
3 int's　　　**Don Hughes**　　Lafayette　vs Lehigh 1967

Most Sacks
5 sacks　　　**Brian Guttman**　Lafayette　vs Lehigh 1982

Lehigh's Jason Cristino holds the record for most yards receiving in a Lehigh-Lafayette game. Cristino's 319 yards in the 1992 game is also a school record.

College Football's Top 10 Most-Played Rivalries

> "It (college football) is a game of ancient rivalries that inspires genuine loathing, not for a weekend but for a lifetime. It is traditional games, whose meaning is deep ... there is a spirit about it, a drawing together."
>
> — John Underwood, _Sports Illustrated_

Rank	Teams	Games Played (including 1994 season)
1	Lafayette-Lehigh	130
2	Yale-Princeton	117
3	Yale-Harvard	111
4	Amherst-Williams	109
5	Albion-Kalamazoo	107
6	Knox-Monmouth (Illinois)	106
7	Minnesota-Wisconsin	104
8	Richmond-William & Mary	104
9	Coe-Cornell (Indiana)	104
10	Kansas-Missouri	103

Anniversary Years

Year	Anniversary	Site	Score	
1895	25th Game	Easton	Lafayette 14	Lehigh 6
1916	50th Game	Easton	Lehigh 17	Lafayette 0
1941	75th Game	Bethlehem	Lafayette 47	Lehigh 7
1964	100th Game	Easton	Lafayette 6	Lehigh 6
1989	125th Game	Bethlehem	Lafayette 36	Lehigh 21

Most Coaching Victories in The Game

Rank	Coach	Team		Victories
1	Herb McCracken	Lafayette	(1924-35)	9
2	Bill Russo	Lafayette	(1981-)	8
2	Fred Dunlap	Lehigh	(1965-75)	8
4	Bill Leckonby	Lehigh	(1946-61)	7
5	John Whitehead	Lehigh	(1976-85)	6

Coach Bill Russo, who is one victory away from tying Herb McCracken for most victories in The Rivalry.

Top 10 Blowouts

Rank	Year	Winner	Score	Margin of Victory
1	1917	Lehigh	78-0	78
2	1944	Lafayette	64-0	64
3	1890	Lehigh	66-6	60
4	1943	Lafayette	58-0	58
5	1905	Lafayette	53-0	53
6	1884	Lafayette	50-0	50
7	1974	Lehigh	57-7	50
8	1935	Lehigh	48-0	48
9	1940	Lafayette	46-0	46
10	1954	Lafayette	46-0	46

Lehigh 50-Game Club

John Latimer '18	(50 games)
George Stutz '22	(73 games)
Russell Rubba '23	(60 games)
Laurence Kingham '25	(66 games)
John Maxwell '26	(61 games)
Alden McFarlan '26	(57 games)
Victor Schwimmer '26	(57 games)
Roger Miller '27	(52 games)
Morgan Cramer '28	(58 games)
Earl Diener '28	(58 games)
Edwin Werley '30	(58 games)
Ben Bishop '34	(66 games)
Edgar Howells '34	(62 games)
Milton Hutt, Sr. '34	(60 games)
Curtis Bayer '35	(67 games)
James Mayshark '36	(54 games)
Robert Reber '41	(62 games)
William Toohey, Jr. '41	(56 games)
Frank Roberts '42	(51 games)
Abram Samuels '42	(59 games)
James Niemeyer '43	(54 games)
Wayne Riddle '43	(58 games)
Carson Diefenderfer '44	(51 games)
Peter Facchiano '45	(54 games)
Michael Drozd '46	(57 games)
Samuel Croll, Jr. '48	(53 games)
Lee Barthold, Jr. '50	(52 games)
Richard Jones '54	(57 games)
Lawrence Sheridan '58	(54 games)
Daniel Bayer '59	(52 games)

Lafayette 20-Game Club

Carl Carlstrom '59
Bruce Drinkhouse '50
Dutch Dworsak '36
Guy Elzey '49
James Farrell '41
Leonard Fox '51
Stanley Kulaitis, Jr. '41
Kermit Green, Jr. '56
Robert Leciston '63
James Madara '50
Charles Morgan '42
Charles Mueller '52
Anthony Noto '41
Hilton Rahn, Jr. '51

Longest Win Streaks In The Series

Team	Streak	Games
Lafayette	10 games	1919-1928
Lafayette	9 games	1943 (2)
		1944 (2)
		1945-49
Lafayette	7 games	1898 (2nd of 2)
		1899 (2 of 2)
		1900 (2 of 2)
		1901 (2 of 2)
Lehigh	5 games	1890 (2 of 2)
		1891 (3 of 3)
Lafayette	5 games	1937-41
Lehigh	5 games	1971-75
Lafayette	4 games	1895 (2 of 2)
		1896 (did not play)
		1897 (2 of 2)
Lafayette	4 games	1904-07
Lafayette	4 games	1930-33
Lehigh	4 games	1960-63
Lehigh	4 games	1977-80

LEHIGH: Top 10 Season Point Totals

Rank	Season	Point Total
1	1977	466 (^)
2	1975	430 (^)
3	1989	371
4	1991	363
5	1971	362
6	1889	359 (^^)
7	1988	351
8	1973	366 (^)
9	1903	331
10	1980	350 (^)

(^) includes playoff games
(^^) 13 regular season games

LAFAYETTE: Top 10 Season Point Totals

Rank	Season	Point Total
1	1988	420
2	1992	382
3	1982	335
4	1927	327
5	1989	319
6	1905	313
7	1986	306
8	1981	300
9	1983	293
10	1948	277
10	1991	277

Lehigh Players In The Pros

ATLANTA FALCONS
Kim McQuilken, QB, 1973-78
Horace Hamm, WR, 1992

BALTIMORE COLTS (CFL)
Jarrod Johnson, C, 1994

CINCINNATI BENGALS
Steve Kreider, WR, 1979-86
Kevin Jefferson, 1994

NEW YORK GIANTS
Reed Bohovich, T, 1962-63
Jack Rizzo, RB, 1972
John Hill, T, 1972-74

NEW ORLEANS
John Hill, T, 1975-84

SAN DIEGO CHARGERS
Jarrod Johnson, OT, 1991

SAN FRANCISCO 49ers
Pete Williams, OT, 1958

TORONTO ARGONAUTS (CFL)
Claudio Bertone, FB, 1994
Dave Cecchini, WR, 1994

WASHINGTON REDSKINS
Kim McQuilken, QB, 1978-80

GREEN BAY PACKERS
Horace Hamm, WR, 1992-1993

CINCINNATI BENGALS
Kevin Jefferson, LB, 1994-

WASHINGTON REDSKINS
Rich Owens, DL, 1995

DALLAS COWBOYS
Scott Sempimphelter, QB, 1995

Note: No former Lafayette football players have been signed to a professional football team.

Lafayette School Records

Career Rushing Yards

	Years	Yards
1. Erik Marsh	1991-94	4,834
2. Tom Costello	1988-90	2,936
3. Ryan Priest	1982-85	2,597
4. Tony Giglio	1971-73	2,519
5. Bruce McIntyre	1983-86	2,169

Career Passing Yards

	Years	Yards
1. Frank Baur	1985-89 (*)	8,399
2. Tom Kirchhoff	1989-92	6,721
3. Frank Novak	1981-83	6,378
4. Ed Baker	1967-69	2,921
5. Mark Jones	1973-76	2,782

(*) did not play 1986 season

Frank Baur — Lafayette's All-Time passing leader and first Leopard to participate in the Hula Bowl.

Career Receiving Yards

	Years	Rec.	Yards
1. Philip Ng	1985-88	152	2,111
2. Frank Corbo	1981-84	136	1,970
3. Dave Baird	1988-90	92	1,681
4. Jamal Jordan	1990-92	99	1,634
5. Bob Donofrio	1968-70	75	1,364

Lehigh School Records

Career Rushing Yards

	Years	Yards
1. Rod Gardner	1972-75	3,188
2. Dick Gabriel	1948-50	2,506
3. Lee Blum	1983-86	2,398
4. Erick Torain	1987-90	2,397
5. Jack Rizzo	1968-71	2,216

Career Passing Yards

	Years	Yards
1. Marty Horn	1982-85	9,120
2. Kim McQuilken	1970-73	6,996
3. Glenn Kempa	1990-91	6,732
4. S. Semptimphelter	1992-93	6,668
5. Mark McGowan	1986-88	4,838

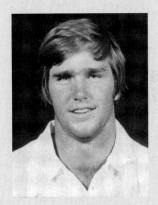

Rod Gardner — Lehigh's All-Time leading ground-gainer.

Career Receiving Yards

	Years	Rec.	Yards
1. Rennie Benn	1983-85	237	3,662
2. Horace Hamm	1988-91	158	2,540
3. Rich Clark	1988-91	160	2,386
4. Rob Varano	1986-89	152	2,383
5. Bill Schlegel	1970-73	139	2,204

Greatest Upsets

1915

Lafayette snaps a three-game losing streak against Lehigh, 35-6, and hands the Brown and White their first loss at Taylor Stadium after 13 consecutive wins.

1929

Entering The Game, Lafayette rode a ten-game winning streak against Lehigh. Over this period, the Maroon won two National Championships and sported a 67-15-6 mark. Meanwhile, Lehigh carried a 36-43-9 record over the same time frame. Behind two blocked extra point by Lehigh's Tubby Miller and a game-ending goal line stand, the Brown and White stunned their heavily favored guests 13-12.

1949

A 1-6 Lafayette squad entered Taylor Stadium against a 6-2 Lehigh team which arguably had the best running back tandem in the east. Dick Gabriel led the east in rushing yards and scoring in 1949, while fellow Engineer Dick Doyne came within 34 yards of shattering his teammate's mark in 1950. Despite being mismatched on paper, the Leopards stunned the Engineers 21-12.

1965

Lehigh, at 0-8, took one of its worst records ever into The Game against a 3-6 Lafayette team. Down 20-0 late in the fourth quarter, Lafayette scored on an 84-yard kick-off runback and a 47-yard interception return. With 2:15 remaining, the Leopards' onside kick was recovered by Lehigh, securing the Engineers' lone win of the season for rookie coach Fred Dunlap.

1968

Lafayette, having its most successful campaign in 20 years at 7-2, sat atop the Lambert Cup poll as it prepared for The Game. In addition, the Leopards were undefeated and unscored upon in the four home games prior to the finale with Lehigh. The Engineers limped in with a 2-7 record, but left with a stunning 21-6 defeat of their ancient rivals.

1981

A national semi-finalist from a year ago, Lehigh brought another loaded team into The Game. At 8-2, the Engineers rested atop the Lambert Cup poll and had a virtual lock on their fourth playoff appearance in five campaigns. Lafayette, under new coach Bill Russo, quietly entered The Game with the same 8-2 mark. In a hard-fought defensive battle, a Roger Shepko fourth quarter touchdown run gave the Leopards a stunning 10-3 victory. Despite the win, Lafayette was not invited to post-season competition and finished only third in the Lambert race.

Legends **Trivia Questions**

Q1. What player in The Rivalry was credited with inventing the football helmet?

Q2. Only once was The Game not played in Bethlehem or Easton. Name the location.

Q3. Have Lehigh and Lafayette ever played more than twice in a season?

Q4. What was the only year that Lafayette and Lehigh did not play?

Q5. Name the quaterback that completed the first touchdown pass in The Game.

Q6. Name the halfback who bested Olympian Jim Thorpe in the 100-yard dash at a track meet in Easton.

Q7. Name the only Lehigh-Lafayette player to be inducted into the College Football Hall of Fame.

Q8. This person was a head coach at both schools, and played eight years of college football, four each at Williams and at Penn. Name him.

Q9. Taking a cue from a "wrong-way" touchdown run, this gridder later played professional baseball for the Detroit Tigers, Philadelphia Athletics, and Brooklyn Dodgers. Name him.

Q10. This Easton native was the only player to tally points for both Lafayette and Lehigh in The Game, and record wins on both sides of The Rivalry. Name him.

Q11. This coach was credited with inventing the huddle.

Q12. Has either school won a National Championship in football?

Q13. Name this quarterback and punter who holds the record for the shortest punt (a negative one-yarder) in The Series' history (Hint his last name is indicative of his punting average).

Q14. This former Lafayette coach holds the NFL single-game scoring record with 40 points and gave up a home run to Babe Ruth. Name him.

Q15. Which school's entire student body was placed on disciplinary probation after the melee of 1959?

Q16. What gridder from the 1950's became a Catholic priest?

Q17. What fraternity owns the longest continuous piece of goalpost from The Game?

Q18. What player was a Heisman Trophy finalist?

Q19. What participant in The Game appeared on the cover of *Sports Illustrated*?

Q20. What losing quarterback passed for 372 yards in the first half of a Game?

(Answers on the following page)

Legends **Trivia Answers**

A1. Lafayette's George Barclay in 1896.

A2. Wilkes-Barre in 1891.

A3. Yes, three times in 1891. Games were held in Easton, Bethlehem, and Wilkes-Barre.

A4. In 1896, due to a dispute over a player's (George Barclay) eligibility.

A5. Lafayette's Edward Flad threw the first TD pass to H. G. Lee on a six-yard scoring strike.

A6. Lafayette's John Spiegel.

A7. Lehigh's triple-threat back and first All-American V.J. "Pat" Pazzetti.

A8. S. B. Newton coached Lehigh from 1902-05 and Lafayette from 1898-1901 and 1911.

A9. In the 1918 Game, Lehigh's Raymond "Snooks" Dowd ran the wrong-way, circled his own goalpost, then completed a 115-yard touchdown run that some say went 160.

A10. The vagabond of Lafayette-Lehigh football — Bots Brunner .

A11. In 1924, Lafayette's Herb McCracken instructed his players to receive signals while "huddling together" several yards behind the line of scrimmage.

A12. Yes, Lafayette has won three (1896, 1921, 1926) and Lehigh has won one (1977).

A13. Paul Short of Lehigh in the 1931 Game.

A14. Ernie Nevers coached Lafayette to a 1-8 record in 1936.

A15. Lehigh

A16. Lehigh quarterback Dan Nolan.

A17. Lafayette's Chi Phi house, with the crossbar measuring 23'4" from the 1964 game.

A18. Lehigh quarterback Kim McQuilken in 1973.

A19. Lafayette quarterback Frank Baur on the 1989 college football preview edition.

A20. Lehigh's Jim Harris in Lafayette's 52-45 victory in 1988.

Colonial/Patriot League Champions

Year	League	Winner
1986	Colonial	Holy Cross
1987	Colonial	Holy Cross
1988	Colonial	Lafayette
1989	Colonial	Holy Cross
1990	Patriot	Holy Cross
1991	Patriot	Holy Cross
1992	Patriot	Lafayette
1993	Patriot	Lehigh
1994	Patriot	Lafayette

Legends "All-Berman" Team

Year	Team	Position	Name
1884	Lafayette	S	Nai Kawn "Camera"
1891	Lehigh	C	D.M. "Nutcracker Suite" Balliet
1900	Lafayette	HB	Harry "Rainbow" Trout
1901	Lafayette	Coach	Silvanis "The Big Fig" Newton
1904	Lafayette	HB	James Van Atta "Boy"
1910	Lafayette	HB	John Spiegel "Catalog"
1927	Lafayette	HB	"Yukon" Jack O'Reilly
1931	Lafayette	HB	Slippery "When Wet" Socolow
1931	Lehigh	HB	Allen "Tupper" Ware
1932	Lehigh	HB	Warren "The Real" McCoy
1934	Lehigh	FB	"Yule" Log Pennauchi
1934	Lehigh	QB	"Fort" Knox Peet
1938	Lehigh	P	Steve "Gun" Smoke
1944	Lafayette	WR/HB	Fred "Baskin and" Robbins
1947	Lafayette	E	Todd "Sinbad the" Saylor
1949	Lafayette	RB	Jack ".306" Savage
1949	Lehigh	C	Robert "Paint By The" Numbers
1951	Lafayette	Coach	"Some People Call Me" Maurice Smith
1952	Lehigh	WR	Tommy "Machine" Gunn
1953	Lafayette	E	Tom "Monty Python and the Holy" McGrail
1956	Lafayette	K	Pat Tidey "Bowl Man"
1957	Lehigh	RB	Charley "Bacon Cheese" Burger
1958	Lehigh	T	Walt "I'm Not Going To Pay a lot For This Muffler" Meincke
1962	Lehigh	QB	Walt "It's Good To Be The" King
1962	Lehigh	WR	Pat Clark "Bar"
1962	Lehigh	E	Harold Milton "The Toaster"
1963	Lafayette	Coach	Kenneth "Hot Dog" Bunn
1963	Lehigh	QB	Les "Ham and Spinach" Kish
1964	Lafayette	T	Douglas Dill "Pickle"
1964	Lafayette	G	Richard Peel "and Eat Shrimp"
1964	Lehigh	T	John Bissett "Hound"
1965	Lehigh	Coach	Fred Dunlap "Tires"
1966	Lafayette	QB	Gary "U.S. Bonds" Marshall
1968	Lehigh	FB	Justin "Time" Plummer
1971	Lehigh	RB	Jack "The Ripper" Rizzo
1971	Lafayette	QB	Tim "Vice" Grip
1972	Lafayette	RB	Tony "American" Giglio

Legends "All-Berman" Team

Year	Team	Position	Name
1972	Lehigh	K	Chuck "Motor" Merolla
1973	Lehigh	RB	Rod "Vegetable" Gardner
1976	Lafayette	DB	Tom "Ruffed" Crouse
1976	Lafayette	QB	Mark "I've Got a Basketball" Jones
1976	Lehigh	K	Greg "Mrs. T's" Pierog
1977	Lehigh	RB	Lennie "Jack" Daniels
1977	Lehigh	RB	Dave April "Showers"
1977	Lehigh	OG	Jim "I Know Nuthing" Schulze
1979	Lehigh	QB	Rich Andres "Fault"
1979	Lafayette	DB	Dave Shea "Stadium"
1980	Lafayette	Coach	Neil Putnam "on the Hits"
1980	Lehigh	WR	Mark Yeager "Meister"
1981	Lehigh	K	Mike Whalen "Guitar"
1983	Lehigh	S	Jim "Bubble" Gum
1983	Lehigh	K	Jim "Great" Scott
1983	Lehigh	DT	Wayne "Rock the" Kasbar
1983	Lehigh	MG	Wes "John Boy" Walton
1984	Lafayette	WR	Jim "My" Johnson
1988	Lafayette	RB	Tom "Abbott and" Costello
1989	Lafayette	WR	Philip "I'd Like to Buy a Vowel" Ng
1989	Lafayette	WR	Mike "Quick Draw Mc" Grau
1991	Lehigh	WR	Horace "Green Eggs and" Hamm
1991	Lehigh	C	Chuck Endicott "& Johnson"
1992	Lehigh	OG	Calvin "and" Hobbs
1993	Lafayette	OG	Dave Pyne "Tree"
1994	Lafayette	RB	Erik Marsh "Mallow"

Philip "I'd Like to Buy a Vowel" Ng,
Lafayette's All-Time leading receiver,
heads up *Legends* "All-Berman" Team.

Legends "All-Time" Team Second Half (1950-1994)

OFFENSE

Lafayette		Lehigh
Frank Baur '90	QB	Kim McQuilken '73
Ryan Priest '87	RB	Jack Rizzo '71
Tom Costello '92	RB	Rod Gardner '76
Erik Marsh '95	RB	Erick Torain '92
Frank Corbo '84	WR	Steve Kreider '78
Philip Ng '89	WR	Rennie Benn '85
Craig Roubinek '92	TE	Bill Schlegel '73
Ed Stahl '82	LINE	Walt Meineke '59
Ed Hudak '93	LINE	Joe Uliana '87
Matt Kujovsky '95	LINE	John Hill '71
Dave Pyne '94	LINE	Keith Petzold '90
Steve Biale '81	LINE	Dave Melone '79

Honorable Mention:
Lehigh — Mike Rieker '77 (QB); Marty Horn '86 (QB); Lee Blum '86 (RB); Horace Hamm '91 (WR); Paul Anastasio '81 (TE); Bill Ciarvino '50 (Line); Thad Jamalu (Line); Mark Orcutt '76 (Line)
Lafayette — Frank Novak '84 (QB); Tom Kirchhoff '93 (QB); Tony Giglio '74 (RB); Don Nickles '59 (RB); Jack Gatehouse '82 (WR); Rich Smith '79 (TE)

DEFENSE

Lafayette		Lehigh
Blake Steele '77	LINE	Greg Clarke '77
Tim Gerhart '79	LINE	Mike Crowe '80
Tony Green '83	LINE	Wes Walton '86
Harrison Bailey '95	LINE	Mike Kosko '86
Joe Skladany '82	LB	Jim McCormick '79
Dick Galbally '76	LB	Bruce Rarig '80
Frank Gaziano '86	LB	John Shigo '83
Bob Rasp '80	DB	Joe Macellara '81
Dave Shea '79	DB	Jim Gum '83
Bob Mahr '82	DB	Blair Talmedge '84
Mike Joseph '87	DB	Shon Harker '90

SPECIAL TEAMS

Dave Brown '65	P	Craig Melograno '93
Jason McLaughlin '95	K	Mike Beattie '86
Ryan Priest '85	PR/KR	Mark Weaver '76

COACHES

Bill Russo (1981-__)	John Whitehead (1976-85)

Honorable Mention:
Lehigh — Mike Semcheski '62 (Line); Art Renfro '67 (LB); Tom Clark '91 (DB); Jason Mack '93 (DB); Erik Bird '89 (K)
Lafayette — Rich Doverspike '83 (Line); Ed Sasso '94 (Line); John Anderson '85 (LB); Gene Denahan '61 (DB); Tom Crouse '76 (DB); Bob Sharr '82 (DB); Jim Hodson '90 (K); Bill Vonroth '66 (PR/KR)

Acknowledgements

In order to bring *Legends of Lehigh- Lafayette* to life, the cooperation and involvement of numerous alumni, former players, coaches, sportswriters, sportscasters, band members, cheerleaders, fans, and others connected with the Lehigh-Lafayette football game was necessary. Without their generous time and assistance, much of this book's material would not be possible.

Dr. Peter Likins and Arthur Rothkopf — the schools' Presidents; Athletic Directors Joe Sterrett and Dr. Eve Atkinson; Alumni Directors (both old and new) Don Bott and Barb Turanchik and Debra Lamb; — thanks for all the help and support.

The Sports Information Departments at both schools, directed by Glenn Hofmann and Steve Pulver — thanks for a great job! Likewise for the schools' archivists and staff headed by Marie Boltz and Diane Shaw. It's amazing how much we all discovered about The Rivalry.

Cover design specialist Dave Stevens, photographer Kris Eckenrode, illustrator Tom Hayes, our editor Evie Ishmael — thanks for a tremendous job by all.

Extra special thanks to our friends and families for providing support when it was needed most.

Without the help of the following, the journey of writing and publishing this book certainly would not have been as enjoyable.

Cindy Adams
Craig Anderson
George Andralis
Rich Aronson
Serena Ashmore
Tom Baldo
Evan Baker
Kyle Baker
John Bloys
George Bright
Gimp Brownell
Tim Cirisoli
Jeff Citrone
Frank Claps
Roger Clow
Beano Cook
Dean Davidson
Merlin Davidson
Patty Davidson
Elva Davis
Gene Davis
John Denoia
Denny Diehl
Sean Dobrowolski

Lisa Donchez
Mike Donchez
Robert L. Donchez
Laura D'Orsi
Melisa Filipos
Barry Fetterman
Cy Fleck
Gary Foltz
Chris Fowler
Jean Fowler
K. Hawkeye Gross
Kevin Higgins
Cliff Ishmael
Evie Ishmael
George Kline
Pam Lott
Doc Lutz
John Marynowski
Caroline McAdam
Jack McCallum
Matt Millen
Pete Miller
Harold Milton
Tom Morgan

Jack Park
Agnes Rednagle
Larry Reisman
Anne Ruh
Bill Russo
Dick Ruthart
David Sacher
Paula Sagerman
Greg Schulze
John Shigo
Lauren Simmons
Cathy Smith
Helen Strus
Lincoln Taylor
Richard Thornburgh
Ron Ticho
Janet Tucker
Thad Turner
Joe Uliana
Joe Whritenour
Mark Will-Weber
Newt Wilson
Lesli Wirth
Joe Workman, Sr.

Photographs used with permission of:

Lehigh University Sports Information Department and Special Collections Lehigh University Libraries.

Lafayette College Sports Information Department and Archives.

Pam Lott.

Lehigh-Lafayette MVP and Game Trophies: Courtesy of Lafayette College.

Patriot League Trophy: Courtesy of Lafayette College.

Lehigh Football Equipment: Courtesy of Ron Ticho and Bethlehem Sporting Goods.

Lafayette Football Equipment: Courtesy of Lafayette College.

To order additional copies of
Legends of Lehigh-Lafayette...College Football's Most- Played Rivalry
simply call toll free:

1-800-FULL MUG

(1-800-385-5684)
Credit Cards Accepted

OR complete and send the mail order form below:

Order Form

Please send _____ copies of Legends ($39.95 per copy) to:

Name: _____

Street Address: _____

City, State and Zip Code: _____

Phone (optional): (___) _____

Cost Calculation:

_____ copies x $39.95   = _____

Pa. residents add
6% sales tax
to above number   = _____

shipping
($3.95 per copy)   = _____

TOTAL   _____

Credit Card Orders:

Credit Card Type (circle one):

Visa   MasterCard

AMEX   Discover

Other: _____

Card Number: _____

Name on Card: _____

Expiration Date: _____

Send completed form to:

D&D Publishing Co.
364 Kevin Dr.
Bethlehem, Pa. 18017

Please make checks payable to: D&D Publishing Co.

Thank You
CALL TOLL FREE AND ORDER NOW!